STORIES

BY FORMER FBI SPECIAL AGENT AND BRONX NATIVE
NEIL MORAN

In accordance with my obligations as a former FBI employee pursuant to my FBI employment agreement, this book has undergone a prepublication review for the purpose of identifying prohibited disclosures, but has not been reviewed for editorial content or accuracy. The FBI does not endorse or validate any information that I have described in this book. The opinions expressed in this book are mine and not those of the FBI or any other government agency.

At the author's discretion, true names were not always used.

Copyright © 2025 by Neil Moran.
All rights reserved.

No part of this publication may be reproduced in whole or in part, or stored in a retrieval system, or transmitted in any form or by any means, electronic, mechanical, photocopying, recording, or otherwise, without written permission of the author, except for the inclusion of brief quotations in a review.

For information regarding permission, please write to:
info@barringerpublishing.com
Barringer Publishing, Naples, Florida
www.barringerpublishing.com

Design and layout by Linda S. Duider
Cape Coral, Florida

ISBN: 978-1-954396-84-5
Library of Congress Cataloging-in-Publication Data
STORIES / Neil Moran

Printed in U.S.A.

DEDICATION

My dear wife, Maureen—The kindest, most generous, caring and thoughtful person I have ever known. A devoted wife and daughter; A shining example of a woman and mother to our three daughters, Meghan, Colleen and Patricia; And now a loving and nurturing grandmother to our five beautiful grandchildren, Kate, Aidan, Kevin, Rory and Maeve.

Maureen sits atop a very short list of those I have known who do so much for others yet expects nor asks for anything in return. Maureen has dedicated her now thirty-five-year career as an RN working with the Little Sisters of the Poor, to care for and preserve the dignity of the elderly in their final stages of life—her compassion, dedication and devotion to the residents are resolute. Numerous families have slept peacefully knowing that their loved ones have been in Maureen's charge.

While on her way to work several years ago, on a snowy morning, Maureen was suddenly struck from behind by another car. Not surprisingly, Maureen was so kind and understanding to the woman who hit her, that a week following the accident, she received one of those overly sentimental Hallmark cards from the woman that began something like, "When God created kind and understanding people...." Enclosed in the card was a set of rosary beads—that's Maureen.

I also would like to dedicate this book to my dear late sister Cathy Moran Graney and her son, our nephew and gentle soul Luke—You both were taken much too soon with so much lying ahead. You are forever in our hearts each and every day.

STORIES

CONTENTS

Foreword vii

Acknowledgements viii

Grandma 5

A Building in a Different Time 9

The Firehouse 14

Memories of a Tile Setter 20

In the Game 25

A Hole in the Cement 30

The Crush 35

The Golden Girls, Dino and Me 38

The Career That Almost Never Was 41
    The Beginning

Smooth As Sweet Cream 49

Arrival in New York 63

A Fallen Comrade 73

Bob Joyce 78

Moving On 87

Jackie O 94

Mr. Brooklyn 97

Etan Patz 105

Lufthansa 113

Crime on the High Seas 123

"I Thought Yous was Looking for Hams"	130
Paulie Gentile	134
Sometimes Money is Nothing But Trouble	143
Model Garage	148
ITSP	157
Patricia	165
The Volvo	169
An Afternoon Sail	174
The Cape	178
The SWAT Team	181
Eddie Joseph	188
Operation Winged Foot	194
Cock-Eyed Anthony and Enzo "The Baker"	203
Frank "Frankie Cadillac" Barone	205
Fat Tommy	209
Winged Foot's Impact	227
Anthony Harper	231
Handsome Tommy	239
Going to the Met Game	243
Philly	249
Mickey Salter	275
Judge John R. Bartels	281
June 5, 1992	287
Crown Heights	301
This Precious Life	308
My Last Stop at the Bureau	314

STORIES

Mr. Chips 320
BDO 325
   The Trip to Turkey 331
It's A Small World 335
Sometimes Travel Isn't So Easy 340
Suddenly a וְאָמסדנאָלל (Lantzman) 345
Someone Else Perhaps 349
The Regift Saga 353
Retirement and Dear Rose 357
Looking Back 361
The Next Generation 364
Afterword 368

FOREWORD

Some might say that Americans of Irish decent, much like their ancestors, have a natural born talent to spin a great yarn. My brother, Neil, has certainly inherited that talent.

As a little kid, I was completely transfixed when he would recite whole scenes from James Cagney films, perfectly mimicking Cagney's voice and mannerisms to a tee. Maybe it was inevitable that he became a G-Man (although we always rooted for Cagney in his bad guy roles). Neil truly enjoyed his work as an FBI Special Agent, and we had the bonus of his story telling ability to enjoy firsthand—as they happened.

Neil's talent to tell a tale expanded into everyday life, in particular, our wonderful family and our connection to the Bronx.

With his keen sense of the spoken word, it was foreseeable that one day he would put these narratives on paper to share with everyone.

Nice work brother!

Ellen Moran

Our family is flush with good storytellers, but none better than my brother Neil.

Through the years, so many family gatherings have been spent with everyone on the edge of their seats, while Neil shared his experiences with us.

Truly entertaining tales told by the man that lived them.

Terry Moran

ACKNOWLEDGEMENTS

There are so many people to thank—the list seems endless.

My late grandparents, parents, aunts, uncles and extended family who, through their examples, instilled in us to always try to do the right thing.

The people with whom I have shared many of my writings through the past few years and have never hesitated to give me feedback—good or bad: my wife Maureen, my sister Ellen Moran, my cousin Brian Murphy, my oldest friend Lenny Frisaro—"Roll Tide," and my Cork cousins, the most literary people I know, Karen Forde, Orla Forde, Gillian Forde, and Daragh Forde.

I extend my thanks to Barbara Novack and my colleagues in our creative writing class for their wisdom, kindness, encouragement and guidance.

The countless people with whom I have been in contact the past few months who pooled their collective memories from the past fifty or so years to help tie many loose ends together and were so generous with their time: Dr. Thomas Lansen, Eric Seidel, Eric Krauss, Harvey Pincus, Kenny Ruffo, John Cable, Jimmy Abbott, Warren Flagg, Ellen Moran, Terry Moran, John Kapp, Ken Lanning, Andy Conlin, John Keenan, George Hanna, Bob Joyce, George Wright, Jim Murphy, Steve Carbone, Richie Mika, George Terra, Kathleen Murray Moran, Ed McDonald, Roze Worrell, John Ligato, Jerri Williams, Dan Rosen, Kieran McNamara and Kathryn Denise Ballew, National Press Operations Unit, FBI Office of Public Affairs.

From the moment I walked into the New York FBI office on East 69th Street, on August 23, 1971, and started as a clerical employee, I met and worked with many people with whom I am still in contact. Many of them had moved on to other professions and I am happy to have continued long-lasting friendships through these past fifty-four years: Tommy Gallagher and his wife, Mary Ann Tolan Gallagher (Mary Ann and I used to ride the Woodlawn #4 train home to the Bronx together every night), Tom Testi, Mike Gildea, John Crimmins (John introduced me to my wife), George Hanna, Bob and Kathy Joyce, John Twiname, Denis Collins, John and Mary Ellen Kapp, Bill Daly, Dennis McManmon, Marty and Ronnie Finn, Bob Curran—and several former colleagues who have sadly passed away, Bill Barry, Bob Shea, Rick Leahy, and John O'Hara.

All the wonderful and dedicated people in the FBI and the NYPD with whom I had the privilege of working. I am especially grateful to the senior and more experienced agents who, in the early part of my career, extended themselves to make the new guy feel comfortable and show him the ropes. I am forever proud and honored to have worked with you all.

The people at BDO USA, where I spent the largest portion of my second career and never imagined that I could find something as challenging, interesting and enjoyable as my years in the FBI.

STORIES

INTRODUCTION

I was never a particularly good writer.

When I joined the FBI, what I captured on paper with respect to what I was told or what I observed, could be the difference between an acquittal or conviction, so attention to detail was critical. How one captures that detail is another story.

Intermittently, Steve Carbone was my supervisor for approximately eight years. Prior to joining the FBI, Steve was, of all things, an English teacher at Brooklyn's Nazareth High School. He was not at all enamored with my writing skills.

Here I was in my late twenties, and he sent back everything I put into his inbox for review like I was still being corrected by Sister Andrew Marie at St. Brendan's in the Bronx:

"*See me re this.*"
"*You're not making sense here.*"
"*This is not on point—you're going off on a tangent.*"
"*You've lost me, you're rambling.*"

These are a random sampling of his often acerbic and biting comments, all highlighted in the margins, in *red pen*, no less. It was mortifying!

Due to unforeseen circumstances, there came a time when Steve was transferred from the Brooklyn-Queens FBI office to the main New York headquarters at 26 Federal Plaza, in Manhattan, over a disciplinary issue with an agent on our squad.

Steve's position was filled by a new supervisor, but on his first day on the job, after I submitted some paperwork, he later stopped by my desk and said, "Nice job on this Moran, your writing is pretty good."

I was on the phone to Steve in a heartbeat and we both had a good laugh.

Had I suddenly become Ernest Hemingway overnight?—hardly.

It probably wasn't until 2005 when I began to write anything of considerable length. I was then working for the accounting firm BDO Seidman, now BDO USA.

My longtime FBI partner and dear friend, George Hanna, had taken a position at Major League Baseball ("MLB"). George called and asked if we were interested in conducting background investigations on companies and people who were applying for an ownership interest in one of MLB's many teams.

We were an accounting firm, and I was part of the consulting group, where we concentrated mainly on fraud matters. However, one thing I quickly learned as I became entrenched in the business world—never say no to new business. My boss, Carl Pergola, seemed intrigued, told me to run with it and just like that, a new business line was born in consulting.

In 2025, *Forbes* estimates that the New York Yankees are valued at $8.2 billion and the Los Angeles Dodgers at $6.8 billion. Anyone who can afford to own even a small percentage of an MLB franchise would be considered a high net worth individual.

At the outset of our new group (only two of us), we conducted in-depth research on some of the most prominent businesspeople and sports personalities in the country. Steve Cohen, current New York Mets owner; Magic Johnson, former professional basketball player and minority owner of the Los Angeles Dodgers; Professional golfer Phil Michelson, San Diego Padres; Businessman Thomas Rickets, Chicago Cubs; and Donald J. Trump, a New York Mets applicant, were just some of the people into whose backgrounds we delved and reported.

Reports often numbered fifty to seventy-five pages in length (one was over one hundred pages) and were reviewed by MLB's Office of

General Counsel and on occasion, the commissioner. Over the years, as our group flourished, we produced hundreds of these in-depth chronicles, and I only wished that Steve Carbone could have seen the product we were cranking out.

When I stopped full-time employment in June 2018, I thought I might like to take a writing class. Nothing too formal, maybe something along the lines of adult education.

Through a simple 'Google' search—"local creative writing classes," I came across the name Barbara Novack, an assistant professor at Molloy College (now University). We exchanged emails, where Barbara explained that she hosts a creative writing class at the local library and invited me to join.

The format was simple—write whatever you want, poetry, fiction or non-fiction, life experiences, tributes to loved ones, etc. I was even introduced to something called a "drabble," a short piece numbering precisely one-hundred words in length, a favorite of my colleague Lloyd Abrams.

I began to tap into my memory bank about things I had been simply too busy all these years to reflect on for any considerable length. My early years in the Bronx; Grandma Moran and other people that have touched my life; working construction in Manhattan; my father's firehouse; tile setting with Uncle Denis; our family in Ireland, and some of my recent trips there and eventually my experiences in the FBI, which I was initially a bit hesitant to share.

I have always enjoyed telling stories and relating experiences no matter how trivial. A popular place to tell those stories growing up was at our dinner table each evening. My parents never seemed to be in a rush to end a meal as long as one of us had more stories to tell. Very often, I seemed to have the most to talk about.

In my recent trips to Ireland, I see more now than ever the love that the Irish seem to have in telling stories, which I have inherited. It's not uncommon for us to still be talking and relating funny narratives at four or five o'clock in the morning.

STORIES

The ability to talk about an experience and hold one's attention is one thing—reducing that story from pen to paper is another.

As I began to write and became more comfortable doing so, it seemed that my creative writing class enjoyed much of what I had to say.

"Neil, you must put some of these stories together. I am telling you there would be an interest in your essays," our instructor, Barbara, told me.

So, what I have done here is put together a combination of personal yarns and experiences, as well as my years with the FBI.

Some of what I've written is deeply personal and much of it I hope you will find to be humorous, probably in some of the most unlikely places.

I am happy to say, even though my professional career choices were serious and important work, I always was fortunate to be surrounded by people who never took themselves too seriously and always had time for a good laugh.

I hope you enjoy my "Stories."

GRANDMA

This was the most remarkable woman I have ever known. When she was only fifteen, Margaret O'Brien traveled alone from her home in rural County Cork, Ireland, to live with her uncle in New York City. One of nine children living in the tiny enclave of Knockbrack, the poverty in Ireland must have been so desperate for her parents to let go of their young and growing family. My grandmother was the first to leave, followed by six of her brothers, who would eventually immigrate to and remain in New York.

Imagine being parents of nine children with eleven seated for meals and suddenly there were only four.

My widowed grandfather also felt there was no opportunity in the west of Ireland and with two small children in tow, Patrick Moran left County Mayo to settle in New York. As is the case with many of the Irish that have come to America, my grandfather was in the bar business, not always the ideal mix for family life.

A short time after they married, for reasons never spoken, but were definitely understood to be grave, that not only did my grandmother boldly leave the relationship, but with three young children, including my three-week-old father, traveled back to Ireland for the first time, where they remained for a nearly a year before returning to New York.

Raising a family as a single parent in the 1920s, in desperate economic times, my grandmother relied on the kind-hearted generosity

A Bronx rooftop in 1922 shortly after the birth of my Aunt Pat, who is being held by my grandmother, Margaret Moran. Three of my grandmother's brothers are pictured: Standing far left James O'Brien, Michael O'Brien, and far right, Denis O'Brien.

of her brothers until she was able to return to dressmaking, a skill she had learned upon arriving in America.

My grandmother's door was always open. I have fond memories of Sunday afternoon dinners in her Valentine Avenue apartment, in the Bronx, with extended family and fellow Cork neighbors in attendance. The crowd was often so large that the men would gather up on the roof. Grandma rarely left the kitchen, was never seen without her apron and always ensured that everyone had enough of everything, when in hindsight she had very little herself.

No article of clothing was ever discarded in our house as my grandmother would package up anything that was no longer worn and send it home to Ireland. Affectionately known by her many nieces and nephews in Ireland as "The Queen," the stories abound about her thoughtfulness and generosity, especially during the tough times. Her late nephew in Cork, Dan O'Brien, related a story that during WW II, when food and even items like tea were in such short supply, they always knew when a parcel arrived from America that Auntie Peg had not forgotten them.

For many years, my grandmother commuted by public transportation from the outskirts of the east Bronx to Washington Heights, where she worked as a seamstress in Messenger's Dress Shop. At eighty-four, when she continued having difficulty working with her arthritic hands, she decided it was time to switch careers.

Responding to a job posting in the *Irish Echo*, a New York weekly Irish newspaper, she requested that I accompany her on an interview to be a daytime companion to an 'elderly woman,' who was seventy-five. When, during the discussion, the woman's son inquired, "Mrs. Moran may I ask you your age?" I was caught off guard when she replied, "I recently turned seventy-two," and sat in near disbelief when she was hired on the spot.

My grandmother had a strong influence on the person I became and am today. Her devotion to God, the church, and her family was steadfast. Today, whether I am with family in New York or in Ireland, it is rare when her name is not invoked, no matter what the topic. My grandmother was incapable of speaking ill of anyone and even in the face of despair was forever optimistic.

"When God closes one door, he opens another," she often said.

Most people would believe that living until age ninety-four was a full life. A 'good run' you might say. There were so many more things I could have learned from my grandmother and there are now two additional generations since her passing that would have benefitted from her wisdom and example.

Yes, in my mind, this was a life cut much too short.

Above: Mid 1960s photo taken in Turners Cross, County Cork, Ireland. Standing far left, my grandmother's brother James O'Brien, seated far left, sister Hanna Forde, seated far right, brother Daniel O'Brien and next to Uncle Dan, my grandmother, Margaret Moran.

Left: My grandmother, Margaret Moran on the left and two of her nieces in Knockbrack, County Cork, Ireland in the mid-1950s.

A BUILDING IN A DIFFERENT TIME

Having occupied a house for over forty-five years, it seems like another lifetime since I lived in the apartment building where I was raised. So many things were different then. It was only a few years after WW II when I came into the world and the country was slowly getting back on its feet. Everything seemed to be at our fingertips.

Peter Reeves' Supermarket, David's Drugs, Saul and Izzy's soda fountain, Hebrew National Deli, Volpp's Bakery, Horn & Hardart (I still miss the rice pudding more than you can imagine), St. Brendan's Church and School, Montefiore Hospital, and the Bainbridge Movie Theater, all were only blocks away. Even my father's firehouse was within walking distance. Few people in our neighborhood, including ourselves, needed a car.

Stickball, Ringolevio, Johnny-Ride-The-Pony, Manhunt, Red Rover, Hide and Seek, and Stoop Ball were some of the many games that filled our days until a parent stuck his or her head out the window to let you know that dinner was ready.

In 1957, I have a vivid recollection of our entire school, St. Brendan's, walking down Bainbridge Avenue to see the movie, *The Ten Commandments* at the Bainbridge Theater. The New York Yankees were playing the Milwaukee Braves in an afternoon game in the World Series. When the movie ended, as we made our way back to school, Sister Marie Pierre, who was carrying a transistor radio gave us an update.

"The Yankees are winning and it's the seventh inning," she said.

STORIES

315 East 206 Street, Bronx, New York, where the Morans called home from the late 1940s through the early 1960s.

Things were a lot more formal then.

On Sunday afternoons, after attending Mass, our excursions consisted of meeting my aunt, uncle, and cousins at Williamsbridge Reservoir Oval, the nearest park. Mothers and daughters wore dresses and fathers and boys, suits and ties. On most Sundays, the visit to the park was followed by a long walk or a short bus ride, depending on the weather, for dinner at Grandma Moran's on nearby Valentine Avenue, which when I was young, seemed the equivalent of a Thanksgiving meal.

Our apartment building was our own version of the Alfred Hitchcock thriller, *Rear Window*. Although we neither experienced quite the drama portrayed in the movie, which ends with the capture of a murderer in an apartment across the courtyard, nor did we have an occupant with the captivating beauty of Grace Kelly, but from a child's eyes, our building appeared as our own self-contained little world.

We lived on the sixth floor and overlooked both the street and courtyard. On hot summer evenings with only a small fan blowing the hot air around, we would join our parents on the fire escape and my mom and dad would have running conversations with our neighbors who were doing the same. In the dead of winter, one is never cold in a sixth-floor apartment. When scientists proclaimed that "Heat rises," it's likely they came to that conclusion while conducting a test in our building. The radiators in the lobby and the hallways forever hissed and were filled with children's woolen hats and mittens and the intense heat and the water-logged clothing from the wet snow, emitted what is still today an unforgettable smell.

Mr. and Mrs. Markham lived in the adjoining apartment and at that time seemed very old but probably were only in their '40s. Their only child, John, had joined the Navy at the end of the Korean War and I remember them being sad. When John came home on leave, he was a hero in our building and I'll never forget him picking me up, tossing me around and placing his white sailor's hat atop my head.

Mr. Goldstein was also on the sixth floor. Mrs. Goldstein had died when I was a baby, and he was all alone. With my bright red hair and a face covered with freckles, Mr. Goldstein always seemed to know when I was coming or going. He would open his door when he heard me and always ask, "Where did you get that curly red hair and all of those freckles?" and proceed to muss my mane.

When I was old enough, I'd run to Saul & Izzy's and buy him the *Journal American* and the *World Telegram and Sun*. He would always give me a dime for my trouble.

On the floor below and across the courtyard, I remember calling out to my mother one Friday evening when I could see the Koppel family gathered around a table and lighting candles. They were singing in an unfamiliar language. Joel Koppel and his father were wearing small white satin beanies and Mrs. Koppel, a small lace fabric covering her head. "The Koppel's are Jewish, son," my mother explained. "We go to Mass every Sunday and sing 'Holy God We Praise Thy Name' and *'Tantum Ergo.'* They're singing Jewish hymns. Tomorrow the Koppel's will get dressed up and pray at their synagogue with other Jewish people just like we'll do when we go to Mass on Sunday."

Our Aunt Julia also lived in the opposite side of the building. Joe, the love of her life, had died several years before and she never had any children or was interested in anyone else. So, unlike most of the women in that time, Aunt Julia "Went to business," as she used to say, working at the International Paper Company in midtown, taking the "D" train every day. Aunt Julia had her sisters, which included my grandmother, living nearby, but she loved having my siblings and me around to perform chores she would invent as an excuse to give us candy or a nickel and I suppose to provide a respite from the loneliness that she undoubtedly felt.

I imagine the closest we ever got to real-life drama in our building was when our downstairs neighbor, Marty Maguire, learned that his seventeen-year-old sister was pregnant at the hands of one of the local make-believe tough guys, who hung out on the corner. I was awakened in the dead of night with the shattering of glass and Marty yelling, "You son-of a-bitch, I'll kill you." My parents, who also were stirred by the calamity, as was probably most of the building, were perched at the window with the best seat in the house.

As the impregnator attempted his escape with Margie Maguire pleading with her brother to stop, Marty grabbed the future father and proceeded to pummel him with the ferocity of then champ Rocky Marciano. Someone had called the police and after pulling the pugilists apart, they were both led away in handcuffs. On our way to school the next morning, my sisters and I closely examined the aftermath of the brawl and stepped gingerly over the shards of broken glass and splats of dried blood.

By far, my fondest memory was awaiting my father's arrival on Sunday mornings after working the overnight shift at the firehouse. Allowing for his walk across Mosholu Parkway and a stop at Volpp's Bakery, my mother timed everything with the precision of a launch from the Kennedy Space Center. The bacon and sausages would be cooked first, and she would await word from us that our father was walking down the block, armed with rolls and what we believed were the best powdered jelly doughnuts and krullers in the Bronx.

"We see him, Mommy," my sisters would scream and with that, you could hear the crackle of the eggs hit the already simmering pan and moments later as the key went in the door, it marked the beginning of our Sunday morning breakfast ritual.

These were precious years for which I feel lucky to have been a part and will be forever grateful.

THE FIREHOUSE

The 1950s were wonderful years to grow up in the Bronx. Things seemed to be far less complicated. Our neighborhood, then known as Bainbridge after one of the main throughfares, is today known as Norwood. Now largely Hispanic, the area was mainly first-generation Irish and Jewish. Calvin Klein, Ralph Lifshitz (Lauren) and actress Penny Marshall were all raised only blocks from our East 206th Street apartment.

When I think about how much freedom we had as children compared to those today, it's difficult to fathom.

"Neil, here's a dollar; take a walk down to Horn & Hardart's and get a medium sized rice pudding," my mother would say.

I was probably seven or eight years old. Sometimes that sense of freedom presents problems.

You would think that in a neighborhood that boasted mostly six-story apartment buildings that people, especially children, could blend in anonymously—no such chance. I recall four or five of us sitting atop a newsstand, where the Woodlawn bus stopped. As it drove off, we would all pound on the windows where the passengers sat. Only hours later, word had mysteriously gotten back to our parents and let's just say the newsstand was, going forward, permanently off limits.

Today, commuting stories are legendary. People often travel over two hours to work. My father had a ten-minute walk to his firehouse just south of us in Bedford Park. Back in the day, most neighborhoods had one particular place where people often gathered or "hung out." Ladder 37 and Engine 79 was such a place.

Like my dad, most of his colleagues fought in WW II and sought the security of a civil service job. Not surprisingly at that time, most of the firemen were first-generation Irish. My first memories of the firehouse were of my mother pushing a baby carriage containing my

Present-day photo of Ladder 37, Matty Moran joined the FDNY in 1948.

newly born sister, Cathy, after just visiting my grandparents around the corner with my other sister, Ellen, and myself in tow.

Pass by any firehouse today and the doors are never open. As a child, I can't ever recall seeing the doors of Ladder 37 closed, even when the bells went off and they answered a call. They never had to worry about their personal belongings or the valuable equipment inside. The neighborhood was there to keep vigil and await everyone's safe return.

As I got a bit long in the tooth at about eight or nine, my friends and I would walk down Bainbridge Avenue across Mosholu Parkway to the firehouse. On a nice day, people of all ages would gather outside and a good many of the firemen could be seen chatting away with the locals listening to the neighborhood gossip. When retirements of some of the older firemen brought in some in their twenties, there was an immediate increase in the complement of teenage girls all polished up. It's fair to say that everyone in the neighborhood knew what shift almost all the firemen worked, even when they were off or on vacation.

A relatively low-crime area, the neighborhood and the firehouse faithful were shocked when an Albanian man in his sixties shot and killed an intruder in his daughter's nearby Valentine Avenue apartment. The shooting was deemed justified and the man was not charged. I remember listening to the people describing the incident and an in-depth description of the shooter. Only moments later, he turned the corner and approached the firehouse.

He stood about 6'4" with a full head of gray hair, a twirling handlebar mustache and the stature of actor Bela Lugosi. The firemen and those gathered stood silent and still as this now accidental neighborhood legend nodded, cracked a mischievous grin, and continued his deliberate stride, passing the small throng.

When I wasn't at the firehouse, perhaps playing stickball on our block, as soon as we heard the sirens in the distance, everyone dropped what they were doing and ran up the block to see Mr. Moran pass. When the sirens stopped, we knew there was a fire or some trouble nearby.

I remember seeing smoke billowing out of an apartment adjacent to the Bainbridge Theater and we all saw my father climb the ladder

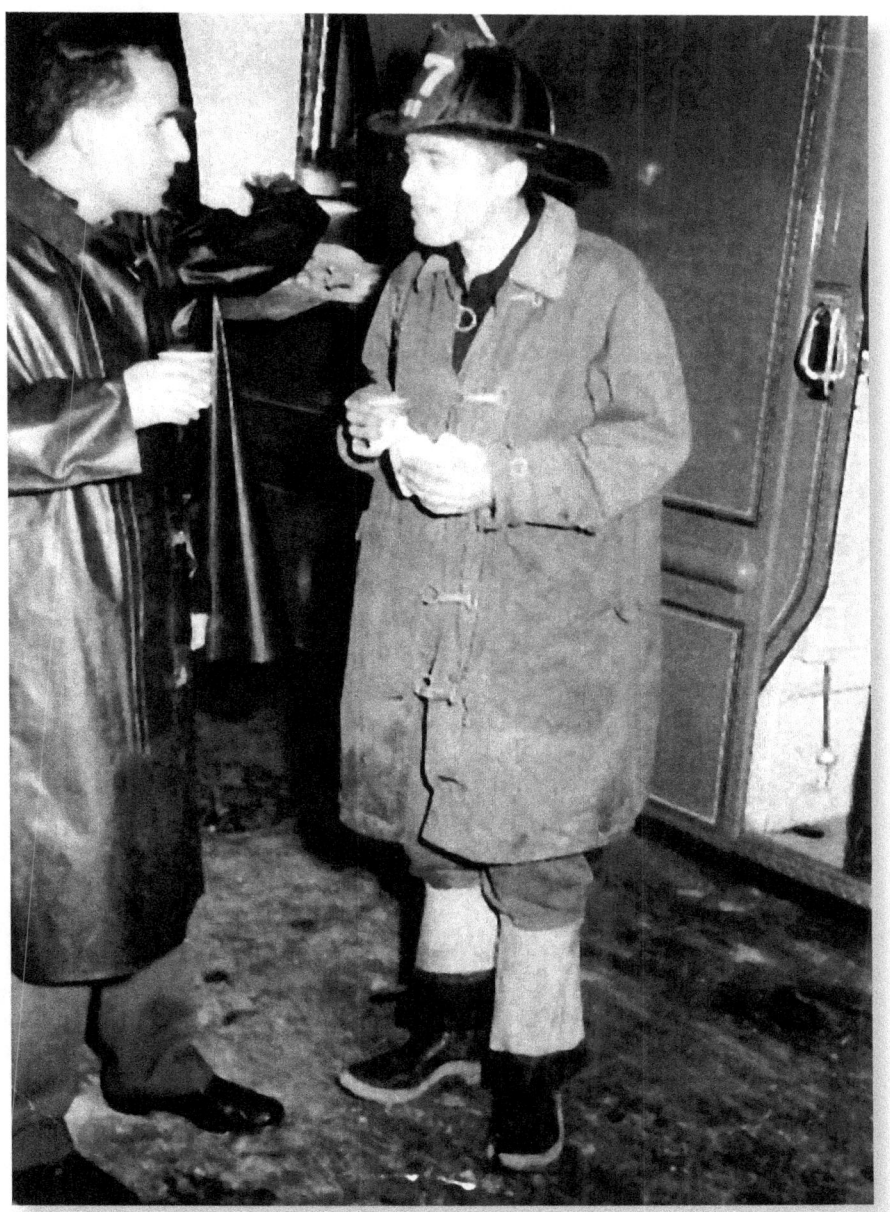

My father at a fire in the Bronx in the 1950s.

with an axe in his hand. With a sizeable crowd gathered across the street awaiting the outcome, there was a collective gasp as my father smashed the window. My dad and his colleagues then assisted a woman as she climbed out the window and down the ladder to safety, much to the delight of the throng below.

"That's Matty Moran," Mrs. O'Neill, my friend Michael's mom said. "That's his son with the red hair with my Michael and the boys."

Following the tragic events of September 11, the term "Brotherhood" was often used to describe the members of FDNY. Although that label may have caught the public's eye at that time, given the massive loss of life, I would argue that it was a "Brotherhood" long before. Yearly picnics, trips to the nearby amusement park, Freedomland, and the annual Emerald Society Mass and Communion Breakfast at St. Patrick's Cathedral were just some of the activities I recall attending as a child with my father's colleagues. They were and are truly brothers.

It was some years later, after our move to the suburbs and I began to work in Manhattan, that I rented an apartment in Bedford Park. I had a standing invitation to join the evening meal at the firehouse. One night as I walked into the kitchen, many of the firemen I had known since childhood were all singing a Latin hymn, *"Tantum Ergo."*

Most of them had been altar boys and challenged each other as to who could sing the entire canticle from memory in Latin. It was truly a sight to behold.

Shortly after September 11, I stopped by the firehouse to pay my respects to honor those who had perished. After explaining my connection, I was invited in for coffee and recounted some of these same stories for the young firemen of a new generation. I was welcomed and treated like one of their own.

Yes, in nearly fifty years, not much had changed at The Firehouse.

Fire Department of the City of New York

CERTIFICATE OF MERIT

PRESENTED TO

FIREMAN

Matthew J. Moran
LADDER CO. 37

IN RECOGNITION OF THE OUTSTANDING EFFICIENT SERVICES PERFORMED DURING ASSIGNMENT AS CHAUFFEUR TO PERSONS IN PARTY OF NIKITA S. KHRUSHCHEV, CHAIRMAN OF USSR, ON OCCASION OF HIS VISIT TO NEW YORK CITY ON SEPTEMBER 17, 18, AND 19, 1959.

FIRE COMMISSIONER

1959—I can recall my father coming home one night prior to the impending visit of then Soviet Premier Nikita Kruschev to NYC. The cold war was raging at that time and the city authorities and the federal government feared for his safety.

A decision was made to have NYC firemen act as chauffeurs for Premier Kruschev and his diplomatic entourage—the reason, they actually were fearful that a NYPD officer might shoot one of them, which sounds absolutely crazy but that's what my father told us. I can remember my dad coming home one of the nights and saying that as they drove past the Empire State Building he pointed it out adding that it was the tallest building in the world to which one of the diplomats in the car said, "For now it is the tallest building."

When the delegation left several days later, apparently my father had driven onto the tarmac at Idlewild (Now JFK) Airport and brought his movie camera—we are probably one of a handful of FDNY families or any family for that matter to have Nikita Kruschev waving goodbye to America as he's boarding at the top of the stairs as part of their home movie collection.

MEMORIES OF A TILE SETTER

My father was among the most talented people I ever knew. He could fix and figure out anything. A high school dropout, who decided to become a welder, he had those plans suddenly interrupted with the bombing of Pearl Harbor. At eighteen, he now found himself fighting the Japanese in the Pacific. After the war, job prospects for twenty-one-year-olds with no education were indeed slim. Enter Uncle Denis.

Uncle Denis, my grandmother's younger brother, was one of six O'Brien boys to leave the family farm in Cork, Ireland, and settle in New York. A skilled craftsman, his assortment of talents included, but were not limited to, woodworking, plumbing, carpentry, and tile setting. Although he mostly worked alone and didn't advertise or have his own business (or website) in the 1940s, Uncle Denis gladly took my father on and gave him work whenever the situation allowed.

As some of my father's cousins returned from World War II, they opted, as many first-generation Irish did in the day, to join the NYPD and the FDNY. Although civil service was never intended to be a path to an apartment on Park Avenue, it was the sense of security that seemed to be paramount. Sadly, these opportunities were non-existent in Ireland for those years, which was why seven of the nine O'Brien children left. These immigrants wanted things for their children they never had.

"You'll get a pension someday if you take a civil service job, Matty," my grandmother was to have said at the time. "At least you'll have a paycheck every two weeks—something steady."

My dad opted for the Fire Department and initially found himself in Manhattan and then several years later, in his own Bronx neighborhood. Marriage to my mother and my birth followed shortly thereafter. The nearest I can guess, my dad was probably making somewhere around $3,500 in 1950. For his entire career with FDNY, as did most of his colleagues, he always worked another job. I can remember from a very young age that a lot of that work was with Uncle Denis.

New houses, older houses, tiling primarily kitchens and bathrooms, my father and Uncle Denis often allowed me to tag along on the weekends as a helper. They worked all over the Bronx and sometimes in lower Westchester, in places like Bronxville, Tuckahoe and Mt. Vernon. My dad might be upstairs tiling the bathroom and Uncle Denis always seemed to have me with him in a kitchen or downstairs bathroom. A big thrill at the time was when Uncle Denis would have me write my name and the date on the back of a piece of tile as we began to set the last few pieces.

In 1958, my father's sister, my Aunt Pat, and her husband, Bernard, a member of the NYPD, decided to leave the Bronx and bought a house in Floral Park, on Long Island. As the construction began, there was little question that the tile work would be handled by my father and Uncle Denis.

I can still remember being in the back seat with Uncle Denis driving from the Bronx out to Long Island. "I think we're lost, Matty," he said, as we now found ourselves on the Southern State Parkway, clearly having overshot Floral Park and about to pay the toll. "Can you tell me are we near Floral Park?" he asked the attendant. Although I can't recall the exchange from that point, I do clearly remember what transpired within a minute or so after we paid the toll. With lights and sirens blaring, my father said, "Uncle Denis, it looks like he wants us to pull over." As the officer approached the driver's side and Uncle Denis rolled down

Photo taken in the mid-1950s in Knockbrack, County Cork, Ireland—My grandmother's sister, Hanna Forde, lower left and my grandmother, Margaret Moran, third from left. Pictured upper far right, the "Tile Setter" Denis O'Brien.

the window, in his thick Cork accent he sheepishly inquired, "Did I do something wrong officer?"

"I'll say you did," he shot back. "You gave the attendant a nickel instead of a dime. The toll is ten cents, not five, sir."

Once again, although the details of the exchange that followed are a bit hazy, suffice it to say, according to the way my father often told the story in the years that followed, Uncle Denis completely charmed the officer, who, after collecting the nickel owed, stopped just short of apologizing for the inconvenience.

I think it probably took my father, Uncle Denis, and their trusted helper, about two or three Saturdays to complete the tile job at Aunt Pat's. As we put the finishing touches on the kitchen, Uncle Denis had me repeat the ritual of signing my name and entering the date.

"Who knows, Neil, someday, if they decide they want to change the tile or put in a different kitchen, someone will see your name and when we finished the job."

Oddly enough, this tender custom from a loving uncle who took great pride in his work, was something I would follow on jobs as an apprentice carpenter in Manhattan during the late 1960s.

The last site I worked in 1970 was known at the time in the construction trades, as the "A" building and the "B" building, later to become One and Two World Trade Center. I can't begin to count the number of times I inscribed my name and date someplace on every floor of both towers I worked. My colleagues often looked on with curiosity and would inquire as to why. Although construction workers are known to often have a rough exterior, after providing the background, there wasn't one that didn't find the practice touching. Sadly, following the tragic events of September 11, 2001, none of my memories have lived on.

I think it was sometime in 2006 when one evening I received a call from Aunt Pat. I hadn't known, as Uncle Denis had speculated some fifty years earlier, that my aunt and uncle decided to remodel their small kitchen.

"Neil, when the tile man was removing the old pieces, he called me into the kitchen. 'It looks like someone wrote their name on the back of the tile. Look at the date Mrs. Murphy, it's from 1958.' My goodness, that's my nephew, who is now in his 50s."

With Uncle Denis and my father both gone, I had great fun recalling the story and the custom introduced by Uncle Denis to my aunt. Who would have known that a simple task would make for such a lasting memory.

Seated: My mother, Beverly Moran, left speaking with Aunt Pat Murphy. Standing: Uncle Bernard Murphy—The back of one of the dark-colored tiles over the stove is where Uncle Denis had Neil Moran date and sign his name.

IN THE GAME

To compete in one's respective sport's National Collegiate Athletic Association ("NCAA") championships, has been the highpoint of the careers of many young American athletes.

It was my junior year and our cross-country team had gone unbeaten. We anxiously awaited word from the NCAA whether we would be one of the teams selected. Our small school, Niagara University, had primarily been known for its achievements in basketball, and had recently enjoyed several successful years lead by its All-American, Calvin Murphy.

As we gathered for practice in the late October afternoon and our coach, Tom Hargrave, approached, he made a failed attempt at shrouding his unreserved delight and said: "Gentlemen, we're the first cross-country team in school history to be invited to the NCAAs. Let's get to work."

We could hardly contain ourselves as we yelled out loud and vowed to continue to maintain our successful season on the sport's grand stage. As a bonus for me personally, the event was to be held at the scene of a number of my boyhood and AAU races, Van Cortlandt Park, in the Bronx. We were going to compete against some of the greatest runners in the world, perennial collegiate powerhouses like Villanova and the University of Oregon in a little less than a month.

An article soon appeared in the school newspaper, followed by another in the *Niagara Falls Gazette*. The team was introduced at a school football game. There were even mentions on the Buffalo television stations. Suddenly, we were campus celebrities.

Although at this stage of our careers, running had become a year round sport, the intensity was undeniably ramped up when the team returned before classes began in August. We had now routinely been logging between seventy and eighty miles a week, which consisted of long and arduous early morning and afternoon sessions.

Once we received word that we were among the twenty-nine teams invited to the championship, our workouts intensified, often to the point of utter exhaustion. Coaching methods and philosophies have changed considerably since the 1960s. Most of today's coaches embrace

The Niagara University Cross Country team in 1969—Neil Moran kneeling lower right.

a "Hard/Easy" approach; one hard practice followed by one that is less stressful. There were no easy days in the month leading up to race day.

With the championship only about a week away, I began to experience pain in my knee, which I didn't share with my coach. *What was happening*, I wondered? *Would this get worse?*

I sought out one of the graduate student trainers, who after examining me and observing some noticeable swelling around my knee said, "It's probably patellar tendonitis. It's an overuse injury. The only remedy for this is rest."

"Rest," I shouted, "the NCAAs are next Monday."

"We can ice this for you and perform some ultrasound treatment, but this isn't going away as long as you guys are out there pounding the pavement every day."

The treatments seemed to help or at least I tried to tell myself so. I managed to make it through the remaining training sessions but following our final practice on Saturday, my knee was killing me. At least, I will have all day Sunday to rest, I thought. Hopefully, that will help.

Race day had come. Only three days before the Thanksgiving holiday, it was an overcast and frosty day with a cutting wind. As I warmed up, I noticed several of the rail thin Kenyan runners from the University of Texas at El Paso, who would go on to capture the team trophy. Many of the notable international stars, including the overall winner Gerry Lindgren and future Olympian Steve Prefontaine, ran past me going through their respective routines. I was consumed by the excitement of competing on this stage. but at the same time, concerned about my now nagging knee pain.

"Runners take your marks," the starter shouted and bang, the gun went off followed by 254 competitors in a furious sprint to the front to gain position before entering the grueling hills. I think the sheer excitement of this spectacle temporarily masked my knee concerns until we entered the hills.

It seemed as though the downhill sprints were aggravating my knee to the point where I began to almost hobble. One by one, runners began to pass me. I came to the halfway mark at three miles passing the crowds, including my parents, siblings, and friends all cheering on the runners. My coach was surprised to see me considerably off the pace and shouted that I needed to make a move soon. As I made eye contact with my father, I looked at him and shook my head signaling that this was not going to be my day.

As I entered the hills for the second time, the pain in my knee caused me to do something I had never done in hundreds of races, come to a complete stop to try and collect myself. I was like a car squirting its final few vapors before stalling and limping helplessly to the side of the road—out of fuel.

I had to keep going. Competing on this stage is why for years I woke when night was at its darkest to get in my early morning workout and the reason I sweltered on sizzling summer afternoons pushing my body to its limits.

"Keep going," I said. As I approached still another downhill, fearing it would intensify the pain, I stepped so timidly that I tumbled and fell. As other runners selflessly helped me to my feet, I knew that any further attempts at jump starting my now stalled engine were hopeless.

As I stood bent over with mud stained and a bloodied leg, hands atop my knees, it wasn't that long before the final runners were passing and I was doing the unthinkable, walking in the national collegiate championships. Humiliation, disappointment, embarrassment, anger, and overwhelming dejection all overtook me at once. I began to wipe away the tears and as I ambled along and looked up ahead, I soon saw my father and then six-year-old brother, Terry, walking toward me in the distance.

"I'm sorry, Dad," I said as he hugged me and took me into his arms as I was now crying with little restraint. "I can't believe this happened. I feel like I let everyone down, my coach, the team, and all of you guys. My knee has been killing me these past few weeks."

"You have nothing to be sorry for or ashamed," my father began. "I know it's of little consolation now, but in life this is what we call a character builder. If this is the worst thing that ever happens, count yourself as one of the lucky ones. There will be many bigger and far greater disappointments. Every runner that puts on a singlet aspires to get to where you were today. You lined up against the greatest runners in the sport. You should be very proud. It's a wonderful accomplishment. The results were not what you had hoped but you were here."

What I suppose he was trying to say was that I was "In the game."

A HOLE IN THE CEMENT

I was a third-year apprentice carpenter working on what would become the world's two largest buildings, the World Trade Center towers. I look back fondly on this time as I was fortunate to work with men who were exceptional craftsmen, took great pride in their profession and instilled those qualities in me by their daily examples. I was a member of carpenter's Local 608, also known in the late 1960s as "The Irish Local," comprised chiefly of Irish-born members.

At the job site, all the trades, which included electricians, steel workers, steamfitters, painters, plasterers, plumbers, and laborers, were assigned small, designated areas in the sub-basement of Buildings A and B, as the towers were then known, where we changed clothes and received daily assignments. "Shanties" as they were called, were also a place where we caught up on the day's events, especially during lunchtime when most of our group was together.

As a nineteen-year-old, I spoke very little during our noon break, but listened attentively as the younger Irishmen spoke about their latest romantic conquests and the older ones about their children or the latest results involving their favorite football and hurling teams in Ireland. The banter amongst the crew could often be hilarious.

One summer afternoon, I recall our shop steward, John Forde, asking for our attention, and his demeanor signaled that the subject was probably serious.

"Lads," he began, in his distinctive and thick Cork accent, "I was chatting it up with the laborer shop steward earlier and he told me that he has a new man in his crew who was just released from Sing Sing (a suburban New York maximum security prison) and served fifteen years for murder."

John added that Mike, the laborer shop steward, fought the union delegate trying not to take on the new man, but ultimately, he had no say and was forced to do so. From some of the delegate's comments, Mike seemed to think that the new crew member was a mob hit man, who was also known on the street as "Mad Dog."

You could have heard a pin drop in the normally very lively shanty. As I looked around, no one was smiling, and several mouths were wide open.

"Oh, and one more thing," John continued, "he has a fierce scar on his cheek and a glass eye as a result of a fight in prison. The chances of any of us running into him are few but be mindful if you do."

As the crew filed out of the shanty, the quiet conversation was all about the man they called "Mad Dog." Pat Leahy, who stood about 6'5", with whom I was teamed that afternoon and looked like someone who could scrap with the best of them, uttered, "Neil, I won't be coming within ten floors of the 'Mad Dog' if I can help it."

Several days passed and other than the revelation from John Forde and chit chat exiting the shanty, no one spoke again about the possible mob hit man lurking in our midst.

One of the responsibilities of an apprentice is to take daily food and drink orders from the crew. Given the vast expanse of these two huge structures, the men could be found on any of the numerous floors of both towers at any given time. It was my charge to ensure that deliveries were made, and in the case of coffee and tea, hopefully while still hot. As I navigated my way between the A and B buildings, my normal custom was to use the stairwells. The elevators were operated by workers and often stopped for lengthy intervals, where building materials were loaded and unloaded, so I always opted to climb the stairs.

One morning, I had only Dan O'Brien's tea and buttered roll left in my box when I flung open the heavy steel door to the stairwell. As I put down both feet, I suddenly felt something collapse beneath me and as I staggered momentarily and looked down, I was nearly knee deep in freshly poured cement. Not only was I immobilized for the moment, but the force of my weight had broken a thin piece of plywood immediately below and created a gaping hole.

The commotion drew the attention of one of the laborers, who, as I looked behind me, stood with his hands at his sides, holding a two by four in one and a nail gun in the other.

"Jesus Christ kid," the man shouted.

As I looked at his angry face, which bore a sizeable scar on his left cheek, one eye that looked directly at me and the other which was lifeless and misaligned, there was little doubt I was in the presence of the man they called "Mad Dog." As he paused and examined the damage, he glanced at my trademark striped carpenter's overalls, nail apron and hammer hanging from my belt loop.

"You fucking Irish carpenters. You are all as fucking dumb as this fucking two by four," he shouted.

There was enough real estate in what were soon to be the world's two largest buildings, that the chances, as John Forde articulated, of running into the "Mad Dog," were quite slim, yet here I stood staring down what I believed to be imminent death. Would he wallop me in the head with the two by four or crucify me with the nail gun and leave me to die undetected in a dimly lit stairwell?

"Sorry, sir," I said, not knowing what or if anything I should say.

"Sir, do I look like a fucking sir to you, you idiot? I just poured that cement and worked on it all morning and you came along and fucked it up in two seconds. Now get the fuck out of here before I kill you."

As frightened as I had ever been in my young life, I said nothing, gathered my box and ran out onto the floor as fast as I could. When I eventually came upon my last delivery, Dan O'Brien, he took one look at my pasty complexion and pants soaked in cement and said, "Neil, did you see a ghost?"

"No Dan, worse than that, I just met the 'Mad Dog.'"

The word traveled fast amid the crew and leading up to lunchtime it was now rumored that Neil was nearly butchered and left for dead in a stairwell by the "Mad Dog."

Several hours later we all gathered in the shanty for lunch and the one person who normally contributed little to the conversation was now squarely in the spotlight.

"Were you scared Neil?" Brendan asked.

"How big is the scar?" Aidan wanted to know.

"Did he have a gun?" Terry inquired.

"Jaysus, you must have been crippled with fear," Kieran said.

I barely had an opportunity to begin to describe the accurate version of what had occurred when Mike, the laborer shop steward, walked in.

He looked at John Forde and said, "I understand that one of your men had a run-in this morning with one of our guys."

"That would be our apprentice, Neil," John said in acknowledgment, nodding in my direction.

"Well, Pete told me that he lost his temper and thinks he scared the hell out of the young kid. I just thought I would come down to make sure there was no harm done. You know Pete's on parole and doesn't want no problems."

"Not at all, Mike, other than some concrete-stained pants, we're good here. You'll have no problems from us," John replied.

As Mike departed, the entire crew was aghast. The "Mad Dog," who we now knew to be Pete, probably was not the only person of several thousand working at the Trade Center who had ever done time in prison. There were some rough characters on every job site and apologies for minor dust ups were few and far between.

The legend of my run in with the "Mad Dog" grew throughout the length of my remaining time at the Trade Center to the point where there was talk that the young 608 apprentice had taken a swing at Pete and he backed down.

I did see him from afar several times after that day and although we never spoke, he would always look with his one good eye, acknowledge me with a slight nod and even sometimes manage to crack what could pass for a small grin, which told me that even a man they call "Mad Dog" can't be all that bad.

The World Trade Center under construction, as it appeared, when Neil Moran worked there in 1970. Designed by Minoru Yamasaki, work on the foundations began in 1966. However, contractors didn't start building the actual towers until 1968. They were opened to the public in 1973. PHOTO CREDIT: INSTAGRAM @ UNKNOWN / DM

THE CRUSH

In July 2010, I attended the Galway Film Festival with my Irish cousins in Galway City, Ireland. *The Crush* was one of the featured short films, and it would eventually be nominated for an Academy Award in 2011 for Best Live Action Short Film.

The story centered around a young Irish boy who fancies his teacher. I adored the film and have watched it many times since. Aboard my flight home, somewhere over the Atlantic Ocean, reflecting on the movie, I recalled my first real crush.

I have wonderful childhood memories of seeing my grandmother and her brothers off at the airport for their many visits to Ireland. In 1960, my grandmother's only sister, our Aunt Hannah, was the first of a series of Irish family visitors to New York. Only three years later, Aunt Hannah's son, John and his beautiful bride Mary visited here on their honeymoon.

I am a child of the 1950s. Growing up and to this day, I have always been an ardent movie fan. At a young age I especially loved gangster films starring tough guys like James Cagney, George Raft and Humphrey Bogart. However, there came a time when glamorous movie stars like Grace Kelly, Elizabeth Taylor and Marilyn Monroe also grabbed my attention.

Naturally, when we were notified by my grandmother that John and Mary were going to be honeymooning in New York there was an exciting buzz throughout the extended family. On the day they arrived, the O'Briens, Murphys, Erbs and Morans were out in full force.

It seems like yesterday (I was thirteen), but I still recall my grandmother saying, "There they are," as the striking young couple walked through the doors at the international arrivals building at what was then Idlewild Airport. As my grandmother and her brothers made the introductions, I met Mary for the first time and recalled her saying, "Hello Neil, nice to meet you."—I was completely smitten—Grace Kelly had just walked into my life.

It was back to my grandmother's apartment in Woodlawn for a family gathering, where it was mainly the adults who were getting to know the young honeymooners. At some point I remember Mary coming over to all the children, where she began to chat with us. Only in her early twenties, as she began to speak, it's fair to say I was utterly enchanted with her beauty and charm.

Most people can recall family get-togethers when they were young, where the extent of a child's conversation with adults might be for them to comment on how tall you had gotten or how pretty you were. From the get-go there was something different about Mary. The first time I met her and the occasions that followed during their stay, she took the time to ask me all about myself—How did I like school? Did I enjoy sports? How was I spending my summer holidays? Did I think I might like to visit Ireland someday? When you're a little guy and an adult takes the time to speak with you, that's something you'll always remember and this little guy certainly did. Yes, simply said, I was hopelessly infatuated.

Fast forward several years and at age nineteen I made my first trip to Ireland. Like all the American relatives that had preceded me, it was assumed I would be staying with Aunt Hannah and her husband, Uncle John. As our plane descended, and I looked out my window seat, even though it was "lashing" rain, for me this was a dream come true.

As I made my way through Irish customs and immigration and finally exited, not having any idea who would be there to greet me, I suddenly heard a woman's voice yell, "Neil, hello Neil, over here." Oh my God, I couldn't believe my eyes when I saw it was Mary frantically waving, and as it turned out, she was alone. It had only been six years since her visit and Mary, now in her late twenties, in my mind was even more striking than I recalled. A "real stunner," as the Irish often say. For the next three hours, I would be escorted alone to Turner's Cross by Marilyn Monroe.

I wasn't aware when we arrived that Mary had devised a plan to literally abduct me from Aunt Hannah's and have me spend my entire trip with her and John. She recognized that staying with the two oldest members of the family was no place for a teenager.

In the days that followed, we took excursions with all the relatives, but on those occasions when people had to work or tend to their young families, Mary would take me around to various Cork landmarks. One of those attractions was the famed Blarney Castle, where, according to Irish folklore, if you kiss the stone atop the castle, you are granted the gift of eloquence. With a relatively short line, as we got closer and I awaited my turn, I observed those before me lying on their backs and with the assistance of a seventy-something-year-old gentleman, being lowered down to kiss the stone. When it was my turn, with Mary, clad in what was at that time, a very fashionable miniskirt and standing beside me with no intention of participating, the man, out of nowhere, suddenly grabbed her around the waist, threw a blanket over her legs, lowered her and called out, "Kiss away," as she loudly screamed in protest.

In the 1970s and 1980s, with marriage, children and a career, my trips to Ireland were less frequent. In recent years, there has been a complete reversal to the point where I now travel there every summer. The one constant throughout every trip has been Mary. Just as in our first encounter some sixty-two years ago, she has always taken the time to get caught up on all the family news from America.

Now in her eighties, Mary is in a senior care facility and sadly her memory has faded. When I talk to her now, she seems to stare at me for a good bit and I'm almost expecting her to blurt out, "Neil, so very nice to see you, how's your summer going and how are all the relatives in America?" I'll never know now if Mary had an inkling about my infatuation years ago, but I certainly will always fondly recall my very first real crush.

THE GOLDEN GIRLS, DINO AND ME

I've previously spoken about my admiration for my brave grandmother, Margaret O'Brien Moran and the poverty most Irish families experienced in the late 1800s.

The struggles in those times must have been unthinkable for parents to say goodbye to their children, still at tender ages. Making the journey alone at sixteen, Grandma boarded the *SS Cadria* in what was then called Queenstown (now Cobh, County Cork), to seek opportunity in a new world.

Fiercely independent, even at this young age, while girls today are celebrating their "sweet sixteen" with elaborate parties and celebrations, my grandmother took a job in a garment factory, where she learned to be a seamstress and later a dressmaker, trades she would continue to hone into her mid-80s.

After years of traveling by public transportation from the Bronx and Yonkers to Messenger's Dress Shop on West 181st Street, in Washington Heights, via a series of buses and trains, Grandma decided to retire. Her cousin, Joe Gleason, owned a house in the East Bronx and another cousin, Nellie Buckley, lived in the upstairs apartment. At the tender age of eighty-five, suddenly my grandmother would have a roommate.

Grandma was the answer to Nellie's prayers. Never married, Nellie "went to business," as they said back in the day, working in Manhattan and had been retired for several years. I recall my grandmother telling us that when she arrived, the cupboard was stocked with canned foods and "TV" dinners that were piled in the freezer. Although she looked ten years older than Grandma, in fact, she was probably a few years her junior. Standing at about 4'10," Nellie couldn't have weighed more than eighty-five to ninety pounds.

There came a time when my family moved from the Bronx to suburban Rockland County. I was working construction jobs in Manhattan and the commute was next to impossible. In conversation with my grandmother, when she asked how I was doing, my father casually mentioned my commuting woes.

"Tell him to come to the phone," she said.

"Neil, why don't you come and stay with us in the Bronx. The #5 train is only two blocks away. You can sleep on the Castro convertible."

It didn't take much convincing and I packed my bags the next day. I was moving in with the *Golden Girls* or you might say a prelude and different version of the hit television series, *Three's Company*.

No bachelor was ever treated better. When I would walk in the door in the winter, still freezing cold from working in buildings under construction with no windows, Grandma would have the hot juice drained from making fresh carrots and celery in the pressure cooker ready for me with a slice of her vintage Irish soda bread.

"That juice needs plenty of salt," she would remind me. "Only take one slice of soda bread or you'll spoil your dinner."

At mealtimes, I would recall the day's events for Nellie and my grandmother and have them roaring at the antics of my fellow carpenters.

I never knew my grandmother to ever take a drink until at a recent family gathering, watching my father making a batch of whiskey sours, she said, "I might try one of those Matty," stunning all those in attendance.

Suddenly, my grandmother realized what she had been missing for eighty plus years and began to enjoy an occasional whiskey sour.

The highlight of each week was Thursday evenings when the *Dean Martin Show* was shown on NBC. Nellie and my grandmother adored

Dean Martin and his regular guests including Rodney Dangerfield, Dom DeLuise, Paul Lynde, Nipsey Russell, and of course, The Golddiggers.

"Oh, I love that Rodney Dangerfield," Nellie would say.

"Neil, would you mind making Nellie and me a whiskey sour?" Grandma asked one night just prior to the beginning of the show.

"Of course, Grandma—two whiskey sours coming up. I might even make it three."

So, there we sat, a nineteen-year-old construction worker and his two eighty plus year-old companions, sipping whisky sours while watching Dino each Thursday. I would look over at their glasses and given Nellie's slight and delicate frame, she had a wooden leg when it came to drink. I wasn't even halfway through, and I could see Nellie wiping the foam from her lips, anxious for a refill.

"I'll have another when you get a chance, Neil."

As I stepped off the train one afternoon, who did I spot walking down the street, fresh from a visit to the liquor store but the "Golden Girls."

"We ran low on whiskey," Nellie said, holding onto my grandmother's arm for dear life.

I am among those fortunate enough to have had a special and loving relationship with a grandparent. I am the person I am today, in large part, due to this very special "Golden Girl."

THE CAREER THAT ALMOST NEVER WAS

THE BEGINNING

We had moved from the Bronx a little north of the city to nearby Rockland County, a migration which was common among families of cops and firemen working in Manhattan and the Bronx, beginning in the 1960s. So, my father traded in a walk across Mosholu Parkway for a twenty-six-mile commute to his firehouse in Bedford Park, in the Bronx.

In our new community, called New City, our neighbors' professions varied condiserably. Mr. Corley worked at IBM. Our next-door neighbor, Mr. Frisaro, was a plumber. Mr. Skelly was a sergeant in the NYPD. Mr. Unger was a high school principal, and Mr. Fishkin owned a Bronx pool hall.

The most well-represented profession in our new development of about fifty or so homes was the FBI. From a young age, I was intrigued.

The Bureau was not only well-represented in our neighborhood, but there was actually a new development in town where there were so many FBI agents living, it was known as 'Hoover Hill,' after then longtime and only director, J. Edgar Hoover.

Of course, my father was a fireman, and we also had members of the family who were cops, so it would have been logical for me to want to follow in their footsteps, but as I grew older, something about the FBI stuck with me.

How many high schoolers and college students actually know what they want to do for the rest of their lives?

For some reason, I did.

It was my senior year of college and nearing decision time as to the best course of getting into the Bureau was concerned. My dad suggested that I speak with a neighbor, Bob Lawson, who was a veteran New York agent.

"I think your best shot at getting in would be to take the test for officer candidate school in one of the branches of service and go that route. The FBI loves veterans and even better, officers," Mr. Lawson began.

"The other option," he noted, "would be to apply as a clerical employee and work in the office for several years. When you become of age and if everything goes well, you will probably be called to attend new agent's training."

In conversation with my dad, a World War II veteran, I opted for joining the service and initially discussed with him that I would like to become a U.S. Marine.

Once my mother got wind of all this, she was not at all happy.

"Why do you have to join the service?" she asked.

"Why not work in the office like Mr. Lawson said would be another option? There are so many people being killed in Vietnam. It's too dangerous. I don't want to see my son killed."

The draft was still in effect at that time, and I had been issued a fairly low number, which meant that I would likely be called, so I held my ground, believing this was the best path.

One thing my mother would not yield on was my joining the Marine Corps. One of our cousins, Denis Flood, had enlisted in the Marine Corps out of high school and had been seriously wounded in Vietnam. For his gallantry, Denis was awarded the Silver Star.

My mother had read that the Marines had the highest casualty rate of all the service branches, and was convinced that if I chose another, it would be better.

So, it was Easter vacation in the spring of 1971, when I traveled to Whitehall Street, in lower Manhattan, to take the Officer Candidate Test for the U.S. Army. I recall being there most of the day and after receiving the news at some point during the Easter break that I had passed, I was called for a physical exam which also went without a hitch.

In the days following my graduation from Niagara University, I again reported to Whitehall Street for my 'pre-induction' physical.

As I stood before the doctor giving me the once-over, he grabbed my hands and twisted my arms with my palms facing up and then down.

He then asked, "Why doesn't your arm straighten out all the way?"

"I dislocated my elbow as a child and apparently the doctor set it incorrectly. It has never straightened out all the way since. It doesn't prevent me from doing anything, really. It's not a concern."

"Well, let me be the judge of that," the doctor replied.

"Take this man to X-ray," he told his assistant.

"Is this necessary, doctor?" I asked.

"I'm volunteering, you know."

Almost totally ignoring me, the doctor yelled, "Next."

So, this sudden turn of events now required a trip back down to Whitehall Street the following day to get the results of my X-ray.

"Young man," the same doctor began.

"See these small things on your elbow? They are floating bone chips. This is a problem. I am rejecting you and exempting you from any military service."

"What!" I yelled.

"Doctor, you can't do this. I'm volunteering. I can't be rejected for physical reasons. I want to go into the FBI. They will never accept me if I'm rejected. Can't I sign some sort of waiver or do something to get this resolved?"

"Not my problem, young man. If you get hurt over there, and it's attributed to your elbow, the government could get sued for millions. You will never serve in the military."

"So, you're saying I'm '4-F'?"

"No, I am classifying you '1-Y,' which means women and children will go before you."

I can still hear the doctor shout again, "Next," as I walked out completely shattered.

My mother was ecstatic, and my father was bewildered and also concerned—would this shocking turn of events prevent me from getting into the FBI?

I put in my application to work as a clerical employee in the New York FBI office almost immediately and in July I was called for an interview.

Maurice 'Moe' Daniels, who was one the agents on the applicant recruiting squad, went through my application thoroughly and all seemed to go well until he reached my draft status.

"1-Y," what's that all about?" he asked.

I related the entire saga, and he even asked me to remove my jacket and roll up my sleeve, so he could have a look at my arm.

"Well, you know, Neil, that if all goes according to plan, and you eventually get called for a new agent's class, you will have to pass a physical exam, and they will definitely focus on your elbow and arm. You are kind of rolling the dice here," Mr. Daniels said.

"I know, I'm willing to take the chance, Mr. Daniels. This means a lot to me."

In late August, I started at the FBI office located on East 69th Street and Third Avenue, in the heart of the fashionable Upper East Side.

Through a friend of my grandmother, an older couple from Sicily rented me a spare room upstairs in their two-family house on Bainbridge Avenue, in the Bronx. I shared a common bathroom with another tenant.

At $25.00 a week, it wasn't exactly an exciting bachelor pad, but it happened to be right around the corner from my father's firehouse, and it was only several blocks to the #4 train to Manhattan.

What a wonderful atmosphere to begin my career. I was working alongside young eighteen to twenty-two-year-old men and women for the most part and enjoying every day. My starting pay: an eye-dropping $4,897.00 per year!

NEIL MORAN

3-159 (Rev. 12-17-69)

UNITED STATES DEPARTMENT OF JUSTICE
FEDERAL BUREAU OF INVESTIGATION
WASHINGTON, D.C. 20535

In Reply, Please Refer to File No.

August 4, 1971

Mr. Neil Francis Moran
31 Mark Lane
New City, New York 10956

Dear Mr. Moran:

    I am pleased to offer you an appointment in the Federal Bureau of Investigation, United States Department of Justice, as a **Clerk** in Grade GS **2**, with salary at the rate of $ **4897** per annum less necessary deductions. This appointment is probationary for a period of one year during which time you will be required to demonstrate your fitness for continued employment. In accepting this appointment you will be expected to remain on duty for a minimum period of one year contingent, of course, upon your maintaining a satisfactory work record. This is necessary in view of the substantial expense involved in the over-all processing of your application and the training which will be afforded you following your entry on duty. Positions in the Federal Bureau of Investigation are excepted by law from the competitive Civil Service, and your acceptance of this appointment will automatically constitute relinquishment during your tenure of any such competitive status you may have acquired. If the date on which you report to this Bureau immediately follows your employment in another Federal agency, you should advise the Personnel Office of that agency the date you will enter on duty in this Bureau, in order to insure that your sick and annual leave is properly transferred or correct payment is made for annual leave. Positions in this Bureau are under the Annual and Sick Leave Act of 1951, as amended.

    Please advise this Bureau at once of your acceptance of this appointment. You should report at your expense and at your earliest possible convenience for oath of office and assignment at 8:15 A.M. on any day except Saturday, Sunday, or a holiday to the Special Agent in Charge, **201 East 69th Street, New York, New York.**

    This letter, which should be considered strictly confidential and given no publicity, should be presented when you report for duty. Evidence to verify the correct date of your birth should also be furnished. It is necessary that you bring your Social Security card with you. If you have had active military service, bring with you a copy of your form DD-214 (Report of Transfer or Discharge). Enclosed are additional instructions which become a part of this appointment offer.

                  Sincerely yours,

                    J. E. Hoover

                  John Edgar Hoover
                  Director

Enc. (5)

Clerk appointment letter, August 4, 1971, signed by J. Edgar Hoover.

Bouncing around to various assignments on different floors of the office, even though there were over a thousand people working there, I liken the atmosphere to the television series *Cheers*, where "Everybody knows your name."

With so many employees, the FBI was a huge presence in the neighborhood. Whether it was the coffee shops in the morning, the delicatessens and restaurants at lunch or the bars like Flanagan's, Gleason's or Sun-Luck Restaurant, there were FBI agents and clerks like me everywhere. Sun-Luck was where, several years later, I would meet my wife.

Every pay Friday, hundreds of employees flooded the Manufacturer's Hanover Bank across the street to cash our paychecks. The tellers never asked for identification, and we knew all of them on a first name basis.

Bank robberies were quite common in New York in those days, and the bank robbery squad was probably the busiest in the office.

One pay Friday, two men, probably most aptly described as, 'The gang that couldn't shoot straight,' thought they would hit the Manufacturer's Hanover on the busiest day for most banks.

As they announced a holdup, no less than ten agents cashing their paychecks immediately pounced on them and foiled the robbery.

I truly enjoyed my clerical years and made lifelong friends in the process. Some of us stayed and waited out what seemed, at times, to be a never-ending process and others left for jobs including the NYPD, FDNY, ATF, DEA, Naval Intelligence, American Express, Kroll Investigations, and what is known in the FBI as the 'private sector.'

In early 1975, I was notified that to fill classes for new agent's training at the FBI Academy, I was being scheduled for a physical exam.

D-Day for me arrived.

To say I was apprehensive was an understatement.

The physical exam was held at a facility in lower Manhattan called, "Public Health."

As I moved from station to station, all the routine things were performed.

I was now standing in front of the standard eye chart and the nurse asked if I wore glasses.

"Yes, I do. It's a slight correction," I began.

"Twenty over forty in one eye and twenty over sixty in the other."

There was no problem as far as the Bureau was concerned, if my vision was correctable to twenty-twenty.

She then took my vision while wearing my glasses. When I was done, she said nothing.

As we moved to the next station, the nurse said, "Okay, now I'll take your blood pressure."

As she wrapped the Velcro around my bicep, the results of what she had completed thus far were in front of me and I attempted to read them upside down. I thought I saw that for my corrected vision I was twenty over thirty in one eye and twenty over forty for the other.

I suddenly felt faint. I could feel my normally low blood pressure elevate instantly.

"Miss," I began, "Does that say my corrected vision is not perfect or am I reading it wrong?"

"No, you're correct, it's not perfect."

"I need my vision to be twenty-twenty. I won't get accepted without it," I continued.

Now somewhat put out by the whole thing but continuing squeezing the ball that tightened the Velcro, the nurse then asked, "Do you suffer from high blood pressure?"

"No, I don't. As a matter of fact, my blood pressure is always very low," I replied.

"Well, it's really up there now."

As the nurse guided me back to the eye chart area, she saw me standing as I placed my hand over my eye and said, "What are you doing back there? That's not the right spot. Move up here where you were before."

"This is where I was standing before when you tested me," I shot back.

"Oh no, you should be up here. No wonder you didn't pass."

I did pass and then the nurse re-did my blood pressure and said, "Wow, your pressure is low. Are you sure you're awake?"

Well, with that hurdle cleared, it was time to see the doctor.

"Mr. Moran, what's this business with '1-Y' and your elbow?"

After relating the entire saga at Whitehall Street years earlier, I was already encouraged by what seemed to be a positive attitude, when he asked if I was looking forward to becoming an FBI agent.

After whacking my arm and elbow area several times, he saw that I was unable to straighten my arm completely and asked, "Does this restrict you from doing anything?"

"No, not at all, doctor. Never has. I can give you fifty pushups right now if that helps."

"No, not necessary right now," he said.

"Okay, I'm going to tuck my elbows into my hips with fists facing up. What I want you to do is try and lift me off the ground by my elbows. I just want to see if you have any problem doing that."

The doctor was probably about six feet tall and weighed maybe 215 pounds. I weighed about 150 pounds with all my clothes on.

I thought, this is the one shot you have, don't blow it.

"Anytime you're ready son, go ahead."

One often hears of episodes of superhuman strength such as when a person is trapped under a car and a good Samaritan comes along and lifts the car right off the ground.

Although this lacked the life and death aspect, I rated this as one of those occasions.

I nearly put the doctor through the ceiling.

"Whoa, easy! Okay, you can put me down. Well, I can see that this injury hasn't hampered you in the least. Nothing the matter with that arm. Best of luck, son. I hope it works out for you."

In April, I received word that I would be in the May 5th new agent's class at the FBI Academy.

Had I never had the curiosity to look at the eye exam results and had the doctor not liked the way I parted my hair that day, this easily could have been the career that never was.

SMOOTH AS SWEET CREAM

It was, at that juncture, the most important day of my young life. The April 24, 1975, letter read, in part:

Dear Mr. Moran

You are offered a probationary appointment in the Federal Bureau of Investigation, United States Department of Justice, as a Special Agent, Grade GS10, $14,117 per annum less 7 and one-half percent deduction for retirement purposes.

Should you accept, you are directed to report for oath of office and assignment to Room 625, Old Post Office Building, 12th Street and Pennsylvania Avenue, Northwest, Washington, D.C. at 9:00 a.m. on May 5, 1975.

Sincerely yours,
Clarence M. Kelly
Director

On May 5, 1975, at age twenty-five, along with twenty-four men who would become my new classmates, we were sworn in as special agents of the Federal Bureau of Investigation.

STORIES

3-302a (Rev. 3-28-75)
OFFICE OF THE DIRECTOR

UNITED STATES DEPARTMENT OF JUSTICE

FEDERAL BUREAU OF INVESTIGATION

WASHINGTON, D.C. 20535

April 24, 1975

Mr. Neil Francis Moran
Federal Bureau of Investigation
New York, New York

Dear Mr. Moran:

You are offered a probationary appointment in the Federal Bureau of Investigation, United States Department of Justice, as a Special Agent, Grade GS**10**, **$14,117** per annum less 7 1/2% deduction for retirement purposes. Following assignment to a field office, additional compensation in the amount of **$3536** per year may be earned for overtime performance in connection with official duties provided certain necessary requirements are met. Your salary will also be subject to the necessary Federal Withholding Tax. Positions in the Federal Bureau of Investigation are excepted by law from the competitive Civil Service, in view of which your acceptance of this appointment will automatically constitute relinquishment during your tenure of any such competitive status you may have acquired. This appointment is subject to cancellation or postponement at any time prior to your entry on duty. In accepting this appointment, you will be expected to remain on duty for a minimum period of three years contingent upon your maintaining a satisfactory work record. This appointment letter, which should be considered strictly confidential and given no publicity, should be presented when you report for oath of office.

Inasmuch as this appointment is probationary for a period of one year, after which it will become permanent, it will be necessary for you to demonstrate during the probationary period your fitness for continued employment in the Federal Bureau of Investigation. It is understood you are to proceed on orders to any part of the United States or its possessions where the exigencies of the service may require and it should be clearly understood that you will continue to be completely available for any assignment whenever and wherever the needs of the service demand. Further, you cannot expect an assignment to an office of your own preference. You should, therefore, so arrange your personal matters before taking oath of office that you will be able to accept any assignment wherever the exigencies of the service may require. Any expenses incurred in proceeding to Washington, D. C., to assume your official duties must be borne by you.

Carefully read the additional information enclosed with this letter and notify this Bureau by return mail if this appointment is accepted, otherwise it will be canceled. Should you accept, you are directed to report for oath of office and assignment to Room 625, Old Post Office Building, 12th Street and Pennsylvania Avenue, Northwest, Washington, D. C., at 9 A. M. on **May 5, 1975.**

Sincerely yours,

Clarence M. Kelley
Director

Enc. (4)

Agent appointment letter, April 24, 1975.

FBI Academy, Quantico VA. PHOTO CREDIT: FBI.GOV

This brief ceremony took place at FBI Headquarters, in Washington, DC, and within the hour, we were whisked away on what looked like an old school bus from the *Andy Griffith Show*. So much for rolling out the red carpet for these newly sworn defenders of America.

Our destination was an hour away, the U.S. Marine Corps Base, at Quantico, Virginia. For the next sixteen weeks, we would receive training at the FBI Academy, housed within the confines of the base.

Physical training, including defensive tactics and arrest techniques, firearms and legal instruction, investigative and interview methods, plus handling of informants were some of the areas that occupied our days. Having attended college in upstate New York, I had never been exposed to people from around the country and our class certainly was well-represented in every region.

My roommate, Tom Olmstead, an attorney, thirty-four with four children, had been an LAPD sergeant and decided he no longer wanted to live in Los Angeles.

My suitemates, Al McCulloch from Charlotte, had worked at a local bank and Parker Taylor from Tennessee, like me, had been a clerk in the FBI office. We also had several classmates from Florida, one from Missouri, a Mormon from Salt Lake City, a few from the Boston area, and others.

The FBI has traditionally hired many veterans, especially those that had served in the Marine Corps. Our class was no different, including several that had served in Vietnam.

The FBI at that time was much the same as any law enforcement agency in that the preponderance of hires were male. Although that has changed significantly since 1975, during my tenure at Quantico, there were very few females filling the class rosters. Our class had no women.

The instructors and counselors were quick to establish an atmosphere of camaraderie and competition within each class and often pitted one against another.

As was my routine at that time, at the conclusion of each day, I went to the gym and changed into my running gear. I would navigate the backroads of the Marine Corps base, often running into small groups of officer candidates and enlisted men.

It didn't take but a few weeks for two of the counselors to get wind of the fact that there were some fair runners amid the new recruits.

Training at the FBI Academy, Quantico, Virginia. PHOTO CREDIT: FBI.GOV

Alan V. MacDonald, Quantico classmate and Neil Moran's first partner pictured in his beloved hometown, Swampscott, Massachusetts.

Several of the counselors arranged for a head-to-head race between Dan Jablonski, from Kansas and Neil Moran from New York. Dan was in the class two weeks ahead of us.

It was America's Heartland v. The Bronx.

The race, which would be two miles, was to be held at 7:00 a.m. on 'Hoover Road,' in the rear of the FBI Academy, which was utilized for each day's physical training.

The buzz began to build during the days leading up to the race. One day, during a firearms session, the instructor located high above in a tower, bellowed out that he had heard that Moran had little chance of winning the two-mile race—again, anything to stir up a little competitiveness amongst the classes.

Days later, as the gun went off precisely at 7:00 a.m., a fair number of other trainees, instructors, and counselors came out to cheer on the competitors for the Race of the Century.

At the first mile, we were neck and neck, and it remained that way until the very end when I was fortunate to come out slightly ahead of Dan.

We both narrowly missed the academy record by a second or so.

It didn't take all that long before people with leadership qualities stepped forward to play a role in supporting their classmates. One such leader in our class was Alan V. MacDonald or what he later became known to those who would work with him, "Alan V."

Al was born in December 1944, in Lynn, Massachusetts.

"Lynn, Lynn, the city of sin," I can still hear him say, whenever he referred to his birthplace.

One of two boys, raised in nearby Swampscott, Al joined St. John's Seminary, in Boston after high school and finished at Salem State College, when he decided that he would put his future as a Catholic priest on hold.

Al joined the Marine Corps, became an officer and was a combat veteran of the war in Vietnam. He attained the rank of captain and was awarded a Bronze Star with a Combat V for valorous actions in direct contact with the enemy.

After leaving the service, Al joined the Swampscott Fire Department and along the way found time to earn his law degree at Boston College. A champion debater in high school, Al had done more at age thirty than many achieve in a lifetime.

There wasn't a day that went by when our class counselors didn't remind everyone that a certain grade (I believe it was 80) had to be achieved on each exam or risk dismissal. This also went for physical training.

"Climb up that rope," or "Pick up that pace."

I can hear our instructor bellowing out orders like these to some of my classmates who struggled in all physical things.

There were a fair number of us who had never received any legal training and Al took it upon himself to hold regular evening sessions in one of the classrooms, to review and clarify items likely to be the focus of the next exam. He had a deep and commanding voice with a heavy Boston accent, one that you might expect to hear doing voiceovers on the radio.

It was our tenth week of training, which traditionally marked the dramatic opening of sealed envelopes containing our field office destination upon graduation.

The amphitheater was packed with counselors from other classes, instructors, and administrative staff, who always seemed to enjoy the shocks on many of the faces when the envelopes were opened.

One of the counselors, a native of Birmingham, Alabama, clearly had an issue with my accent during my sixteen weeks and there wasn't a day that went by that he would utter, "Moran, they are gonna love that New York accent in Tupelo, Mississippi."

He did have me scared half to death.

In alphabetical order, Al proceeded me and didn't seem at all upset when he announced that New York City was his destination.

With the counselor from Birmingham smoking his pipe looking on, I couldn't resist when I opened the envelope uttering, "Birmingham, Alabama."

There was a collective gasp from the attendees, and I thought the counselor would swallow his pipe. I then smiled and said, "Sorry, I couldn't resist, actually I'm headed back to New York City."

So, Al and I, joined by three classmates, fellow New York clerk Don Weber, Bill Doherty and Cape Cod native Larry Ferreira were off to New York for our first assignment.

At the outset, our supervisor had us paired with senior agents who would take us out on 'leads' in cases they were working.

We began to work many investigations where members of the armed forces had 'deserted' or went AWOL. Not exactly glamorous as far as the seasoned agents were concerned, but for people like Al and me, we thought we won the lottery. It wasn't before long, at our urging, that the senior agents were reassigning many of the deserter cases to the two of us.

Al was assigned one such case on a deserter from the 101st Airborne's Air Assault Team, the Screaming Eagles.

We tracked him down to a sixth-floor apartment on Sedgwick Avenue, in the Fordham section of the Bronx, only a short distance from where I grew up. The two of us scoped out the building the day before and surprisingly, there was no fire escape for him to make his getaway. We convinced our supervisor the two of us could handle this alone, so the next morning we appeared at his door at 5:00 a.m.

Al in his unmistakable voice uttered, "This is the FBI, open the door and come out with your hands above your head. You are surrounded; there is no means of escape."

There was clearly someone in the apartment as we could hear some shuffling followed by silence. We then sought out the superintendent of the building, (he wasn't pleased at 5:00 a.m.), who let us in with a master key.

The search of the apartment failed to locate anyone. While checking the back bedroom, we saw the window fully open and the curtains blowing from the incoming breeze. As we looked out the window into a vacant lot, we thought there was no way that he could jump out a window six stories and get away.

Al then pointed to the Screaming Eagle jacket draped over a chair. "Could it be possible?" I asked.

A search of some papers on a nightstand revealed a notation that the subject had an appointment in Manhattan at 1:00 p.m. that day to receive his public assistance check. We later made our way to the location and when his name was called, we approached him. Al, acting as though he was about to arrest John Dillinger, blurted out, "It's all over, Douglas."

We obviously were curious as to Douglas's means of escape.

"I jumped out the window, what do you think?"

"How do you feel?" I asked.

"My neck hurts, but I'll live."

It was New Year's Eve and 1978 was about to end.

Only several weeks earlier, the Lufthansa Airline terminal at JFK Airport, in Queens, had $6.2 million stolen by armed thieves, which at that time was the largest cash robbery in U.S. history. All Christmas vacation days were cancelled, and a full court press was applied on those we believed to be suspects.

I was assigned to the 10:00 p.m. to 6:00 a.m. shift, along with Al, George Hanna, Bob Joyce and Andy Conlin. We were waiting for our subjects to move, which, on a terrible evening with sleet and light snow falling, was unlikely.

George Hanna and Al had the 'standby' duty which meant that anything that occurred in the off hours would require them to respond.

With no cellphones in the 1970s, the radio operator requested that Al call the office. Within a few minutes, he returned and announced that an anonymous caller had stated that several men were unloading what was believed to be stolen liquor into a basement of a hardware store in Brooklyn. The two of them would have to break off our surveillance.

George and Al, with some additional assistance from the office, arrested four men, including one future Lucchese LCN (*La Cosa Nostra*—Italian for "Our Thing") Crime Family capo, Peter 'Fat Pete' Chiodo.

It was about a year later that the four men went to trial before U.S. District Court Judge Jacob Mischler. Judge Mischler, who sat in Brooklyn's Eastern District of New York, was a no-nonsense jurist who was very familiar with our squad which exclusively handled truck hijackings, then the 'bread and butter' of organized crime. Each of the four defendants had their own attorneys, and were joined by many family members, which led to a circus type atmosphere.

Among the government supporters in the courtroom were colleagues of the assistant United States attorney handling the case, members of our squad and what are known as 'courtroom buffs.'

These were mostly groups of men who had retired from many professions and came to the courthouse each day looking for interesting trials to attend and often lending their observations to agents and prosecutors during breaks. Our squad, a fixture at the courthouse, was a favorite of the buffs, who were very pro prosecution.

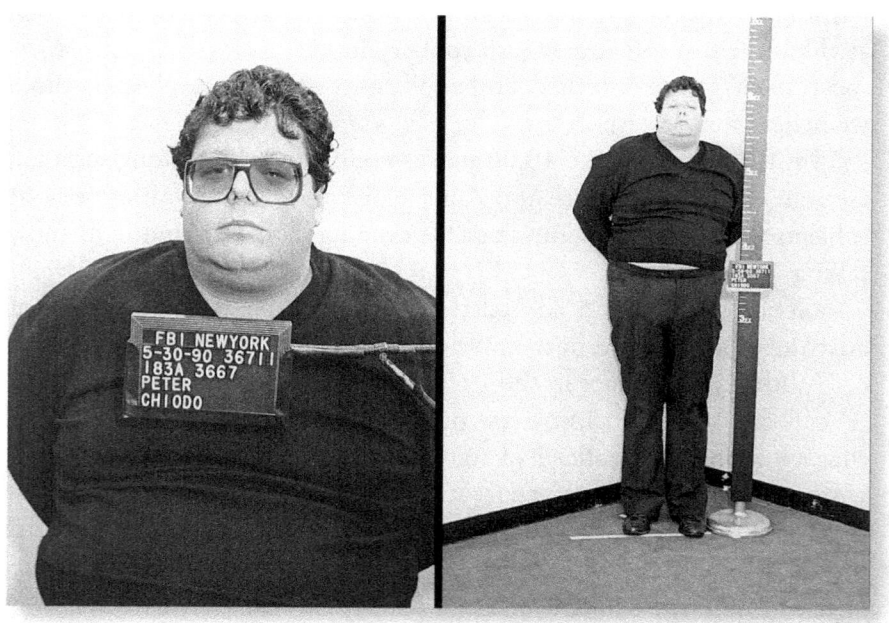

Peter "Fat Pete" Chiodo

Where Al was legendary amongst his peers was testifying in court. Whereas many agents, especially when they are new and inexperienced, are terrified of cross examinations by defense attorneys, who relish the opportunity to trip up an FBI agent, Al loved the challenge and could spar in a highly professional, erudite and respectful manner with the best.

On direct examination, Al MacDonald was masterful. Looking square at the jury in a calm and measured tone, he walked them through that evening and the events leading to and including the arrest, as well as the observations he made.

When asked to describe the weather conditions, rather than simply state that it was a combination of sleet and snow, Al spoke about the dangerously slippery conditions that had formed a "thin glaze" of ice on the streets of Brooklyn that evening, seemingly with the knowledge and expertise of a seasoned television meteorologist.

Now it was the defense counsel's turn.

Try as they might, one by one, each attorney attempted, in vain, to trip Al up and establish one lone inconsistency in his testimony. When asked to describe a schematic that the government had introduced depicting who was where on that evening, in response, Al asked if he might leave the stand to further clarify the scenario.

"Sure, agent MacDonald, why don't you educate us all."

What a mistake.

With the skill of a college professor, standing before an easel with a pointer in hand, Al walked the judge, jury and onlookers, seemingly hanging on his every word, through every step, as defense counsel collectively held their heads in hand in disgust.

Judge Mischler could not hide his approval.

This was the late 1970s and smack in the middle of the mini-skirt era. Several of the defendant's wives, who faithfully attended trial each day, were quite attractive and shall we say, dressed very stylishly.

One appeared to lack the focus to sit for testimony for more than fifteen minutes at a time and continued, from her front row seat, to get up, walk across and out of the courtroom. Full disclosure, she had the eyes of just about everyone, including all the agents, on each of her trips.

In another five to ten minutes, everyone could hear her four-inch spiked heels getting closer as she would re-enter and take her seat. The judge had had quite enough.

"Young lady, who are you?" Judge Mischler yelled, exploding out of his chair and now standing behind the bench with both hands on his hips.

"I'm, Angelina Greco, Mario Greco's wife."

After identifying herself as the wife of one of the defendants, the judge retorted, "Mrs. Greco, up and down, up and down, you've been 'sashaying' back and forth in this courtroom all morning. I can't have this, the jury can't have it, and the gallery can't have it. Either you wait outside or make your trips less frequent. Most of all you are distracting the witnesses. Isn't that right Agent MacDonald?"

The normally unflappable Al MacDonald was now completely flummoxed.

Judge Mischler, perhaps not wanting to appear too heavy handed with his admonition of Mrs. Greco, may have been looking for some support and now dumped this in Al's lap.

Completely red in the face and now visibly nervous, Al meekly uttered, "Yes, I suppose so your honor."

We later learned from Al, that defense counsel, whose cross examination had been interrupted, with a hand covering his mouth whispered to Al, "Would you have dared to say no?"

During the next break, as our squad encircled Al outside the courtroom discussing the morning events, the 'sashayer' approached us.

Glaring at Al, she said, "Was I bothering you, Agent MacDonald?" and promptly walked away in a huff.

In summation, one of the defense attorneys recalled Al's testimony.

"And then there was Agent MacDonald, ladies and gentlemen, a professional witness if I've ever seen one. His testimony was as smooth as sweet cream."

It was as if he was asking the jury to discount Al's testimony because he was essentially a 'hired gun' and a cut above everyone else. The jury deliberated for only an hour: guilty on all counts.

Al later went on to join a task force with the NYPD that was formed to investigate the sexual exploitation of children. He had great success there, but he expressed frustration at what he felt was a lack of support from our senior management.

In 1987, Al took a transfer to the FBI office in Boston.

A confirmed bachelor, he was very devoted to his mother, who was in her 80s, and wanted to be closer to her.

We were all in shock and saddened when, in May 1989, we learned that while vacationing in Scotland with his mom, Al succumbed to an aortic aneurism at only age forty-four.

It was a proud moment when I was asked by the family to serve as a pall bearer at his funeral in Swampscott, which was attended by several thousand people, including members of many law enforcement agencies across New England.

Retired Supervisory Special Agent Kenneth V. Lanning was in the FBI for more than thirty years before he retired in 2000. He specialized in the study of the sexual victimization of children after being transferred to the FBI Academy in Quantico, Virginia, and was assigned to the FBI Behavioral Science Unit.

Movie enthusiasts were introduced to the Behavioral Science Unit in the 1991 chilling thriller, *Silence of the Lambs*, where new agent trainee, Clarice Starling, played by Jodie Foster, is recruited by Jack Crawford, a BSU supervisor, to assist the unit in solving a string of murders, by attempting to match wits with a psychopathic cannibalistic killer, Hannibal Lecter, played by Sir Anthony Hopkins.

"During the time I was assigned to the BSU, I organized training at the FBI Academy concerning sexual victimization of children and interacted with the Missing and Exploited Children's Task Force in New York City," Mr. Lanning began.

"This Task Force was made up of a group of FBI agents from the New York Field Office and detectives from the NYPD. As I interacted with the NY Task Force, the unanimous feedback I got from all the members was that Al MacDonald was in essence the heart and soul of the group, the glue that held it together and made it work better. He was respected and admired by all the agents and detectives."

"I was devastated to hear the news," Mr. Lanning recalled, upon learning that Al had passed away.

"The FBI lost an agent with important, rare, and refined investigative skills. More important, those who knew him lost a good, kind, and caring person who was always willing to share with and help others. Not sure how I could honor two such special agents in Boston, I decided to add a special dedication to a training monograph I had just written for the National Center for Missing & Exploited Children. The two editions of my monograph *Child Sex Rings: A Behavioral Analysis* are dedicated 'To the memory of two FBI agents who devoted their professional lives to helping sexually exploited children: Leo E. Brunnick, FBI Boston and Alan V. MacDonald, FBI Boston.'"

Yes, there was only one "Alan V."—He was truly as "smooth as sweet cream."

ARRIVAL IN NEW YORK

On August 20, 1975, in a ceremony at the FBI Academy, in Quantico Virginia, twenty-four classmates and I received our 'credentials' or identification as duly sworn special agents of the Federal Bureau of Investigation. In between that time and my first day reporting to what New York agents like to think of as the Bureau's 'Flagship office,' I must have read the inscription on my identification fifty times:

> *This is to certify that Neil F. Moran whose signature and photograph appear hereon, is a regularly appointed Special Agent of the Federal Bureau of Investigation, United States Department of Justice, and as such is charged with the duty of investigating violations of the laws of the United States collecting evidence in cases in which the United States is or may be a party in interest, and performing other duties imposed upon him by law*
>
> *Office of the Director*
> *Federal Bureau of Investigation*
> *By Order of:*
> *The Attorney General*
> *Of The United States*

Top: Graduation Ceremony and receipt of credentials, FBI Academy, Quantico, VA, August 20, 1975. Bottom: My credentials.

I had just completed sixteen weeks of training and enjoyed every single day. I had to pinch myself each morning thinking I was getting paid to go to class, attend firearms and fitness training and eat three very decent meals. Frankly, I would have done it for nothing!

It was only until recently that FBI headquarters began assigning those graduating from new agents training to New York. The office had worked out a program that the new people would spend six months on the prestigious criminal division, where most of the new agents hoped to land. Bank robberies, airplane hijackings, fugitives, truck hijackings, kidnappings, bombings, and extortion were just some of the violations that lay ahead for all of us. There were five of us from our class dubbed '75-6,' who were sent to New York. Al MacDonald and I were assigned to a very active squad whose primary responsibility was terrorist bombings.

The *Fuerzas Armadas de Liberación Nacional* or Armed Forces of National Liberation, better known as the FALN were the most active group. This Puerto Rican separatist organization advocated independence from the U.S. Earlier in the year, they had claimed responsibility for the noontime bombing of historic Fraunces Tavern in lower Manhattan, killing four patrons as they ate lunch. They were linked to 120 bombings throughout the U.S. during their terror spree from the mid-1970s to the mid-1980s.

We never knew what we would be doing from one day to the next. I think our supervisor, George Tempro, was a bit nervous having such young agents on the squad and insisted that we be with a senior agent at all times.

Bank robberies were rampant in New York at that time. It wasn't uncommon to have five or six in one day. At any given time, groups of agents would be flying out of the office with vests and shotguns in hand to respond to a situation.

On my second day, George Tempro summoned me into his office and asked, "How would you like to work bank robbery rover today?" Bank robbery rover was a team of two agents who drove around the city waiting for a bank alarm to come over the air. It made more sense than having agents always responding from the office and arriving at the scene ninety minutes after the fact.

As soon as I introduced myself to the two agents who had duty that day, I could sense that they weren't all that thrilled about having me ride with them in the back seat. It wasn't more that an hour after we crossed over the Brooklyn Bridge into tony Brooklyn Heights, that we heard, "Ten thirty-seven, Manufacturers Hanover Bank, Hylan Boulevard, Staten Island—Bank robbery rover responding?"

"Ten-four, Rover enroute."

One of the agents threw the light on top of the roof and the driver started the siren. With a lot of road ahead, it was like the parting of the Red Sea. New Yorkers, who have often had the reputation of not being cooperative at the sound of a siren, seemed to be making every effort to dispel that notion.

It was probably a good twenty-five minutes before we arrived. As we pulled into the parking lot, there were at least five NYPD marked cars and several unmarked vehicles. As we entered the bank, one of the agents recognized an NYPD sergeant from the Major Case Squad.

"What do we have, sarge?" he asked.

"Two guys with guns. One vaulted over the counter and the other put a gun to the teller's head. They're not sure how much they got away with. One of the tellers did get a partial plate, so we do have something. The uniforms got here first and basically just tried calming everyone down. We haven't asked for statements yet. We figured we'd wait for you guys."

"Well, you are in luck today. We have a new guy here, and this is his second day on the job. I'm sure he'll have this solved in about thirty minutes," one of the agents said.

Admittedly, I was nervous enough without the smart-ass remarks, but my parents always taught us that a smile, even in awkward and uncomfortable situations, generally is the best course.

After introducing myself to the sergeant, he suggested that I begin interviewing the tellers while his detectives and the agents begin speaking with the customers, which numbered about ten to fifteen.

I was surprised when the first teller didn't know if the gunmen were black or white.

"I think one of them was about 6'1" and the other about 5'10"," said one teller. Another had them both at 5'6" to 5'7." Stress will do that to you as I began to learn.

One senior member of our squad, Tom O'Hara, took a liking to me and asked if I would like to join him to pay a visit to one of his informants up in the Bronx.

"Sure, Tom, I would love to, thanks."

Before heading to the Bronx, we had to run down a lead in Brooklyn.

Now for Bronx born people, Brooklyn and Queens are foreign territories, much the same as the Bronx is for them.

"How well do you know Brooklyn, Neil?" Tom asked, as we navigated the Interboro Parkway and eventually onto Eastern Parkway in Mike Tyson territory, Brownsville.

"About as well as I know Egypt," I replied.

Tom, a proud Brooklynite, pointed out all the landmarks as we worked our way to the Prospect Park section.

"Brooklyn is known as the borough of churches," Tom noted. "Supposedly, with more houses of worship than any other borough."

Tom knew the names of every one of them, Catholic, Episcopal, Lutheran, Presbyterian, as well as every synagogue.

As we later arrived in the Bronx, I found myself in familiar territory, on the east side of the Bronx River Parkway, across from the Bronx Zoo.

"I spent my early years not too far from here," I said.

We spent about thirty minutes with his informant and then Tom asked me to direct him to my old neighborhood. That's the type of guy he was, very interested in everything New York, especially things with which he wasn't familiar.

"That's my father's firehouse," I pointed out, as we drove across Bedford Park Boulevard and onto Briggs Avenue. "Too bad he isn't working today. He would love to meet you."

With that, I saw three or four of my father's colleagues chatting with people from the neighborhood standing out in front of the firehouse. "Pull over, Tom, I know all those guys."

As I exited the car, complete with suit and tie, I had known most of these firemen since I was a child. They all knew I was in the FBI and had just completed my training.

"Oh my God, look who it is, Neilly boy, how are you doing?" Neil Flanagan yelled.

"Good, Mr. Flanagan, really good." I had known Neil Flanagan for my entire life, and it was always Mr. Flanagan, so in that regard, that's the way it would remain.

"Your dad has been keeping us up to speed on Quantico. Sounds like you were enjoying it last I heard."

I introduced Tom to everyone, and we turned down their gracious invitation to have coffee with them in the kitchen.

Tom wouldn't leave the Bronx until he saw my old parish and school, St. Brendan's.

"Not bad," Tom said as we drove past, "but nothing like the Brooklyn churches." *Typical Brooklynite*, I thought.

It was only days later, on September 5, 1975, that there was an attempted assassination on the life of President Gerald Ford, in Sacramento, California, which he survived. The assailant was identified as Lynette "Squeaky" Fromme, an avowed member of the Charles Manson Family, who in 1969 murdered actress Sharon Tate and several others.

Ms. Fromme and other members of the Manson Family started a group called the International People's Court of Retribution, which targeted executives who they felt were operating companies, believed to be harming the environment.

Ms. Fromme said she tried to kill President Ford to win favor with Charles Manson.

Presidential assassination attempts don't occur that often but when they do, the statute is one that is the FBI's responsibility.

Lynette "Squeaky" Fromme. YOUTUBE

In this instance, the Sacramento office would be known as the 'Office of Origin,' or where the crime occurred. During their investigation, the originating office sends out 'leads' to any of the FBI offices where further investigation is required, to put a prosecutable case together.

I recall sitting in the office, days after the assassination attempt, when Tom O'Hara came over and asked, "Want to work on the President Ford assassination attempt, kid?"

"You're kidding," I replied.

"No, no, apparently Sacramento pulled the home phone records of the defendant Squeaky Fromme, and we have a lead to go interview somebody on the Upper West Side (Manhattan) and see what the connection might be. Are you ready?"

"Wow, of course, let's go!"

As we wound our way through Central Park, we parked somewhere in the west 70s, near the park, in other words, the high rent district.

We walked up to the address and were greeted by the doorman.

"Help you gentlemen?" he asked.

As we took our credentials out of our jacket pockets, Tom said, "Yes, Tom O'Hara and Neil Moran, FBI."

Admittedly, I still had to pinch myself thinking I'm about to work on something the whole country is talking about.

As was the case for the thousands of times I was to repeat this process for the remainder of my career, it always did get a rise out of people.

"FBI, my goodness, is everything okay? What's this all about?" he asked, very typical of New York doormen, who were often the eyes and ears of neighborhood 'goings ons.' Just watch any *Law-and-Order* episode and count the number of doormen who provide tips to the NYPD.

"Does Macy's tell Gimbels?" Tom replied in typical New York fashion.

"I suppose they don't, fair enough," the doorman said.

I can't recall the party's name, but the phone was listed to a woman and the doorman immediately knew the apartment and directed us inside.

"And we would appreciate you not calling upstairs to warn her we're coming," Tom said.

"I won't," the doorman said.

We knocked on the door, a woman asked who we were, and Tom put his credentials up to the peephole and said, "FBI, can we have a moment please?"

The woman, probably in her early to mid-40s, appeared a bit nervous as we walked in.

"What's this all about?" she asked.

Tom explained that the FBI was investigating the recent attempt on President Ford's life and the telephone records of her alleged assailant reflected a telephone call to this apartment, sometime in the very early a.m. hours. We asked quite a few questions, but nothing seemed to resonate. The woman was completely at a loss, and it appeared as though she was telling the truth.

"Who lives with you here, if I can ask?" Tom said.

"I'm divorced, so just my daughter and me."

"How old is your daughter?"

"She just turned sixteen."

"Is she by any chance here?"

"Honey, would you come out for a second, please," she called.

As the young girl walked into the living room, the woman said, "These gentlemen are from the FBI. They are trying to track down a phone call they say came from California at about 3:00 a.m. one morning last week. Do you remember getting a call that early?"

"According to the phone records, the call only lasted two minutes so it wouldn't appear that it was a wrong number, but somebody here talked to someone at that number for sure," Tom said.

"Oh, mommy wait; remember I told you I answered the phone and there was a woman on the line who had read my article that was published in the magazine and complimented me? I was half asleep and when I told you the next day you said you never heard it. The woman asked if she could have my address, so she could write me a thank you note."

"Did she ever write that note," Tom asked.

"Yes, I have it inside," she said.

As her daughter left the room to retrieve the note, the woman explained that the daughter had submitted an article to a conservation magazine outlining how the environment was being slowly harmed. With that, the woman retrieved a copy of the magazine and directed us to the article. As we looked at the magazine, the daughter reappeared with a postcard.

The message apologized for waking the young woman at such an early hour and complimented her for drawing attention to the environment. It ended with asking that she keep up the good work. The post card was signed "Squeaky."

"We're going to have to hold on to this for possible evidence in the case. We would also like a copy of the magazine. I presume you have others?" Tom said.

Lynette "Squeaky" Fromme was ultimately convicted of the attempted murder of President Ford and was sentenced to life in prison in West Virginia. Ms. Fromme was released from prison in 2009.

A little over two weeks after Squeaky Fromme's failed attempted assassination, another California woman, Sarah Jane Moore, tried to assassinate President Ford in San Francisco. Although Ms. Moore's attempt failed, she did manage to get off a shot but was thwarted by another onlooker.

Tom O'Hara, now the squad's 'go-to guy' on presidential assassinations was assigned all the leads and I was fortunate in covering them with him. Some of our stops included the psychiatric ward of Bellevue Hospital, where Ms. Moore had been committed for a time, following a suicide attempt in the 1950s. We then tracked down an NYPD lieutenant, who, as a young beat cop, had responded to Ms. Moore's attempted suicide. The shock on his face when we informed him of the connection was something I wouldn't soon forget.

Ms. Moore was sentenced to her full term in the same facility as Squeaky Fromme. In 2007, she was released from prison after serving thirty-two years.

A FALLEN COMRADE

The primary responsibility of my first squad was the investigation of terrorist bombings, which were quite common in the 1970s.

As previously outlined, our primary nemesis was the *"Fuerzas Armadas de Liberacion Nationale Puertorriquena"* or the FALN.

Among the FALN's targets were financial institutions, federal buildings, military installations, and even NYPD headquarters in lower Manhattan on New Year's Eve.

It was late fall and Saturday night had turned into Sunday morning as I drove my '69 Volkswagen under the Broadway elevated train tracks in the shadows of Van Cortland Park on my way home in the Bronx, after an evening with friends.

My AM radio, tuned to WCBS News Radio 880, reported that bombs had exploded at the corner of West 57th Street and Seventh Avenue in Manhattan. NYPD and FDNY were on the scene. I spotted a phone booth just opposite Gaelic Park, double-parked my car and called the office.

"Yes, we are in the process of calling everyone on your squad," the night switchboard operator began.

"You should head down to the scene in midtown. Other agents will join you. That's about all we know now."

I wound down the Henry Hudson Parkway, onto the West Side Highway, got off at West 57th Street and made my way east toward midtown. At the ungodly hour of 3:00 a.m., I encountered little or no traffic.

I arrived at a chaotic scene of police vehicles and fire engines everywhere I looked, as well as dozens of uniformed personnel. There are few cities in the world, while most of the country sleeps, where thousands of its public servants go about their business in an almost cavalier fashion, no matter how tragic or dangerous the circumstances. It's what these unusually brave and dedicated men and women do.

I parked my Volkswagen at the first available space I could find, which just happened to be on the sidewalk. With perimeters yet to be set up, I literally could have been anyone as I wandered toward the heart of the action. Two banks on opposite sides of the intersection had suffered significant damage with smoke everywhere as the FDNY finished up with what little fires remained.

"Can I help you?" an officer looking to be in his late twenties, clad in an NYPD Bomb Squad jacket asked.

At twenty-five, and probably at the time a quite boyish twenty-five, still not really believing that I was doing this for a living and no doubt failing very much to look the part, I replied, "Neil Moran, FBI. I'm with the squad that handles bombings."

Fumbling for my identification, the officer said, "You're the first 'fed' to arrive, Brian Murray's my name. Nice to meet you, Neil. Do you want to tag along with me for a bit until your guys show up?"

With police officer Murray's kind offer, for at least the next forty-five minutes, I was the lone representative of the U.S. Government investigating a terrorist bombing, later claimed by the FALN.

Even as the senior members of our squad trickled in, once they saw that I was working with police officer Murray, they suggested I continue as they went about their business.

As we combed through debris, searching for evidence with members of the NYPD's Arson and Explosion unit, Brian couldn't have been more affable and welcoming. Happily married to a girl from the Bronx (good taste in women I thought) and living on Long Island with two little boys, he peppered me with questions about my training in Quantico and how I was liking the FBI so far. He had served in Vietnam and specialized in working with explosive devices.

When things wound down and the city awakened and onlookers began to gawk, I felt as though I had met a friend I hadn't seen in a few years and just spent the night catching up. The two of us had really hit it off.

"I'm sure we'll see each other again at the next bombing, Neil," Brian said, shaking my hand.

"Good luck."

He was indeed correct. Anti-Castro Cubans planting a bomb at the Cuban Mission to the United Nations, the Jewish Defense League planting pipe bombs at Soviet installations, including their mission to the U.N. and Aeroflot Airline offices on Fifth Avenue were just some of the events where Brian and I would again meet, mostly at times while the city slept.

As I knew my tenure working on my first assignment would soon come to an end, in the spring of 1976, I was transferred to the squad handling national security matters, but which also included keeping tabs on the Jewish Defense League, which had been quite active.

My wife, Maureen, and I had gotten married, and we were still honeymooners living in the Riverdale section of the Bronx.

While watching television on a Friday evening in September, regularly scheduled programming was interrupted with news that a TWA flight had been hijacked shortly after takeoff from La Guardia Airport and was taken over by a Croatian terrorist and his wife.

In addition to the claim of having a bomb on board, the hijackers said there was a second bomb located in New York City. That device was subsequently found in a locker in Grand Central Station by the NYPD Bomb Squad.

I wonder if Brian is working the 4 p.m. to midnight shift, I thought to myself?

Without the 24-7 multi-channel news coverage of today, in 1976, once the bomb had been located, coverage concluded with the commentators explaining that the device would be transported to the NYPD's facility in the Bronx, called Rodman's Neck, where it would be properly disposed. *Another routinely successful job by the Bomb Squad*, I thought as I went to bed.

It wasn't until the next morning that my wife and I turned on the radio while still in bed to learn the outcome of Friday evening's events.

"Tragically, an NYPD officer, Brian Murray has been killed while attempting to dispose a bomb in the Bronx planted in a locker at Grand Central by Croatian terrorists," the reporter said.

My heart sank. Brian was gone. He was only a few years older than me with his whole life ahead of him.

How could this have happened?

The Bomb Squad guys are the best in the business. They don't make mistakes. What would become of his wife and two little boys?

Days later, I counted myself amongst the thousands of uniformed police officers from across North America who turned out for Brian Murray's funeral. With the mournful sound of the bagpipes and brave grown men and women reduced to tears, an NYPD funeral is a spectacle to behold. It was my first memorial for a fallen police officer, but it was not to be the last.

Many years later, in the fall of 2017, I read a newspaper article entitled, *The True Story of a Cop's 9/11 Death—From 1976*.

The piece went on to talk about Brian Murray's death (coincidentally on September 11) and his wife Kathleen's (remarried and now Kathleen "Moran") soon to be released book.

It stirred such emotion after reading the article that I sat down and emailed the reporter. After reading my story, he asked if he could pass my comments on to Brian's widow.

Only a day or so went by when I received the most heartfelt email from Kathleen Murray Moran. It had been forty-one years since Brian's death. Her boys were now middle-aged men. She had moved on, having remarried and giving birth to a daughter. There weren't many people who recalled the tragedy of that early Saturday morning when her life took an ill-fated turn or could speak to having known Brian, as casual as our brief and limited friendship had been. But it was clear from her words that the brave and gracious man that had me by his side and showed the 'new guy' the ropes at our first chance meeting was the man that she had known and loved.

Brian Murray, with wife Kathleen, at 240 Center Street in lower Manhattan, May 1971, after graduation from the NYPD Police Academy.

BOB JOYCE

Although I knew of Bob Joyce when I worked as a clerk in the FBI office on East 69th Street, in the early 70s, he was assigned to another section of the office, and we never really traveled in the same circles. He graduated from the FBI Academy several years behind me and, like many of us, was assigned to return to New York and to the newly opened Brooklyn Queens office, in mid-1978, to work truck hijackings.

Our squad was the largest in the office. Stolen coffee, cigarettes, frozen shrimp, sesame seeds, Romanian suits, Hartz Mountain flea and tick collars, Perego Super Bye-Bye baby strollers, Este Lauder perfume, stereo equipment, Kodak film, televisions, liquor, and Benjamin Moore paint were some of the more interesting stolen items that we investigated and successfully prosecuted.

A lot of us were in our late twenties and early thirties and loved what we were doing. These cases could be very demanding.

An informant, as a prospective buyer, would receive a call from an associate to look at a stolen load of merchandise normally stored in a warehouse, and make an offer if he was interested. Piecemealing it out by the seller was too risky.

The informant would then call us with the details, and we would track down the origin of the merchandise and determine whether it was a load traveling in interstate commerce.

At that point, a team would begin to discreetly surveil the warehouse around the clock, to record the comings and goings of the people in control, attempt to identify them, and obtain details for a search warrant.

To protect the informant, we would have to wait until we had a 'go ahead' when he or she felt comfortable that enough potential buyers had seen the goods, and the source would not be singled out as providing the tip to the FBI. This would sometimes take days and just recalling the dozens of times we performed this ritual is still exhausting.

Bob and I were often paired together on surveillance. At eight or more hours at a clip, you truly get to know one another.

Bob was Jesuit educated at Brooklyn Prep, in the Crown Heights section of Brooklyn. From a very close family, he and his two brothers and sister were raised on Long Island.

After high school, it was off to St. John's University, in Queens where Bob became a second baseman on several of St. John's more successful baseball teams.

When we began to work together and make our way back to the office in the late afternoons, I recall a time when we stopped by St. John's when the baseball team was playing.

As we parked the car, the late legendary basketball coach, Lou Carnesecca, was standing nearby taking in the game. As we approached, Coach Carnesecca immediately recognized Bob and said, "Hello, Bobby. How's the FBI treating you?"

"Good coach, all good. So nice to see you," Bob replied.

I thought to myself, pretty sharp for the coach to remember Bob, who didn't play basketball and knew that he worked for the FBI after probably not seeing him for at least the last ten years.

I can best describe Bob as a 'no nonsense' guy. At times, he wouldn't always have the highest tolerance level. We would often be out in the car in the afternoon listening to all-sports talk radio's WFAN show, *Mike and the Mad Dog*.

"These guys don't know what they're talking about," Bob would blurt out at least several days a week. God forbid, they strayed off sports and began to weigh in on political or social issues. Bob would have a fit.

"These clowns should stick to sports, where they're wrong half the time anyway."

Where Bob began to really hit his stride is when our boss, Steve Carbone, tapped him to be the administrative case agent for our very successful undercover case entitled, 'Operation Winged Foot.'

No easy task, George Hanna and I, while working in an undercover capacity, were often recording four or five consensually monitored conversations with subjects each day. In addition, over the course of nearly a year, we obtained approximately 150 'give ups' or 'insurance jobs.' These were cars that were fraudulently reported stolen by the owner to collect the insured value, which we stored at an airplane hangar at Brooklyn's Floyd Bennett Field. Each one of these cars needed to be documented thoroughly, which included identifying their respective insurance carriers, etc.

Duplicate copies of keys and registrations to all the cars and many additional administrative tasks all fell on Bob's shoulders. Truly not a job for someone who was not highly organized, Bob had an acute sense of attention to detail and with the successful prosecution of all the defendants, proved to be the ideal candidate for the job.

As if he wasn't busy enough, Bob also tried to at least take a pass through most of our recorded conversations to see if there was anything we may have neglected to share and determine if something required immediate attention.

When I think back to all the recorded conversations we made and the length of some of them, I wonder how Bob remained friends with George and me.

One evening, the informant reached out to us and indicated that a neighborhood guy, who went by the nickname, 'Al Rocks,' was at his house in Ozone Park and he was a potential target for some 'give ups.'

"Get over here right away," the source told us.

A short time later, we pulled up to the informant's home and he was chatting with none other than 'Mr. Rocks.'

"Al, this is George and Neil, the guys I was telling you about. Maybe yous can do some business." Al greeted us and simply nodded.

"Al is known in the neighborhood as a DJ and does a lot of break dancing. He's one of the best around," the source continued.

"Hang on one second," the informant said as he ran inside and retrieved a boom box. With that, he turned up the music and Al dropped down to the sidewalk and spun around like a top. Michael Jackson, on his best day, would have been envious. Al Rocks was truly masterful and ahead of his time.

Seemingly not one bit exhausted after nearly several minutes, the source then put on Al's favorite song, and he continued for what seemed like forever. With the tape recorder going in my boot, all I could think of was that once Bob listened to this George and I would be toast.

Al concluded his performance and literally bowed as we tried to show our appreciation with some light and polite applause. No further mention of any business was discussed when Al said, "Sorry dudes, I gotta run."

It was several days later, after I had turned the tape over to Bob and didn't have the heart to forewarn him about what he would hear.

"Tell Hanna that if he thinks transcribing a tape of Al Rocks breakdancing is so hysterical, he can do it himself," Bob began.

"All I heard in the background, *when I could actually hear anything*, was George hysterically laughing."

Wow, I thought, *I escaped easily from that one*. For some reason, George was taking the brunt of Bob's fury, and I was more than happy to pile on a bit, "Yea, Bob, I'll tell him, you know George."

Like several people the hijacking squad arrested, many started out as small timers and later became significant figures in the five LCN families. One such figure was Thomas 'Huck' Carbonaro.

Bob and I were tasked with executing an arrest warrant for Mr. Carbonaro in connection with his participation in a truck hijacking in 1979. We surprised him at his Brooklyn home in the pre-dawn hours.

Say one thing about most of these guys, treat them as you would want to be treated, and they will reciprocate and not give you any trouble. In those days, no one, and I do mean none of their ilk, ever offered any smidgen of cooperation, but they generally had good senses of humor.

We had arrived back at the office and Bob and I had taken 'Huck' into the room to be photographed and fingerprinted.

Carbonaro was not tall by any stretch of one's imagination and was quite portly in appearance. As Bob was to learn, he would prove difficult to fingerprint.

"Tom," I began. "Been hitting the pasta a bit heavy lately, you think?"

"I'm Italian, agent, what can I tell you, it's the culture."

Bob then weighed in.

"You are built like a human bowling ball, Tom. You have the fattest fingers I have ever seen. Look at this. This is the third fingerprint card I've tried. Your fingers don't even fit into the little boxes."

"What can I tell you. Fat body, fat fingers. And what are you guys, Abbott and Costello with the jokes? And as long as we're on the subject, yous two look like you could stand a good home cooked Italian meal yourselves. Yous both look Irish? You're probably married to Irish girls. Everyone knows they can't cook."

Huck's career blossomed as the years went on. In 2005, Thomas Carbonaro was sentenced to seventy years in federal custody for plotting to kill his former boss, Sammy 'The Bull' Gravano, the former underboss of the Gambino LCN Family, as well as several additional mob related killings. He is eligible for parole in 2063, when he will be about 115 years old.

We ran into another comedian, Lenny DiMaria, while arresting five people at one of the Brooklyn piers, on a Saturday afternoon, in February 1981. "The Conductor" was DiMaria's street name, attributed to his former profession as a conductor on the Long Island Railroad. Apparently, the pay and benefits for LIRR employees weren't as lucrative as dealing in swag.

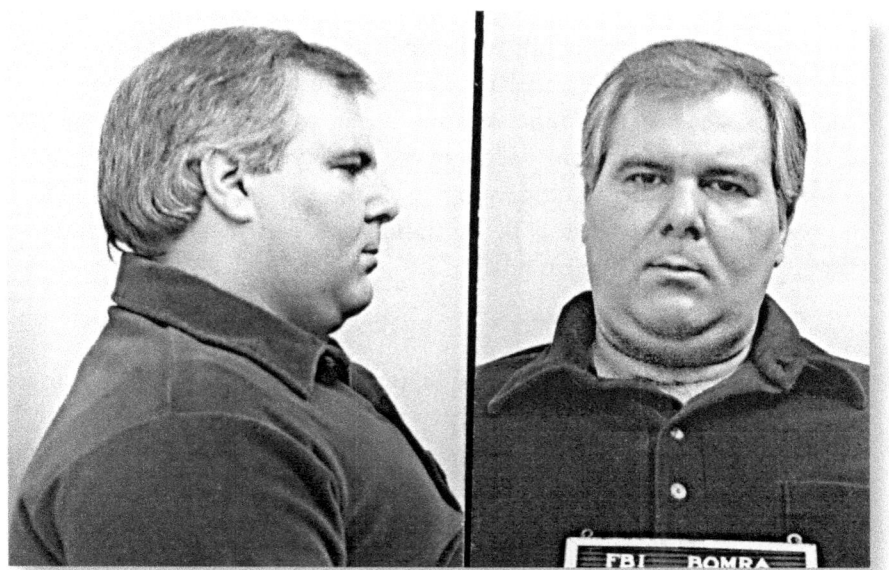

Thomas "Huck" Carbonaro—March 20, 1981
Arrested by Bob Joyce & Neil Moran

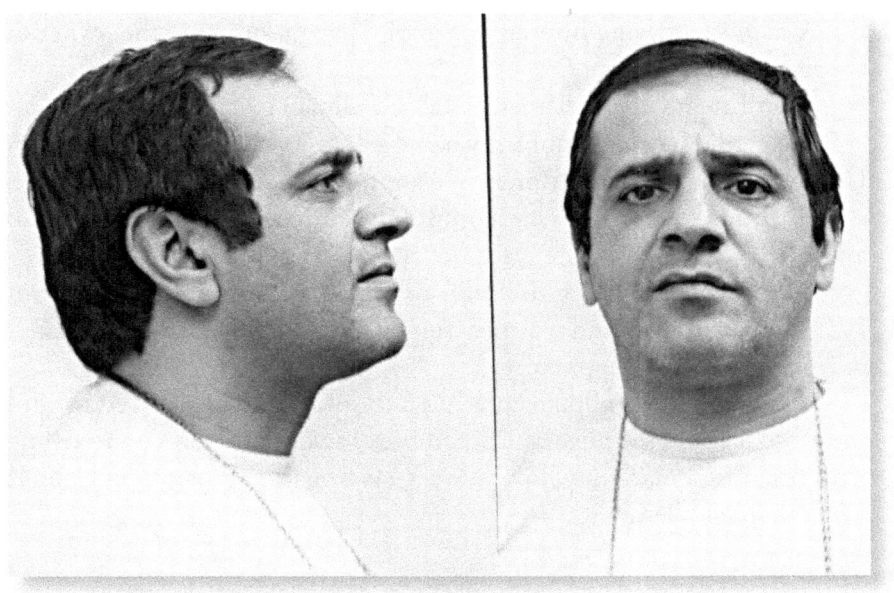

"Lenny the Conductor" DiMaria following his arrest on
February 21, 1981—"I didn't know you guys worked weekends."

It was like something out of a movie as about ten agents converged onto the pier where the bad guys were loading contraband onto rented trucks. As we sped through everyone began to run, which was a sight to behold. Some of them didn't make it fifty yards when they were suddenly out of breath and gave up.

As Lenny DiMaria was being handcuffed, he uttered, "I thought you guys didn't work weekends."

On one occasion, George Hanna and I joined Bob Joyce in doing a 'walk-in,' or attempting to gain entry to the premises without a search warrant, at a matzah factory, in Brooklyn's Williamsburg section, which is largely populated by the Satmar sect of Hasidic Jews. We had received information that a stolen load of JVC Stereo Speakers, valued at $1.1 million, was being stored at that location.

As we walked in, we observed dozens of Hasidic men doing what else? Making matzahs. I recall vividly, not one person looked up at us, but everyone continued about their business—time is money I suppose.

A man identifying himself as Rabbi Chayim Fullman, the owner of the factory, greeted us.

"Can I help you gentlemen?" Rabbi Fullman began.

"Yes, good morning rabbi, my name is Bob Joyce and these are agents George Hanna and Neil Moran. We are from the FBI," Bob began.

"FBI, my goodness, what could be the problem?" Rabbi Fullman asked.

"We are investigating the theft of over a million dollars' worth of JVC Stereo speakers and we are acting on information that the speakers may be located on the premises."

Bob and Rabbi Fullman continued to speak, and as I looked behind the rabbi, I could see huge cardboard boxes stacked almost to the ceiling with bright red markings "JVC." Every investigator's dream—talk about being in 'plain view.'

"Mr. Joyce, this is a matzah factory, we don't know anything about speakers. What would we be doing with stereo speakers here?—we make matzah," Rabbi Fullman said.

George had directed Bob's attention to the far wall, and Bob snapped, in somewhat of an agitated state, "Yeah, then what the hell are those boxes marked JVC behind you—is JVC some type of new matzah ingredient?"

Rabbi Fullman very calmly turned his attention to the boxes and said, "Mr. Joyce, calm down, please calm down, you're going to have a heart attack. Such a nice young man, we don't want any heart attacks on the premises. Let's talk about this. I don't know where these JVC things might have come from or how they got here. They must have arrived when I wasn't here, but I'll get to the bottom of it, I promise."

In addition to Al MacDonald and George Hanna, Bob Joyce was the only other longtime partner I had during my career.

I was privileged to serve as the emcee at Bob's retirement dinner as he moved on to a successful career in the private sector. Prior to leaving, he had been promoted to supervisor of a drug task force with the NYPD and then as the senior resident agent at the FBI office at JFK Airport.

Among the many things I recall pointing out about Bob was an analogy that has often been made about Michael Jordan, arguably the greatest professional basketball player ever. The pundits say that part of Jordan's greatness was that he had the unique ability to make those around him better. Take apart the successful Chicago Bull teams, which he led to six NBA championships, put many of those players on other teams and they may have been only moderately successful. It was Michael Jordan who made them strive to want to perform at a higher level.

The same can be said about Bob. I know on many occasions during our undercover case, no matter how much I was juggling, I was extra careful to dot my 'I's and cross my 'T's because in not doing so, I might hear it from him, and I didn't want to add to his already heavy burden or disappoint him.

I also spoke about the fact that Bob is simply not a chitchat type of guy. You don't call him up and anticipate being on the phone for an hour. I no longer see Bob daily. When we do see each other, however, we immediately pick up where we left off, catching up on our children and now grandchildren.

I know that if I called Bob at 3:00 a.m. and asked for his help with anything, he would be at my door in minutes, not requiring any explanation.

This is a true friend, and I count Bob as one of my dearest.

MOVING ON

My tenure in the criminal division, which was supposed to only last six months, had stretched into the spring of 1976.

I received word that I was being transferred to a squad that handled 'Internal Security' matters or in other words, investigating possible threats on the domestic front as opposed to 'Foreign Counterintelligence,' which concentrated on potential external threats from foreign nations and groups affiliated with those nations.

As it turned out, I was much luckier than many of my new agent colleagues.

I had just left the squad which devoted a considerable portion of its manpower to investigating bombings. My new squad was actively investigating a group called the Jewish Defense League (JDL), whom had been involved in planting bombs targeting various locations occupied by Soviet diplomats. This was in protest against what the JDL felt was persecution of Jews in the then Soviet Union.

In addition, under a fairly new statute, called 'Protection of Foreign Officials,' the new squad would be responsible for liaison with the U.S. State Department, Secret Service, NYPD, and scores of other agencies when a high-profile figure from a foreign country visited New York.

The JDL kept us busy right from my first week on the squad, which was loaded with respected veteran agents including, Jim Ohlson, the late Lenny Cross, Jim Kenny, Ed Madden and our boss, Vince Milaccio.

The group had taken credit for a shooting that occurred in the early morning hours at the residence for all New York-based Soviet diplomats. This was a high-rise building, coincidentally located in the Riverdale section of the Bronx, not too far from my old neighborhood and only blocks from our first apartment when my wife, Maureen, and I married in July of 1976.

Three of us, all recent transfers and new agents, were assigned the glamorous duty of working a 10:00 p.m. to 6:00 a.m. shift at the location where the NYPD had determined the shots were most likely fired.

We split up and were instructed to talk to anyone who was on foot in the neighborhood in the hopes that they might have seen something on the evening of the shooting.

Riverdale Avenue was the main throughfare in the neighborhood and a stop for regular NYC buses and what was called the 'Express Bus,' which traveled to and from Manhattan each day for those who opted not to take the subway.

We did this for three consecutive nights. Many people spoke with us but there were always some who, in typical New York fashion, couldn't be bothered.

Yes, a glamorous assignment.

As my father used to say, "It builds character."

We believed that the JDL continued to have responsibility for planting mostly pipe bombs in places like the Soviet Mission to the United Nations, only blocks from the FBI's East 69th Street office and at the time, only steps away from the NYPD's 19th Precinct, Amtorg Trading Corporation, a Soviet trade organization on Lexington Avenue, and Aeroflot, the Soviet airline on Fifth Avenue.

Months later, we managed to arrest five JDL members on bombing and weapons charges. All were sentenced to various terms in federal prison.

Every time a diplomat visited New York, I managed to get assigned to many of the cases.

Former prime ministers of England, Edward Heath, and Harold Wilson, were not exactly high-profile visitors, but their trips to New York required meeting with various federal, state, and local agencies to assess any potential threat.

Given New York's vast size and history of political activism, even the most low-key visit by these former prime ministers had to be taken seriously. No agency wanted to be blamed for an international incident occurring on their watch.

The most exciting case of a visiting diplomat to which I was assigned was that of Queen Elizabeth II during the celebration of the 200th anniversary of U.S. Independence, in July 1976. It was called 'Operation Sail.'

Queen Elizabeth was certainly a high-profile visitor and the meetings in preparation for her arrival began months in advance.

I was hoping that my supervisor, Vince Milaccio, had faith in me that was not misguided.

"Are you sure you're okay with me doing this alone, Vince?" I asked.

"You think one of the older guys should come with me?" I added, hoping he would agree.

"Neil, you'll bang 'em dead," he countered.

Of major concern with someone like the Queen, was the ongoing situation in Northern Ireland and relentless bombing campaigns by the Irish Republican Army (IRA). New York City and the surrounding area have for decades been the home to the largest concentration of Irish born and Americans of Irish descent, in the U.S.

It was no secret that there were Irish and Irish Americans based in New York assisting with financing of the IRA.

A series of meetings were held at NYPD headquarters, One Police Plaza, in lower Manhattan, which for me was an easy trip on the #6 train from East 68th Street to the stop at the Brooklyn Bridge.

Every agency imaginable was in attendance including, New Scotland Yard, the State Department, NYPD, Secret Service, U.S. Customs, the U.S. Coast Guard and others.

Thankfully, all went well with "Op Sail," as the Bureau dubbed it for the celebration and several months later, once again, I moved on to another squad. This time on the Organized Crime division.

The case was entitled 'UNIRAC,' an acronym for union racketeering.

Our squad, headed by Bob Ruetter, was investigating labor union officials and shipping executives who were alleged to be taking kickbacks. Members of organized crime were also alleged to have heavily influenced union activities and to have received payoffs to keep labor peace.

Queen Elizabeth II pictured on July 4, 1976 with then New York Governor Hugh Carey taken by Neil Moran while on duty during "Operation Sail," America's 200th anniversary.

Future FBI Director Louis Freeh, who had graduated in the class ahead of me at the FBI Academy, was also assigned to this squad and was actually acting in an undercover capacity off and on.

The case was an overwhelming success, and it was also where I met and worked with John Keenan, John Pritchard, who had been a NYPD detective, Nick Gianturco, and Joe Spinelli. All solid guys and adding to the many wonderful people with whom I would work in the ensuing years.

UNIRAC produced more than 110 convictions, including that of Anthony M. Scotto, vice-president of the International Longshoreman's Association, and reportedly a member of the Gambino LCN Crime Family.

In late 1977, I was transferred for a brief time to a squad that handled all surveillance requests from the organized crime division.

I wasn't on the edge of my seat every day, but more often than not it was quite fun.

I had always been an organized crime buff of sorts and to see many of these high-profile characters that I knew only from photos or from television, and to record their comings at social clubs and meeting places up close was exciting.

On February 3, 1978, we were pulled from our regular assignment to provide surveillance coverage for the abduction of the daughter of fashion designer, Calvin Klein, eleven-year-old Marci.

Ms. Klein, who was living with her mother following her divorce from Mr. Klein, had been on her way to the Dalton School, on the Upper East Side, when she was met by a former babysitter.

Kidnapping of Marci Klein, daughter of Calvin Klein, February 3-4, 1978.

February 1978 news coverage following sensational kidnapping and release of daughter of fashion designer Calvin Klein.

The babysitter, Paule Ransay, informed Ms. Klein that her father was ill, and she had been asked to take her to him.

Instead, she took her to an apartment where Ms. Klein was bound and gagged while Ms. Ransay and two accomplices phoned Mr. Klein demanding $100,000 be paid to ensure her release.

The crew directed Mr. Klein to a series of telephone booths in midtown before he was instructed to personally deliver the ransom to a location inside the Pan Am building atop Grand Central Station, in busy midtown Manhattan.

Working with the NYPD and with an FBI agent posing as Mr. Klein's driver, the surveillance group was assigned to take up various locations around this very high traffic and pedestrian area.

After the drop was made, Mr. Klein was initially directed to the incorrect address, and it was hours before Ms. Klein was found unharmed.

Ms. Ransay and her two accomplices were arrested and charged with kidnapping.

All of the ransom money was also recovered.

Later that month, I was transferred to the Brooklyn Queens office.

JACKIE O

I am undeniably "star struck." This was probably a bit more pronounced when I was younger, but I admit to keeping up on the comings and goings of prominent personalities, things of which most people wouldn't give a hoot.

When I began working at the FBI's New York headquarters in the heart of Manhattan's Upper East Side, I was like a kid in a candy store. Celebrity sightings were quite frequent in and around the neighborhood and all over Manhattan.

Woody Allen and Mia Farrow, often with children in tow, seemed to be out and about quite frequently, as was famed broadcaster Howard Cosell. Actors from Hollywood's "Golden Age" of the 1930s/1940s, including Joan Crawford, Greta Grabo and one of my very favorites, Myrna Loy of *The Thin Man* fame, all lived in the neighborhood. Add author Truman Capote, comedian Rodney Dangerfield, Henry Kissinger, and former President Richard Nixon to those who called the Upper East Side home.

Swing over to the 'west side' and you were likely to spot Dakota (One West 72nd Street) residents, Lauren Bacall, comedian Gilda Radner, and Beatle John Lennon and Yoko Ono. There were also frequent sightings which included singer Carly Simon, actors Liza Minelli, Diane Keaton, and Dustin Hoffman.

One former colleague, a frequent visitor to the famed Elaine's Restaurant and Bar, on East 88th Street, was invited to have a late-night snack by the famed husband and wife comedy team of Anne Meara and Jerry Stiller.

As I was stopped for a light one afternoon while weaving my way through Tribecca, crossing in front of me were Harvey Keitel and Robert DeNiro. I would run into Mr. DeNiro again, this time with actor Mickey Rourke on the Lower East Side, where they were filming a movie called *Angel Heart*.

Imagine my surprise when I was using the men's room at the Manhattan Criminal Court Building one morning and the guy relieving himself next to me was none other than actor Jerry Orbach, aka Detective Lenny Briscoe, taking a break from filming the television series *Law and Order*.

But it was the most unanticipated sighting one afternoon that stood above the rest.

My supervisor, Vince Milaccio, had a lengthy commute and generally beat everyone into the office. Upon seeing I was getting settled one Monday morning, he motioned for me to come in and have a seat.

"See the guy sitting at the desk right outside my office? He just transferred in from Cleveland, and he doesn't seem very happy to be here. Apparently, he had problems selling his house and had to leave his wife and children behind. He's a quiet, soft-spoken guy who was blindsided by the transfer. If you don't have anything special planned, I'd like you to bring him with you, show him the sights—you know, try to build up his spirits."

I told Vince I had several leads to cover in Manhattan and the Bronx and was happy to have the agent tag along and give him the cook's tour.

Vince was right—the agent barely said two words as I pointed out such famous historic Bronx landmarks as the Willis Avenue Bridge, the Grand Concourse, Fordham University, and two of New York's most gridlocked expressways, the Major Deegan and the Cross Bronx. As we headed up the Major Deegan, he barely flinched when I said, "Over on your right is Yankee Stadium."

As we walked up several flights of stairs at our first stop, a typical six-story apartment building on Creston Avenue, in the Fordham section, and approached the apartment where I had hoped to locate and interview a witness, the agent drew his revolver.

"What the hell are you doing?" I asked. "This woman is a potential witness. I'm not anticipating any trouble. Put that thing away before she comes to the door. I'm looking forward to her cooperation. The last thing I want to do is frighten her and start a riot."

I suppose it's not everyone who feels comfortable in the Bronx.

I figured he would like a trip down New York's historic Fifth Avenue, which borders Central Park, so I thought we would eventually work our way down that famed street, and I would point out the sites. As we approached the high 80s, I could see the Metropolitan Museum of Modern Art ahead on our right and at East 85th Street, I saw, on our left, a green awning marked '1040' which any self-respecting *"Page Six"* gossip devotee knew was the home of Jacqueline Kennedy Onassis.

"Now, up ahead up on your right," I began, "you see the Metropolitan Museum of Modern Art and on the left, that green awning marked '1040' is where Jackie Kennedy lives."

As we drew closer, I saw a woman standing on the corner, exquisitely dressed, donning sunglasses with oversized frames and dark leather gloves, hailing a cab. Even those who are vision impaired, could recognize who it was—effortlessly elegant, I thought.

I had barely gotten out the words, ". . . that green awning marked '1040' is where Jackie Kennedy lives," when in the calmest and most impassive tone imaginable, trying to contain my own excitement, I said, "As a matter of fact, there she is right now."

"Jesus Christ," the agent yelled as he jumped up, banging his head on the roof. "I can't believe we just saw Jackie Kennedy—oh my God, wait until my wife hears about this. On my first day—wow that was something else!"

Yes, it took a former first lady and one of the most famous women in the world to bring this guy around, who never came up for air for the rest of the day.

MR. BROOKLYN

I first met George Hanna in 1975 when he 'entered on duty' as a clerical employee at the FBI office, then located on East 69th Street and Third Avenue, in Manhattan's fashionable East Side.

A graduate of LaSalle Academy and the John Jay College of Criminal Justice, count George among the many support personnel who patiently waited his or her turn on the path to becoming FBI agents. I had graduated from the FBI Academy, in Quantico, Virgina, in August 1975, and had been working in the office's criminal division.

Standing about 6'2" and at that time probably 240 pounds, George seemed to favor trim fitting suits that accentuated his well-muscled physique. He would often draw the assignment of standing in the lobby checking the identification of the employees as they arrived for work, which is where I first met him. As a twenty-two-year-old, two of George's loves were body building and tinkering with antique cars in the driveway of his parents' Windsor Terrace, Brooklyn, home with his father, George Sr.

It was only two years later, in 1977, that George was sworn in as a special agent and successfully completed his training at the FBI Academy.

Hoping to get back to New York, he got the shock of his young life when he was assigned to the FBI office in Jacksonville, Florida. Only married a short time to his childhood sweetheart, Debbie, who

STORIES

News coverage following the shooting involving George Hanna on April 3, 1978.

was born and raised only blocks away, George took his appointment in stride as the young Brooklyn couple prepared for life south of the Mason Dixon line.

Toward the latter portion of training at the FBI Academy, the instructors instill the importance and the responsibility of carrying a firearm.

I can still hear our firearms instructor announcing to our class, "Once you strap on that weapon, you always have to expect the unexpected. Anything can happen at any time and the split-second decisions you make may save your life and the lives of others."

What transpired next, as twenty-three-year-old George Hanna prepared to begin his career, is a story line one only reads in a thriller by James Patterson.

Staying at his parent's home, in the shadows of Brooklyn's Greenwood Cemetery, and preparing to leave for Florida, George had dropped off some clothes at the neighborhood dry cleaner the day before. In late morning the following day, he walked up the block to collect them. As he was returning with the clothes draped over his shoulder, George had promised the day bartender at the Terrace Café, he would stop in to say goodbye.

As George walked through the door, he was confronted by a man who put a gun directly to his head.

"Okay big guy, hands up and don't even think about trying anything," he announced.

"No one gets hurt unless you do something stupid."

George was told to take a seat at one of the tables as he draped his dry cleaning over his lap.

The bartender was now in the basement with the gunman's accomplice, where George knew the safe was located.

Now, given that George was only walking a short distance to run an errand and say his goodbyes, this could have easily been a time when any law enforcement officer would have left his or her weapon at home.

Although there is never an opportune or ideal time to be confronted with a situation like this as it occurred, having just left the firearms range at the FBI Academy only days before, and having listened to instructors stress the importance of carrying one's weapon, this was *that* time.

George had fully complied with the assailant's instructions, but out of the corner of his eye, he could see that he seemed to be focused on the entrance to the basement, as he spoke back and forth to his partner.

Seizing the opportunity and instinctively feeling the element of surprise was in his favor, George drew his revolver and pumped two shots into the gunman's chest, and he dropped to the floor.

After securing the gunman's weapon, George recalled hearing frantic shouting from the accomplice who wondered what had transpired.

"Your partner is dead and unless you want to join him come up the stairs slowly with your hands above your head."

The second gunman surrendered, and George disarmed him, holding him at gunpoint until the police arrived.

Sirens blared and police cars from several bordering precincts now filled the normally quiet streets of Windsor Terrace, as the 911 call of shots fired went out over the air.

Identifying himself as an FBI agent to NYPD officers, the police reached our office in Queens and his future supervisor, Steve Carbone, responded to the scene.

As things got sorted out in the latter part of the day, word had filtered down to Washington, DC, that a new agent had interrupted and foiled an armed robbery, in Brooklyn. The two gunmen had been identified as associates of the Colombo LCN Crime Family. This prompted then FBI Director, Honorable William H. Webster, to put in a call to George.

After commending him for his quick and decisive actions, Judge Webster asked if there was anything he could do, which was undoubtedly the most stressful day in George's twenty-three years.

"Judge Webster, I would be greatly appreciative if I could stay in New York. I am a Brooklyn guy and I'm not so sure my accent will go over that well in Jacksonville. Is there any way you can kill the transfer orders?"

Unhesitatingly, Director Webster told George he should consider it done and wished him luck in his career.

It was on the truck hijacking squad, supervised by a veteran agent, Steve Carbone, where I first worked alongside George. For anyone who has seen Martin Scorsese's *Goodfellas*, hijacking trucks during the late 1970s was the 'bread and butter' of organized crime.

To paraphrase the late actor, Ray Liotta, who played the role of mob associate, Henry Hill, "Whenever we needed money we'd rob the airport (a reference to John F. Kennedy International Airport, in Jamaica, Queens). To us, it was better than Citibank."

Although George quickly established himself as a capable, enthusiastic and dogged investigator, it was one of the first big cases, a stolen load of coffee, where George put out over the air something that follows him to this day.

As about a dozen of us waited on Father Cappadonna Boulevard in the shadows of the Verrazano Narrows Bridge, in Staten Island, in the pre-dawn hours, George, who probably had the shortest distance to travel from Brooklyn, was nowhere to be found.

"2864, on the air?"

The number, 2864, was George's 'signal' number, to which every agent is assigned and part of his or her identification, rather than using actual names over the airwaves.

"I'm five minutes away," was George's terse reply.

Five minutes, ten minutes, fifteen minutes go by, and George is nowhere to be found. With senior agents not having any of this from a twenty-three-year-old, as the decision was made to hit the warehouse without "2864," George came careening into the staging area.

It was probably eighteen to twenty years later, when George and I were on the Belt Parkway one evening, approaching Coney Island. We had a date to meet a federal prosecutor and longtime friend for dinner, Mark Feldman, at Don Pepe's Restaurant, in south Ozone Park, Queens.

We received a call over the air indicating that Mark was asking what our arrival time would be as we were already twenty-five minutes late with a good fifteen miles to go.

"Tell him we're five minutes away," George replied.

Old habits do indeed die hard.

It was 1983 and George and I were now working on the Joint Auto Larceny Task Force ("JALTF") comprised of agents from the Brooklyn-Queens FBI office and NYPD detectives from the Special Operations Division/Auto Crime Unit of the police department. This ushered in a new era for the FBI, which in the past, under the late director J. Edgar Hoover, was mistrustful of local police and established a reputation of a 'one-way street' philosophy.

"We will gladly take any information you might like to share, but we're not sharing anything," was basically the philosophy of the old Bureau.

Task forces, under the direction of then New York FBI boss, Ken Walton, had already been formed in the areas of terrorism, bank robberies and organized crime. The formation of the FBI/NYPD task forces laid the foundation for a model that was to be copied in scores of other Bureau offices around the country.

George and I would work together, initially as undercover agents, in a highly successful auto sting and then operate a series of informants, which led to many successful prosecutions.

As imposing a figure as George was some forty years ago, possessing Arnold Schwarzenegger type strength, I never saw him mistreat any of the bad guys, even when it was probably warranted.

He always exercised sound judgment, exhibited a calm and professional demeanor, never raising his voice, and had a knack for speaking to people and gaining their trust, whether he was chatting with a longshoreman or a bank manager.

George was one the most successful developers of informants in the history of the New York office, illustrated at the conclusion of his career, by gaining the cooperation of Joey Massino, then boss of the Bonanno LCN Crime Family, also known as the 'Last Don,' and Vincent 'Vinnie Ocean' Palermo, the de facto boss of the DeCavalcante LCN Family of Northern New Jersey.

We are such complete opposites.

George and I have often been compared to Jack Klugman and Tony Randall, better known as Oscar Madison and Felix Unger of the television series, the *Odd Couple*. In every partnership, someone has got to be, as my late father used to say, 'the fusspot' and one who doesn't sweat the small stuff.

Take a moment to ponder who was who.

One of the more humorous ongoing controversies George and I continue to have, to this day, is Brooklyn *v.* The Bronx.

As with a good number of Bronx people, I count myself among them having never set foot in Brooklyn until I became an FBI agent. On the flipside, George had never been in the Bronx. George considers any trip over the Whitestone or Throggs Neck bridges to be close to the Canadian border.

"Tell me you never visited Coney Island as a kid," George put forth one day while were riding in the car.

"No, never, we had Freedomland and Rye Playland. Why would we need to go to Coney Island?" I snapped back.

"As far as I'm concerned, they should annex The Bronx and make it part of upstate New York," George countered—and so it goes, even today.

I count myself as those fortunate to have known and worked with George for an extended period.

This is a man who has a heart of gold, and as his family, friends and colleagues will readily attest, he gives to everyone and expects nothing in return. In all the years we worked as partners and encountered uncomfortable and often dangerous situations, I always knew that having George by my side, everything would be fine.

Living only blocks from each other during the 1980s, in suburban Long Island, we always socialized with George and Debbie's extended families and continue to do so today.

My daughter, Colleen, even at a young age, was always quite fond of George, so whenever I announced that I needed to run over to his house for a minute, she was likely to join me.

It was a Saturday morning as we pulled up to the Hanna house and rang the bell. Colleen was probably seven years old and easily the most observant of my three daughters, had already announced, "I don't see his car, Daddy, he's probably not here again."

Debbie answered the door and confirmed Colleen's suspicions, "I don't know where he is but he's probably in Brooklyn."

After a brief chat, as we began to pull away, Colleen, obviously disappointed, uttered, "Daddy, how come every time we go to George's house Debbie says that he's in Brooklyn?"

Fumbling for an explanation, the best I could come up with was, "I don't know what to say, honey. George is a busy guy. He's probably working."

"You know what, Daddy, instead of George, I think we should call him Mr. Brooklyn because he always seems to be there."

ETAN PATZ

On the morning of May 25, 1979, a six-year-old first grader, Etan Patz, left his home at 113 Prince Street, in the SoHo (South of Houston Street) section of lower Manhattan. It was a two-block walk to the bus stop and was the first time he walked alone, after convincing his mother, Julie, he could do this by himself. After Julie Patz walked her son downstairs, she briefly watched as he walked away, went back upstairs, and never saw him again. Stan and Julie Patz were understandably alarmed when Etan failed to come home at the usual time and learned that he never boarded the bus, nor had he shown up at school.

The police were notified and hundreds of uniformed and plainclothes NYPD officers flooded the streets of SoHo. Etan's disappearance resulted in a media firestorm and soon his image was seen in every newspaper and newscast. It was said that this was the most intense manhunt for a missing child since the kidnapping of the Lindbergh baby in the 1930s.

It was early in 1978 that Congress passed the Sexual Exploitation of Children Act. The FBI was given authority to investigate crimes that fell under this new federal statute. In addition, following the kidnapping of Charles Lindbergh's son, Congress passed the "Lindbergh Law," in 1932, which gave the FBI the authority to investigate any reported mysterious disappearance or kidnapping involving a child twelve years old or younger. No ransom demand was required, and the child did not

STORIES

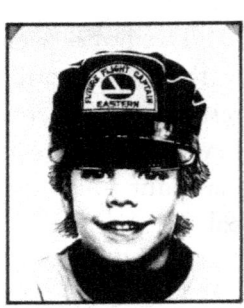

Missing Person poster issued by NYPD following the disappearance of Etan Patz May 25, 1979.

have to cross state lines or be missing for twenty-four hours before an investigation could be initiated.

This new violation was assigned to our squad in the Brooklyn Queens office. Kenny Ruffo, a Baltimore, Maryland native, began working these cases.

It wasn't until sometime after the disappearance of young Etan, when the FBI officially opened a case, that we began a series of 're-interviews,' hoping that new information might be developed.

"Neil, would you come with me today? I have an appointment with Mr. and Mrs. Patz," I recall Kenny asking one morning.

"Sure Kenny, I'm happy to," I replied.

In about forty-five minutes, we were through the Queens Midtown Tunnel and driving through SoHo and onto Prince Street. The media had been set up for weeks out in front of the Patz home, a two-story loft apartment. As we reached the second floor and knocked on the door, Stan Patz greeted us.

"Hello Ken, please come in," Stan said.

"Stan, this is Neil Moran from our squad. He's been helping me out with several leads."

Mr. Patz was very businesslike and simply nodded.

"Please sign the book gentlemen," he asked.

Lying on a table was a book containing the date, time, name, and agency of every person who had visited since their son's disappearance. As I finished signing my name I glanced to the rear of this very spacious apartment, which boasted at least a fourteen to sixteen-foot ceiling, I noticed Julie Patz. I recall her long hair which stretched to her lower back. She was small in stature, wearing a blouse and jeans. She looked at us, gave a faint smile and disappeared to the rear of the apartment. I thought about the hundreds of people like us that had been in and out of their home since their little son's disappearance and how she undoubtedly hoped that today was going to be the day for good news. I suppose when you've repeated this process endlessly, one's optimism begins to wane.

In conjunction with the Missing Person's Squad, Kenny had arranged for us to interview some of Etan's friends in the neighborhood. All these people had already been spoken to by the police.

Mr. Patz provided us with the names and addresses, and we were on our way.

Nothing remarkable occurred following the last of our interviews that day, but one thing was clear: the sudden disappearance of Etan Patz, an adorable young boy, had and still shocked the collective conscience of this tight community. There wasn't one discussion we had with any of the children that their parents failed to tear up.

Kenny Ruffo recently provided the following comments on the Etan Patz investigation.

"In 1979, I attended an in-service training at the FBI Academy, in Quantico, relating to Sex Crimes & Sexual Exploitation of Children investigations.

"It wasn't long after, I soon began working a series of cases involving the sexual abuse of young children at the hands of adult males.

"One such case being investigated by the Nassau County Police Department (NCPD) involved an organization known as the North American Man Boy Lovers Association (NAMBLA). According to the NAMBLA website, www.nambla.org:

> *We believe sexual feelings are a positive life force. We support the rights of youth as well as adults to choose the partners with whom they wish to share and enjoy their bodies.*

"In July 1981, the NCPD arrested Martin Swithinbank, reported to be a trustee of NAMBLA and several associates, charging them with various sexual exploitation-related offenses.

"As a result of the volume of information being developed regarding the Sexual Exploitation of Children in this and other cases, as well as the attention that had been afforded to some nationwide missing persons/kidnapping cases, which included Etan Patz and Adam Walsh, a Sexual Exploitation of Children Task Force Squad was initiated at the Brooklyn Queens FBI office by then boss Jim Murphy. Included as part of this task force were detectives from NYPD, NCPD, Suffolk County PD and FBI agents.

"As an outgrowth of the NCPD case against Mr. Swithinbank and his associates, numerous photographs of young boys were seized. One specific photograph bore a strong resemblance to Etan Patz.

"Etan Patz was six years old when he disappeared walking to his school bus stop. The discovery of this photograph resulted in the case being re-opened by the FBI and assigned to the newly formed task force.

"Previously, when the NYPD had initiated their missing person's investigation into young Etan's disappearance, the New York FBI office had only assisted with out-of-state interviews of Patz family relatives. Now, with re-opening of the case, in about 1982, we began to focus on leads of reported nationwide sightings of Etan, possible involvement of pedophiles as suspects and international investigation reporting that young Etan might be in either Germany or Israel.

"One of the stronger leads developed was that a woman named Susan Harrington had been hired by the Patz family, as well as other parents in their SOHO neighborhood, to walk their children to and from school during the NYC school bus strike in 1979.

"Reportedly, Ms. Harrington was occasionally accompanied by her boyfriend, Jose Antonio Ramos. Investigation revealed that Mr. Ramos was a pedophile, with previous criminal convictions. Further investigation disclosed that Mr. Ramos had sexually abused Ms. Harrington's son, who at the time was eight years old. When interviewed, Mr. Ramos admitted to having had contact with someone who fit the description of Etan Patz.

"The continued investigation regarding Mr. Ramos' involvement with Etan Patz did not develop enough probable cause to make an arrest. However, following my transfer to the FBI office in Baltimore, in November 1987, the Patz family brought a wrongful death suit against Mr. Ramos and a judgment of two million dollars was awarded to them with Mr. Ramos being found liable for Etan's death.

"In May 2012, having been long retired since 2005, I was contacted by the New York FBI office, who advised that Pedro Hernandez, a former bodega worker in SOHO had confessed to killing Etan Patz.

"The bodega, which was about two blocks from the Patz home on Prince Street, was young Etan's destination the morning of May 25, 1979. He had planned to buy a soda to bring with him to school. At that time, Pedro Hernandez was seventeen or eighteen years old and was employed by his uncle, who owned the shop.

"In mid-2012, the Manhattan District Attorney's Office requested that I travel to New York to be debriefed on the FBI's investigative files, which had been turned over to them.

"After providing me with an overview of their identification of Mr. Hernandez as a suspect, his interview and confession, they had concluded that after thirty-three years, they felt they had identified the person responsible for the disappearance of Etan Patz.

"I attempted to highlight segments of the FBI's investigation that I believed had never been completely resolved, but they did not seem to be interested.

"Following the trials of Mr. Hernandez in 2015 and his conviction in 2017 and reviewing as many of the details available, I must admit that the circumstances regarding the investigation, especially into his time employed at the bodega, the lengthy unrecorded portions of Mr. Hernandez's interview and his confession have left me with doubts that he was indeed responsible for Etan's disappearance."

During the trial, which was covered extensively by the media, Julie Patz testified. Both her and her husband's pictures were in the newspapers and on the evening news. I could not believe the change in both their appearances. So, this is what happens to parents, who on the first occasion their son is allowed to walk by himself to the bus, they never see him again.

After the first trial ended with a hung jury, in February 2017, Pedro Hernandez was retried and found guilty of kidnapping and murdering Etan Patz. He was later sentenced to life in prison.

On November 24, 2025, the Manhattan District Attorney's Office announced that it intends to retry Pedro Hernandez for the kidnapping and murder of Etan Patz. Their statement reads:

"The District Attorney has determined that the available, admissible evidence supports prosecuting defendant on the charges of Murder in the Second Degree and Kidnapping in the First Degree in this matter, and the People are prepared to proceed."

In 1983, President Ronald Reagan established National Missing Children's Day, to be celebrated every May 25th, the day Etan Patz disappeared. Since that time, this custom has spread to many other countries. Etan's disappearance has elevated public awareness of the abduction of children and has encouraged making child safety a priority.

Media coverage of the Lufthansa Robbery December 1978.

LUFTHANSA

The Christmas holidays were almost here. I had been married for two years, and we recently welcomed our first child, Meghan.

There is a special buzz at Christmastime in New York and many of us with young families were looking forward to taking a few days off.

The best laid plans are often interrupted by the unforeseen.

On Monday morning, December 11, 1978, sometime around mid-morning, several of us were directed to the Lufthansa cargo terminal at JFK Airport in Queens.

Prior to our departure, I recall overhearing Supervisor Dave Steckler say, "They may have gotten away with a lot of money."

The New York FBI maintains a small office at JFK and for years, it was headed by an old timer, Walter Yoos, commonly known in the office as the 'Big Guy.'

Walter was your quintessential poster boy—1950s, James Stewart, Bonnie and Clyde era 'G-Man.'

Standing a good 6'4" and never without a cigar, I don't think I ever saw Walter when he wasn't sporting his dark-colored fedora, emblematic of the John Dillinger/Pretty Boy Floyd era of the legendary early FBI days. To round out the perfect ensemble, raining or not, he always wore a Brooks Brothers trench coat.

As we arrived on the scene, I can recall seeing Walter holding court with several of the other agents assigned to JFK and a flock of

Port Authority Police Department detectives and brass, who had responsibility for JFK and LaGuardia Airport.

At some point, we learned that a group of armed men had overpowered several employees in the early morning hours and made off with approximately $6 million in cash and jewelry. If this proved accurate, it would be the largest armed robbery in U.S. history.

"We don't know if we'll be needing you guys today," Walter began.

"We're going to work on this with the Port (the PAPD). They have some very positive information as to who may have pulled the job."

As the days followed and the media continued with articles about the case, an agent in the Brooklyn Queens office had a reliable source who tentatively identified the participants and the engineer of the heist.

When we learned that members of the Paul Vario crew of the Lucchese LCN Crime Family were responsible for pulling this job, it ultimately proved bigger than originally believed and the case was transferred to Steve Carbone.

Suddenly, almost every available agent who wasn't working on something critical was now assigned some role in what FBIHQ dubbed 'LUFROB.'

Many of us, including Al MacDonald, George Hanna, Andy Conlin, Bob Joyce, and me were assigned to the 10:00 p.m. to 6:00 a.m. shift and at first were directed to follow suspects in and around the south Ozone Park/Howard Beach areas.

Working the overnight shift is the worst assignment for keeping up on what's developing in any case. You are never in the office and generally, when you are relieving the prior shift, those agents can't wait to get home so the conversation is often minimal.

A longtime member of our squad with whom I worked for many years was Richie Mika. Richie had a great reputation with agents and detectives as a crack investigator who specialized in any and all things involving stolen cars.

Richie recalled his involvement in the early days of the Lufthansa robbery.

"Like many of my colleagues, I was involved in the surveillance of some of Jimmy Burke's crew including Tommy DeSimone, Angelo Sepe and others.

"Information had been developed that Tommy DeSimone had played a significant role in the heist and early on a decision was made to place him under twenty-four-hour surveillance. One of the steps in that process was to obtain a court order to place a 'beacon transmitter' onto DeSimone's car so we could track his movements.

"After obtaining the warrant, the first problem was trying to locate his car since it had disappeared for a time. The warrant was good for only thirty days and time was of the essence. If the thirty-day period expired, it would require us to return to court and obtain another warrant.

"Agents made repeated attempts to locate the car at several different locations known to be frequented by DeSimone, but the car could not be found. As the weekend approached just before Christmas, Steve Carbone tasked Andy Conlin and me to take turns every four hours to try and locate the car.

"Sometime in the late evening hours of Saturday, December 22, or the early morning hours of Sunday, December 23, I spotted the car, parked and unoccupied, near Tommy DeSimone's residence in Queens. I radioed the office to advise Steve Carbone that the car was located.

"Before Carbone arrived, DeSimone exited the residence, entered the car and drove away. Not wanting to lose him, I followed alone.

"He initially stopped at a bar or club on Liberty Avenue. After several minutes, DeSimone exited and I then followed him to Jimmy Burke's residence in Howard Beach, where he lived on a dead-end street adjacent to the swamp.

"Steve Carbone soon arrived with several agents serving as backup.

"It was our intention to place the beacon transmitter onto DeSimone's car that morning. However, it wasn't exactly parked in an ideal spot for the installation. DeSimone parked off the street and on the grass between Burke's house and his next-door neighbor's.

"After hours of waiting for the ideal time to perform the installation, we were afraid that if we waited too long it would soon be light. It was our guess that Burke, DeSimone and others were involved in an all-night card game.

"Finally, sometime between 4:00 a.m. and 5:00 a.m., Steve decided we had to make an attempt to install the transmitter.

"Steve and I walked toward the car parked next to Burke's house. I got down under the car to affix it to a place where it would be secure. I could see Steve standing about ten feet away with his gun drawn. I joked with him afterward and asked, 'What were you going to do if someone came out, shoot them?'

"Luckily everything went fine, and the beacon transmitter was affixed to the car without much difficulty. As I crawled out from underneath, I noticed a large dog peering through a sliding glass door from inside Jimmy Burke's residence with eyes locked in on me. Miraculously, the dog never barked or signaled that strangers were prowling about at 4:00 a.m.

"Steve and I walked away, and the beacon transmitter worked fine.

"About a week later, no signal from the transmitter could be received by any of our units.

"Both the car and Tommy DeSimone were never heard from again."

Another suspect that we soon learned was the subject of an effort to gather enough probable cause to install a listening device in his car was Angelo Sepe.

"Didn't I say not to go buy anything for a while . . . Johnny are you nuts . . . are you stupid. We got a million fucking bulls out there. Everybody's watching us and you get a fucking car."

These were the words of Jimmy Conway, in the role of Jimmy 'The Gent' Burke, played by actor Robert DeNiro, who we believed had engineered the Lufthansa heist talking in a scene from *Goodfellas* where he reads the riot act to Johnny who, against Conway's wishes, bought a pink Cadillac and an expensive fur for his wife.

Angelo Sepe apparently didn't get the memo from Jimmy Burke as he went out and, presumably with his share of the loot, purchased a new 1979 Ford Thunderbird.

The new ride, at that time, was the most popular car in the south Ozone Park/Howard Beach area—a navy-blue body with a rust-colored, vinyl top.

Much like the scene in the movie, our information was that Jimmy Burke was none too happy with Angelo for splurging on the new car.

Angelo Sepe lived in the shadows of John Adams High School, in Ozone Park. He was reported to have relatives who were members of the Colombo LCN Crime Family. He was also a friend of Tommy DeSimone, the character in *Goodfellas* played by Joe Pesci. The two had met in prison and had become fast friends.

Weeks went by trying to establish enough probable cause to install the listening device into Angelo Sepe's car and finally the warrant was signed.

Now, the hard part—installing it.

Apart from the FBI agents that conduct investigations, there are those who are highly trained in gaining entry into a social club, house, or a car undetected and then installing listening devices.

Of course, this is not as simple as it seems.

Painstaking surveillance of the comings and goings of the hours and activities in the social club or the occupants of a house needs to be established so that these technically trained agents can do what's necessary quickly and then leave without a trace.

Very often, in the case of a social club or installing a device in a car, the most opportune time for this covert activity is during nighttime hours.

Although Angelo Sepe at times seemed like he never slept and often kept us hopping until the wee hours. Once he called it a night, he was unlikely to surface until sometime in the middle of the day.

We weren't talking about nine to five guys here.

One final hurdle had to be cleared.

Once the tech agents gained entry to Angelo's car, with amazing precision and speed, a short time after, a listening device had been successfully installed in the car of one of the prime suspects of the largest cash robbery in U.S. history.

So now that we were about to monitor one of the prime suspect's conversations, the big question was, 'Were we too late?'

The 10:00 p.m. to 6:00 a.m. shift had very few nights when we were just sitting around. Angelo was definitely a 'night guy,' and liked to bounce. On our rare quiet nights, we always managed to entertain ourselves or had agents assigned to the shift who kept us laughing. Richie Rogers was someone who always managed a story or two at 3:00 a.m. when our eyes started to close. Although nearly fifty years have passed, I have a vivid image of Richie passing out White Castle hamburgers and French fries from a huge shopping bag at the ungodly hour of 5:00 a.m.

We were all over Brooklyn and Queens and it seemed like at least once a week, Angelo and his wife, Hope, travelled to her parent's home to Mattituck, in Long Island's Suffolk County.

The car was easier to follow than most. The Thunderbird had long, horizontal taillights that stood out amongst the hundreds of cars we would see on the Long Island Expressway on our frequent trips east.

The challenge was capturing conversations that would provide evidence to make a case against those responsible for the Lufthansa heist.

The technical equipment in 1979 was nothing like it is today.

In order for those surveilling Angelo to be able to record a conversation, we often would have to pull up so close that at times we felt we were on his bumper to gain the best reception.

We all had cassette recorders lying on the passenger seat and when one agent dropped off, feeling that he or she was in danger of 'getting made' or recognized by Angelo, another car would pull up and begin recording.

Unfortunately, Angelo was neither a Dean Martin or Frank Sinatra fan, nor did he play anything by Percy Faith and his orchestra.

Angelo was a devotee of The Grateful Dead.

Everyone on our shift began to learn the words of their hit "Casey Jones" by heart, as Angelo would blare it on his tape player.

"Driving that train, high on cocaine. Casey Jones you better watch your speed," the tune began.

Some forty-six years later, I can still hear that song in my sleep.

Violent arguments with Hope riding back and forth on the LIE and blaring music seemed to be the rule rather than the exception.

Several veiled references to "Lufthansa," were about all we captured, and it certainly wasn't enough to make a case against Angelo and the other suspects.

We arrested Jimmy Burke and Angelo Sepe several months after and needless to say, neither cooperated. We just didn't have enough to nail them for the Lufthansa job.

"Yous has gotta do what yous gotta do," I recall Angleo saying when confronted with possible jail time and what might lie ahead unless he cooperated.

Following the arrests, many of us were transferred from Steve's squad but the case continued.

With Jimmy Burke reportedly killing many of the people connected to the robbery, Henry Hill, played in *Goodfellas* by actor Ray Liotta, came forward, cooperated, and testified.

Among the cases Hill cooperated on and later testified was the Boston College point shaving scandal. Jimmy Burke was convicted in connection with the Boston College case and while in prison, he was convicted of murder. He died while incarcerated.

Paul Vario, who oversaw the crew who reportedly engineered Lufthansa was convicted in two separate cases in which Henry Hill testified. Vario died in prison in 1988.

Tommy DeSimone disappeared in 1979 and was never heard from again. It has been reported and as was depicted in *Goodfellas*, he was murdered for killing a Gambino soldier.

In July 1984, Angelo and his girlfriend were murdered in their apartment in Brooklyn's Bath Beach. Reportedly, it was a mob hit in connection with Angelo's involvement in drug trafficking.

Only a small amount of the stolen money and jewelry were recovered from Lufthansa.

STORIES

Left to right: Mickie Burke, James "Jimmy the Gent" Burke (portrayed by Robert DeNiro in *Goodfellas*), Henry Hill, Karen Hill, Tommy DeSimone and unidentified woman.

Left to right: Karen Hill, Henry Hill; center: Mickie Burke, Jimmy Burke, immediately next to Burke is Tommy DeSimone.

Paul "Paulie" Vario—Lucchese Family capo played by Paul Sorvino in *Goodfellas*.

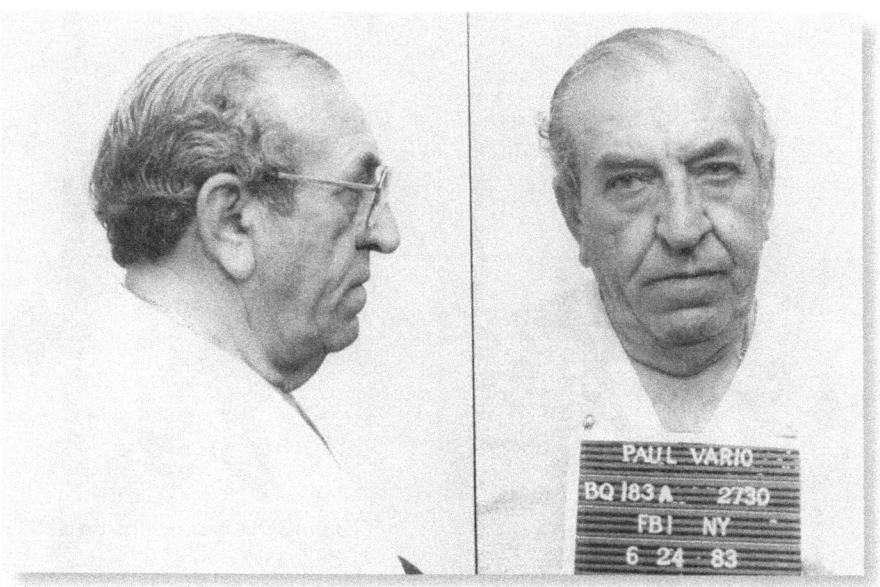

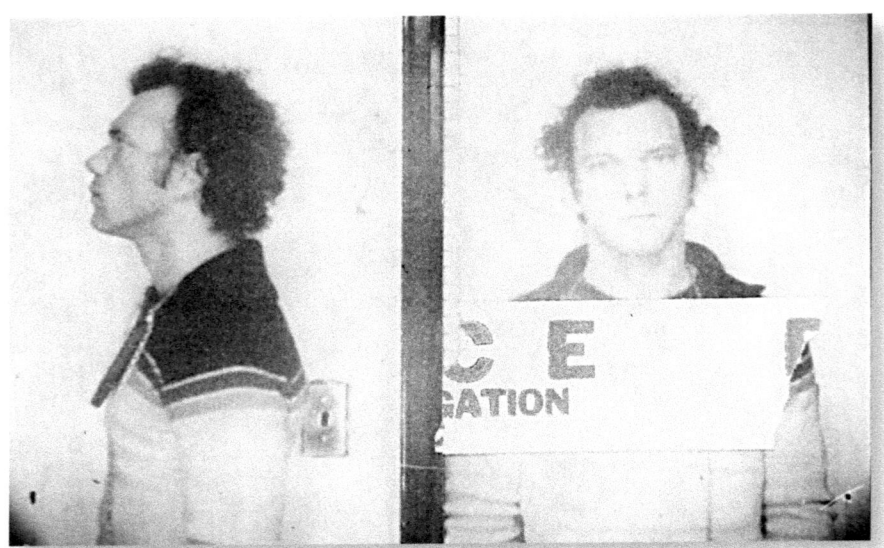

Angelo Sepe

Henry Hill, portrayed by
Ray Liotta in *Goodfellas*.

Tommy DeSimone, portrayed
by Joe Pesci in *Goodfellas*.

CRIME ON THE HIGH SEAS

Of the tens of thousands of current and former special agents of the Federal Bureau of Investigation, one can probably count only a very small percentage who have investigated a 'Crime on the High Seas' case. However, when you are assigned to the New York office, as we all continued to learn, anything was possible.

Jerry Cox and I had the standby duty beginning the third week of June in 1979.

It was about 2:00 a.m. on the morning of June 11, that I was awakened by Jerry's always energetic and enthusiastic voice.

'Bugs,' Jerry always called me and a reference to George Clarence 'Bugs' Moran, a prohibition racketeer, whose gang was gunned down in the infamous St. Valentine's Day Massacre, in Chicago, in 1929.

"I just received a call from the office. It seems there has been a possible murder/suicide aboard a South African flagship somewhere off the coast of Bermuda and it's on its way to Pier 6 in Brooklyn. The NYPD has been notified, and we are supposed to meet them at the ship to try and sort this out. The ship arrives at 5:30 a.m."

Jerry Cox was one of the finest agents with whom I ever worked. A proud Chicagoan and a former clerk in that office, he was always great company, forever enthusiastic and all business when it came to investigations.

"Bugs, let's throw some powder around," a reference to dusting for fingerprint evidence, was a favorite expression of Jerry's at the scene of a recovered tractor trailer in an armed hijacking.

Although the FBI rarely worked homicide investigations per se, Jerry jumped at the opportunity when offered, to attend the NYPD two-week homicide investigation course.

You knew when you were working with Jerry, you were going to get everything he had.

We were all saddened in January 2002, when we learned that Jerry, who had taken a transfer to Detroit, had suffered a heart attack and passed away not long after retiring at only age fifty-four.

With jurisdiction over LaGuardia and JFK Airport, the Brooklyn Queens office was generally kept busy after hours and we frequently received a standby call to respond to one of the airports to meet a flight where a passenger had groped a flight attendant or interfered with the flight crew in some fashion, but this was a first.

"Okay, Jerry, I'll see you shortly," I replied.

We both arrived at Pier 6 about 4:30 a.m. and were met by 11th Homicide Zone Sgt. Thomas O'Connell and Detective Pete Versakos, a veteran NYPD detective and someone who George Hanna and I would collaborate with in future mob related killings.

We were joined by a representative of U.S. Customs Service, who at this ungodly hour was smoking one of those Sherlock Holmes-type pipes or 'Gourd Calabash' pipes as they are known. The Immigration and Naturalization service was also represented.

With a heavy fog rolling in on a warm June morning, fog horns occasionally blaring in the distance, the NYPD and FBI standing by and the silent U.S. Customs fellow puffing on his pipe, you had the makings of a 1940s 'film noir,' setting.

One expected to see Sydney Greenstreet and Peter Lorre pop out from behind one of the large containers stacked on the pier.

At about 5:30 a.m., the South African *Constantia* slowly made its way into Pier 6, where it began to berth.

The ship's captain, Master Alan M. Smaldon greeted us, and we were escorted to his cabin.

Master Smaldon advised that the ship had been enroute to Cape Town, South Africa, and on the morning of June 9, with only about two days remaining in the voyage, the body of the first cook, Rabbiduth Singh, had been found on board. At that time, the ship was approximately 125 miles north of Bermuda.

Depiction of the arrival of the *Constantia* at Pier 6, in Brooklyn, New York, on the morning of June 11, 1979, by Ellen Moran.

Master Smaldon also advised that a member of the crew, Vincent Michael Mostert had been discovered missing at about the same time. Efforts to locate Mr. Mostert at sea had proved negative.

Master Smaldon had notified the U.S. Coast Guard, which sent out a plane to search for Mr. Mostert, and believed they may have seen something in their initial pass through, but those efforts also failed.

We informed Master Smaldon that we would like to speak to members of the crew and obtain statements.

He explained that many South Africans have a very low regard of the police and view many of them as being corrupt. In advance of the ship berthing, he had informed the crew that the New York authorities were likely to request that they cooperate and each one declined.

We fully realized that we couldn't force anyone to speak to us against their wishes but we were anxious to get to the bottom of this, so we asked Master Smaldon if we could take a random sampling of the people on board and determine their willingness to cooperate.

After speaking with about ten to fifteen crew members, no one expressed an interest in speaking with us.

We were then provided copies of statements furnished by crew members, who had interacted with Messrs. Singh and Mostert at the time in question.

What we learned, in summary, was that on the evening of June 8, 1979, several crew members gathered in Mr. Singh's cabin aboard ship. From statements overheard, it was apparent that Messrs. Mostert and Singh were in a relationship. Several of the crew reported that they had received advances, sexual in nature, from Mr. Singh and that he could be "very aggressive."

No one reported anything unusual for the remainder of the evening.

The following morning, a ship's trainee recalled seeing Mr. Mostert, who appeared visibly upset and felt that he had been crying.

The ship's purser's statement revealed that a strange note had been found in Mr. Mostert's cabin, which read:

Dear Friend,

Sorry that this must happen to me. Sorry Whitey that I can't go on with you. I've got problems of my own ahead of me so I have to bid you goodbye.

Your friend
Mossie

We were informed that 'Whitey' was crew member and friend of Mr. Mostert, Edward Clive Stewart, who admitted knowing Mr. Mostert, but disavowed any knowledge of any problems he was having, which may have caused him to leave the note.

A search of Mr. Singh's cabin by the ship's purser, upon learning that a note had been left behind by Mr. Mostert, revealed the body of Mr. Singh lying in his bunk. It was covered by a pillow and traces of blood were evident on the wall.

The purser then immediately notified Master Smaldon that Mr. Singh was dead.

Master Smaldon said that the ship's doctor, Denis Broome, was summoned and he pronounced Mr. Singh dead.

Dr. Broome identified a heavily blood-stained pillow over Mr. Singh's head, as well as additional blood stains near his right ear and his face. A broken drinking glass lay nearby. Dr. Broome said that apparently Mr. Singh's death was "of a violent sort."

Master Smaldon ordered a complete search of the ship, which failed to locate Mr. Mostert.

It was believed that he jumped overboard.

On the morning of June 11, a special team of U.S. Customs Service conducted a search of the entire vessel while it was berthed at Pier 6 and failed to locate Vincent Michael Mostert.

Master Smaldon was so detailed in his inquiry, he must have been a fan of *Kojak* or *Perry Mason* at the time.

In addition to taking thorough statements from the ship's crew, he sealed off the rooms of Mr. Mostert and Mr. Singh until the NYPD

Crime Scene Unit joined us that morning, to conduct forensic examinations.

Master Smaldon had Mr. Singh's body removed from his cabin to a freezer locker on board.

We were all allowed entry to view the remains and witnessed removal of the body by the Kings County Morgue. As I looked at the frozen corpse, a first for all of us, this added new meaning to the word, "stiff," when referencing a dead body.

In a statement to *The New York Times*, Sgt. O'Connell said, "The captain was a very efficient fellow. He did a good job for us prior to his arrival."

In addition, Sgt. O'Connell told the *Times*, "We gathered the steward was a sensitive person. Quiet, reserved . . . I feel satisfied that he did go overboard. There is nothing more to handle now if the South Africans are satisfied with our conclusions. He's gone with the fish now."

As we wrapped up what turned out to be a long day, as was our usual practice, Jerry Cox spoke with Assistant United States Attorney Marilyn Gainey Barnes at the Brooklyn's Eastern District and appraised her of what we had learned.

AUSA Barnes opined that given the apparent murder of Rabbiduth Singh occurred while the *Constantia* was at sea and the fact that the ship was not owned or partly owned by an American corporation, the U.S. Government had no jurisdiction over the matter.

South African Cargo Ship Docks With a Murder Mystery Aboard

By ROBIN HERMAN

The cargo ship South African Constancia pulled into Brooklyn's Pier 6 at sunrise yesterday, her chief cook dead and a 19-year-old steward missing. The youth was presumed to have drowned in the shark-infested waters 150 miles north of Bermuda.

Waiting on the dock was a team of Brooklyn homicide detectives and agents of the Federal Bureau of Investigation summoned by the ship's owner, the South African Marine Corporation. The company had asked for the American assistance, although New York authorities are still not sure what nation has jurisdiction over the crime.

Aboard the Constancia, the investigators found the body of 41-year-old Rabbiduth Singh, punctured with stab wounds and wrapped in sheets, in the ship's freezer. The captain had ordered the body stored there after it was discovered Saturday morning. Mr. Singh was a veteran sailor born in India and an excellent cook, according to the crew.

Missing Steward Is Suspected

The 12,000-ton ship, with 45 crew members on board, had been bound for New York from Capetown carrying dry cargo and bulk liquids. At breakfast time Saturday morning, two days short of the voyage's end, Mr. Singh was discovered dead in his cabin.

When the steward, Vincent N. Mostert, did not report for his duties that morning, crew members went to Mr. Mostert's cabin and there on his desk found a handwritten note. The police said the note implicated him in the alleged murder, but would not elaborate.

Capt. A. M. Smaldon ordered a shipwide search for the South African steward and, when that failed, called in the Coast Guard, which cruised the dangerous waters along the ship's course. The Coast Guard spotted a red object floating on the sea but was forced to turn back for refueling before it could be reached. The teenager had been wearing a red T-shirt when he last was seen.

The police could not immediately determine the cause of Mr. Singh's death because the body was frozen. "The captain was a very efficient fellow," said Sgt. Thomas J. O'Connell of the 11th Homicide Zone. "He did a good job for us prior to his arrival."

When the police removed the body yesterday afternoon only a small piece of sheeting could be stripped away – enough to reveal some stab wounds and a head injury. The police said no murder weapon had been found.

Crew Afraid to Talk

The Brooklyn District Attorney's office and the United States Attorney's office are working on the question of jurisdiction. For now, the body remains in the New York City morgue.

The mostly South African crew members were afraid to talk about the incident to the American investigators, according to Sergeant O'Connell, but a few of them said there had been a personal disagreement between the cook and the steward Friday night in which the cook made a remark that irked the youth.

"We gathered the steward was a sensitive person," said Sergeant O'Connell. "Quiet, reserved. He was a powerful individual, about 5 foot 7 but well-built. I think we are pretty satisfied this fellow did do it, and I feel satisfied that he did go overboard. There's nothing more to handle now if the South Africans are satisfied with our conclusions. He's gone with the fish now."

New York Times article, dated June 12, 1979, covering the NYPD/FBI investigation of a murder/suicide aboard the South African flagship *Constantia*.

"I THOUGHT YOUS WAS LOOKING FOR HAMS"

It was sometime in early 1980 when Bob Joyce and I received information from an agent on another squad that his informant had been offered a stolen load of Johnny Walker Scotch Whiskey, valued at approximately $300,000.

The agent had saved us some leg work and confirmed the the theft originated with a liquor distributor in Philadelphia, Pennsylvania, who was the victim of an armed hijacking several days prior. The load had been traveling enroute to several spots in Connecticut. The agent explained that his informant felt comfortable in giving us the go ahead to proceed to a warehouse in the Canarsie section of Brooklyn, as several other buyers had already viewed the load and failed to negotiate the asking price.

We identified the location as International Poultry, a wholesale warehouse specializing in poultry products. We further identified the owner as Tomasso 'Tommy Sausage' Abbatiello, a cousin of a high-ranking Colombo LCN Crime Family member.

Bear in mind that even though a confidential source provided this information and the agent had followed up confirming that we had a federal violation, we had nowhere near enough for a search warrant.

We were learning this second-hand. We needed to provide a lot more detail before we could travel that often exhausting and sometimes frustrating route with no guarantee a magistrate or judge would sign it.

One alternative we found a lot easier and most of the time with successful results was a 'consent to search' or a 'walk in.'

Plain and simple, the owner or owners of a particular location gave the FBI permission to search the premises. We would identify ourselves, explain what we were specifically looking for, and ask permission to search for that item or items. We even had a form, an 'FD-26,' which explained that the FBI wished to search the premises without a warrant.

The property or business owner could then sign the form, thereby giving consent, decline to sign, but allow the agents to search or decline outright and not allow us entry.

I had never been denied entry when requesting a consent to search. My general standard stock pitch was, 'If you have nothing to hide, what possibly could be the problem?' It always seemed to work.

We pulled up to International Poultry and asked to speak with 'Sausage.'

"My favorites, the FBI, what brings you to Canarsie today and what can I do for you gentlemen?"

"Tommy, strange as it may sound, although I know you are a poultry wholesaler, we received a tip that you are in possession of a stolen load of hams," I began.

"Hams," he replied. "We deal strictly in poultry. What the hell would I do with hams. I have no outlet for that. Plus, I don't deal in stolen goods. I run a legit operation here. I have a clean record. I don't need no aggravation. You know what I'm saying?"

"I'm sure you do, Tommy, but we're just doing our job, and we have an obligation to act on any information we receive. If you don't have any hams, you can show us the door and we'll be on our way."

"Do yous have a warrant?"

"That's where the hitch comes in Tommy, we don't. The information we have isn't specific enough to obtain a warrant, but we do have a form you can look at that allows us to search the premises with your consent. Would you like to read it?"

I handed Tommy the FD-26 and he proceeded to read it aloud.

"Hams huh, well I know there's no hams here, so I don't see why not, but I ain't signing nothing."

Tommy began to give us the grand tour of the entire operation where the sausage, or chicken rather, was made. Trying to generate conversation, I discussed the price per pound of chicken cutlets and roasted chickens and Tommy was impressed.

"Wow, who knew the FBI was up on the sale price for chicken cutlets."

Now, one thing that has not been discussed regarding the consent to search.

Our information was that there was a stolen load of Johnnie Walker Scotch Whisky on the premises. We told Tommy that we were looking for hams, which the courts have held is perfectly permissible in using a ruse and thereby not violating anyone's Fourth Amendment rights.

As we came across an unlit back room, I could see a large tarp on top of something.

As I pointed it out, Tommy quickly said, "Oh there's no light back there, it's just some junk that's been back there forever. It was an eyesore, so I had one of the guys throw the tarp over it. Just junk, believe me."

"Tommy, we're going to have to take a look. Suppose that's where you have the hams?" Bob Joyce said.

Whatever his thought process was we'll never know, but he retrieved a flashlight and gave it to me. I walked over to the tarp, grabbed the bottom and flung it back. Bingo! Case after case of Johnnie Walker.

"What the hell is this, Tommy?" I asked.

"I thought yous was looking for hams," was his reply.

We placed handcuffs on Tommy, and he was charged with violating Title 18 USC Section 659, possessing stolen items traveling in interstate commerce.

Several months later, we received a big blow at a hearing before the trial judge. Tommy's attorney was attempting to have what he called an 'inflammatory statement' ruled inadmissible when Tommy blurted out, "I thought yous was looking for hams."

After about an hour of very spirited sparring between the assistant United States attorney and defense counsel, the judge agreed and threw out the statement.

I was and still am furious after over forty years.

The trial ended in an acquittal for Tommy. I was stunned, as was the AUSA and members of our squad. It was my first of two career acquittals, but it still actually hurts.

The guy got caught red-handed, but in several brief conversations with jurors willing to speak with me outside the courtroom, they felt that Tommy presented the image of a working guy and essentially, the FBI was picking on him.

"Why don't you go after the real hijackers," one juror ordered.

"They're the real bad guys. This guy is just trying to make a buck."

Sometimes you can't fight City Hall, as the expression goes.

PAULIE GENTILE

When the Joint Auto Larceny Task Force with FBI Agents and NYPD detectives formed in the early 1980s, it added a different and much better dimension to the Brooklyn Queens FBI office.

Danny Pisculli regularly brought in Italian pastries from a Brooklyn bakery.

We established a 'coffee club,' where on Friday's we would supply an assortment of bagels for our faithful.

We always ran 'pools' for any of the major sporting events like the Super Bowl or March Madness.

Another thing we were never short of was regularly having a good laugh. The source of many a laugh on our squad originated with an FBI agent—Warren Flagg.

About the only way to describe Warren is that he was then and continues to be a larger-than-life figure. Now, approximately twenty-five years into retirement, one never knows if you'll turn on the evening news and see him being interviewed on a wide range of topics.

Nutty as many of believed Warren to be, he always seemed to develop quality informants that developed good cases.

One of Warren's longtime sources was Michael, who could often be seen with both feet on Warren's desk reading the *New York Post* or the *Financial Times*, reviewing how the international markets were faring.

As any law enforcement officer who has ever operated a confidential source fully realizes, you have to have eyes in the back of your head or your teeth will be stolen in an instant—Michael was no exception.

When Michael wasn't scheming, he had a side business where he wallpapered and painted. How he advertised or landed business was beyond me, but somehow he was hired by former New York football Giant defensive back Carl 'Spider' Lockhart to paint his Teaneck, New Jersey, home.

I'm not sure how satisfied Mr. Lockhart was with the quality of Michael's work, but he couldn't have been happy when Michael helped himself to some of Spider's New York Giant memorabilia. Michael was quickly tracked down and prosecuted by New Jersey authorities.

None of us will ever forget the first New Year's Eve when Warren Flagg appeared in the office wearing nothing but an adult diaper, a pacifier in his mouth, and a 'Happy New Year' hat.

Upon seeing this, I asked the NYPD supervisor, Sgt. Jim Torrens, "Jim, when you got the word that you were being assigned to the FBI task force, did you ever imagine you would see anything like this?"

A man of few words, Jim's only reply with a smile was, "No."

Practical jokes were many and often and I happened to be on the receiving end on one occasion.

We had learned that the FBI was initiating random drug testing and a list of the first wave would be coming out in the next few days.

Yes, I was selected.

One morning, as Sgt. Jim Torrens sat down at my desk and pulled up a chair he asked, "So is it true that you are on this drug testing list the FBI just put out?"

"Yes, sarge, I'm afraid so," I replied.

"Are you concerned about it?"

"I'm not crazy about it and would rather not have to do it but I certainly don't have anything to be concerned about, that's for sure."

"Have they spoken to you or given you any instructions about how to prepare for the test?" he said.

"Prepare, what do you mean, Jim?"

"For instance, if you are taking any medication perhaps they should be notified and what kinds of foods to maybe stay away from that might have an adverse effect on the results."

"What types of foods. I'm not sure what you mean. Are their foods that might affect the results?"

"Well, for instance," he began.

"Did they tell you to stay away from things like poppy seed bagels? Supposedly, they say poppy seeds might make you test positive."

I would say it was well known that I ate a poppy seed bagel at my desk every morning and had for years. Sesame, salted, garlic and onion, or everything bagels were not for me. I just preferred poppy seeds.

I felt faint and could feel my heart rate skyrocketing.

"You must be kidding, Jim. Where the hell did you get this? Are you serious? Did you know I eat a poppy seed bagel every day and have for years?" I uttered.

"Wow, I didn't know that. Maybe, you should think about postponing the test if they'll let you or cutting out the poppy seed bagels for a while."

Little did I realize that everyone was in on this.

Sgt. Torrens was the perfect candidate to pull this off. A serious, soft-spoken guy who was never in on any of our pranks and basically kept his mind on his work and wasn't known as a real 'chit-chat' type of guy.

I started to make a few phone calls.

The first was to my wife, Maureen, who is an RN to get her take on it, and then when they overheard me say I was calling the folks who were overseeing the testing they decided that the prank had been successful.

"Boy, did we have you going," I recall Detective Bob Soricelli saying.

Jim Torrens later reassured me and said that I would have to consume several pounds of poppy seeds in order to adversely affect a drug test.

I did wind up passing but from that day forward, I couldn't look at a poppy see bagel ever again and switched over to plain.

A few of us on the task force joined a nearby gym, the BQE Racquetball Club, in Woodside, Queens.

Open 24-7, every day of the year, the place never closes. None of us were racquetball players, but we were fond of the Stairmaster, elliptical, and stationary bicycles, while others like George Hanna, liked to hit the free weights.

There were six of us who originally joined: detectives, Danny Pisculli and George Terra and agents, Hanna, Warren Flagg, John Cable and me.

George Terra, who was partnered with George Hanna, was literally bullied by Hanna to show up each weekday at the ungodly hour of 5:00 a.m. I recall the first few times George and I pulled up at 4:55 a.m., being quite proud of ourselves, while most of the country was still asleep and we were about to give it our all.

As we walked in, two or three business types were on their way out dressed in suits and ties, probably on their way to Wall Street. There are few places around that boast 1:00 a.m. volleyball leagues, catering to nurses, bartenders, and cops working evenings.

Besides ourselves, there was a wide variety of attendees, including some airline employees (LaGuardia Airport was about a mile away), cops, firemen, and business types, but there were also a fair amount of truck drivers and construction workers who were among the regulars. We were very low key about our respective professions and were very businesslike when it came to our workouts as far as fraternizing with others.

It wasn't long before that we learned that several union leaders in the building and construction trades were frequent attendees. Among them was the business agent for one of the electrical unions, Paul 'Little Paulie' Gentile. Paulie was a well-known Colombo LCN Family associate and was rumored to be the subject of an ongoing RICO investigation with the Colombo Family hierarchy, allegedly accepting payoffs from companies.

Paulie was primarily a racquetball player. He and members of his union would play three or four days a week. To no one's surprise, Warren

Flagg could occasionally be seen playing with the group. Paulie was often observed smoking on the court in between games, obviously in violation of the 'no smoking' policy. The young overnight guy in charge wouldn't even dream about telling him to stop. Why did Paulie blatantly do this? Because he could and he knew no one would challenge him.

My first run in with Paulie occurred in the locker room as I was changing into my gym clothes one morning.

I've had my share of unpleasant run-ins with dogs through the years and like a blind person with an acute sense of smell, I could sense a dog was nearby. Sure enough, it was Paulie bringing a Rottweiler, with a head as big as the Brooklyn Bridge, into the locker room. I was startled.

"What's the matter, you don't like dogs?" he asked.

"As a matter of fact, I don't. What is this, a dog kennel? You've got a lot of nerve bringing that thing in here," I shot back.

I don't believe I rattle that easily and in social situations with strangers I don't become visibly upset over nothing, but I was having none of this bullshit from this smart ass. A bully was all he was, and I never had the stomach for it. I wasn't one of his union workers who blatantly kissed up to him.

"Whoa, easy pal, let's not fly off the handle. I won't bring the dog anywhere near you," he said.

"It's not a matter of not bringing the dog near me, there are a lot of other people here who probably feel like I do but won't speak up. The dog doesn't belong here, period," I added.

Surprisingly, Paulie backed off and uttered in a lower tone, "Boy, some people are touchy, touchy," and walked out with the dog, which I never saw again.

When some of the agents and detectives stopped going to the BQE, I often went alone and enjoyed my anonymity. I had become friends with a guy who worked at a cargo company at JFK Airport and was a real gentleman—Joe Napolitano. He was one of the few who knew I was an agent, and we often spoke about Paulie and the daily nonsense occurring with him and his entourage.

"Do you think he knows what you do?" Joe would ask.

"I really don't, Joe. I don't think a guy like that can keep it in. He would have to let me know that he knows and what a sharp cookie he is. Like saying, "You think the FBI is going to fool somebody like me?"

"No, I don't think he knows."

In June 1992, I was involved in an automobile accident while making an arrest and my injuries kept me out of work and away from the BQE for over a year. Now, suffice it say, that people who frequent gyms at 5:00 a.m. are creatures of habit, so when I didn't show up suddenly for days and now weeks, my friend, Joe, became concerned.

While recuperating at home, I received a call from my boss, Steve Carbone.

"Do you know a guy named Joe Napolitano from the BQE? He called here and he's genuinely concerned. Here's his number, call him. He really sounds worried about you."

"Neil, is everything all right? Your boss was very cryptic, what the hell happened?" Joe asked when I phoned.

After going through a blow by blow for Joe, he said, "Well I'm glad you're okay but I have something to tell you. You know how we always wondered whether Paulie knew where you worked? Well, the good news is that he didn't, but the bad news is that he does now. About two or three days ago, he was in the locker room with his pals and says, 'Whatever happened to the skinny Irish kid that comes here? The guy vanished into thin air.'"

One of his crew then said, "Oh, you mean the agent?"

"Agent," Paulie said. "What agent?"

"The FBI, he's an FBI agent that guy."

"Are you kidding me, that guy's an FBI agent. Jesus Christ, I can't believe it."

It was about a year later when I resumed my gym membership, and Paulie wasted not one second.

Seemingly out of nowhere, he saw me and said loudly, "Neil, good to have you back. What the fuck happened to you?"

Neil, I thought. He had never known or addressed me by name and now all of a sudden, we're on a first name basis.

I really didn't feel like I wanted to give Paulie a rundown on the hospital menu when I was laid up, so I was polite, but not overly.

It was only a short time one morning thereafter, as I was leaving the club and walking past Paulie's car, when it suddenly started. I had seen him inside when I left, so I knew no one was in the car. This was thirty years ago and unlike today, no one had a remote starter in his or her car.

The next day, I saw Paulie and asked, "What's with the remote starter? I got quite a surprise yesterday when I left."

"You like that huh," he replied.

"Hey, in my line of work you can't be too fuckin' careful. Better the FBI gets blown to smithereens than me."

I had learned through the office grapevine that the heat was on Paulie. A grand jury was hearing testimony on union affairs and their relationship with organized crime. Paulie had been subpoenaed to testify.

The showers at the BQE were communal. There were often ten people showering at once and there was literally no privacy, which I was to learn this morning was where Paulie wanted me.

I was alone with no one in close proximity, when Paulie not only walked over to get closer, but took the shower right next to me.

"Feeling a bit lonely this morning, Paulie? I think I'll sit this dance out," I said, wondering what was the motive behind this sudden and awkward closeness.

Obviously, he was comfortable that I wasn't wearing a wire and in fact I wasn't wearing anything, as I stood completely naked, holding only a bar of Dove soap.

"Can I ask you a question?" he began. "Do you know an agent, Graham Murray?"

"Yes, I know him,"

"You know this guy could learn some manners. He doesn't know how to treat people. He comes to my door the other day at 6:00 a.m., upsets my whole family, got heavy-handed, and I didn't like it."

"Paulie, look, I've been coming here for years and for a long time you had no idea what I did for a living. That's the way I live my life. I don't advertise what I do. I come here because I'm a workout guy. I've been active all my life. It's my hobby, my outlet. I don't come here to talk shop. I love what I do but I don't need to do it here, *capiche?*"

"I get it, and I respect that and even though I barely know you, I do know people, and I know you would never treat or embarrass anyone like he did to me in front of my family."

These guys are all the same, I thought. 'Respect, respect, respect—too much *Godfather*. Just like one of the classic lines from *Goodfellas* when Ray Liotta's Henry Hill said, "One day, one day some of the kids from the neighborhood carried my mother's groceries all the way home. You know why? It was outta respect."

"Paulie, I don't know what to tell you. Everyone's got their own way of doing things," and left it with that.

I did track down Graham Murray in the office and briefly spoke.

"I'm sure it's no secret that Paulie has been going to the BQE Racquetball club where I've been a member for years," I began.

"Sure, we all know Paulie goes there."

"Well, he approached me the other day and said he wasn't happy with the way he was being treated. You know the respect nonsense. Now, take this any way you want, but think about this guy as a potential bombshell of a source. He gets convicted and after two years gets tired of playing pinochle and fighting off lunatic inmates and reaches out to you because he felt you were a gentleman and treated him fairly. You may hate the guy but just think about the end game here. Give it some thought."

This could have easily gone bad, but it didn't. Murray seemed to be appreciative of the information, and we left off fine.

It was weeks later while finishing, when my shower pal walks over and says, "You talked to Murray didn't you?"

"What in the hell are you talking about Paulie. I didn't talk to anyone."

"Bullshit, I know you did. He sat in at a meeting with my lawyer and the prosecutor and acted like my best friend. What a turnaround. You can deny it all you want but I know you spoke with him."

Paulie's troubles continued and eventually he pleaded guilty to RICO-related charges and was sentenced to five years' incarceration. It was shortly before his surrender date when, once again as I was enjoying the solitude of a nice long warm shower after my workout and with soap on my face, my eyes were closed. I could sense someone was close by and as water splashed on my face, I saw it was Paulie.

"Paulie, *what*, come on?"

"I got a bone to pick with the feds and you're the only one I can talk to."

"Paulie, please, how many times have I told you I don't mix business with pleasure. Come on."

"Two minutes and I'll leave you alone. I'm surrendering and we'll never see each other again."

"What?" I said.

"What's with this deal with Sammy Gravano?"

Sammy 'The Bull' Gravano, the reputed underboss of the Gambino LCN Crime Family, had just cut a highly publicized deal with the U.S. Attorney, in Brooklyn, that in exchange for his testimony, he would not be charged with the nineteen murders to which he admitted participating.

"Neil, nineteen fuckin' murders this guy does and he's fuckin' walking around and I'm away for five years. Tell me that's fair, will you."

"Paulie, life isn't fair," I retorted, "but who's to say. A lot goes into these decisions. I'm sure it wasn't reached easily."

Paulie went on and on for a bit but ultimately, he did his time.

A far as I know, he didn't tire of playing pinochle and never cooperated.

SOMETIMES MONEY IS NOTHING BUT TROUBLE

Most people, at one time or another, have probably played the lottery in some form, hoping that the numbers or scratch-off results would make for an instant millionaire. Imagine the feeling of winning all that money and the thoughts about what you would do with your newfound wealth? But very often there's a downside to instant and unexpected riches.

On February 26, 1981, while riding through the streets of South Philadelphia, an unemployed longshoreman named Joey Coyle and two friends, stumbled across several canvas bags on the roadside. A short time before, the bags had been picked up from the Philadelphia Reserve Bank by Purolator Armored Services and had fallen out of the back of one of their trucks.

Coyle and his pals were stunned when they discovered $1.2 million in one-hundred-dollar bills in the bags. In broad daylight and in full view of several witnesses, the loot was loaded into the car and the trio drove off. The Chevrolet Malibu they had driven was soon being broadcast by the police as being connected to the missing money and Joey's friends urged him to return their newfound wealth and surrender to the police. Joey was having none of it, and much like Robin Hood of Sherwood, he began doling out the loot to family, friends, and even strangers whom he had just met.

STORIES

Top photo: Al MacDonald, foreground, and Neil Moran escorting Frank Santos out of the FBI's JFK Resident Agency enroute to his appearance in Brooklyn Federal Court. Bottom photo: Joey Coyle, wearing sunglasses, pictured on the left and Frank Santos on the right.

One group you can always count to come crawling out of the woodwork in these situations, no different than cockroaches and rats in a tenement, is *La Cosa Nostra*. Mario "Sonny" Riccobene (Isn't it funny that in tales like this there is always a Sonny), a member of the crime family of Nicodemo "Little Nicky" Scarfo, tracked down Joey and told him he would solve all his problems if he would part with $400,000 of the newfound loot. Riccobene promised he would launder the money at a casino and return it in smaller denominations. He probably also asked Coyle if he wanted to make a sound real estate investment and buy the Brooklyn Bridge, he could also broker the deal.

In only a matter of days, amid intense media publicity, pressure from family and friends, and now bobbing and weaving from the entire Scarfo crime family, Joey and his friend, Frank Santos, fled Philadelphia and traveled to New York City. There they bought plane tickets to Acapulco scheduled for departure the following day, March 3rd.

As people filed into the FBI office on Queens Boulevard, that morning, our supervisor had popped out of his office and told the squad not to go anywhere. About ten minutes later, he waved everyone in and told several of us to head out to JFK Airport. The Philadelphia FBI office had just called and had received a tip that the local longshoreman in the news, tied to the missing money from the armored car, was booked on a 10:00 a.m. flight to Acapulco.

"Hurry up and get out there before he boards the plane," our boss said.

"He may have someone with him. I was told they may be disguising themselves."

For anyone who has traveled the city day-to-day, the last place on the entire planet you want to be when you are in a rush is the Van Wyck Expressway. Whether it's 10:00 a.m. or 10:00 p.m., it's a glorified parking lot. Lights and sirens blaring made little difference, but at about 9:30 a.m., we screeched into the terminal and ran inside. In a clip right out of the final scene of the 1968 Steve McQueen film, *Bullitt*, we scanned the passengers in the process of boarding.

"I think that's them," I said to my partner Al MacDonald. "That one guy looks like he has something running down the side of his cheek."

As we approached, they immediately spotted us and the duo quickly spun around to avoid eye contact. There was no blending in with the crowd, our dress shirts, ties, and trench coats told them we were the law.

"FBI gentlemen, step away from the other passengers and please, no sudden movements," Al said. The two immediately complied and as we walked to the counter to search them, I noticed that Joey Coyle, with no known experience as a beautician, had dyed his hair as it trickled down his face.

"I'm happy that you guys are here. I was hoping it would be the FBI if we were arrested," Joey said. "I guess I can stop running now."

As we searched them, money was everywhere. Even Joey's knee-high boots were hemorrhaging one-hundred-dollar bills. The final count amounted to $105,000.

Joey and Santos (who was not charged) gave full statements.

"You guys are great," Joey said, "I thought you'd be hard-asses and try and beat a confession out of me. Please give me all your names. If I ever write a book, you'll all be in it."

The following March, Joey stood trial in state court in Philadelphia. I was the sole witness for the FBI with regard to his arrest.

Interestingly, Joey had mounted a defense pleading temporary insanity, claiming that when he came upon the money, he lost the ability to think straight. Leading up to the trial, there was a public outcry to dismiss all charges. Joey had officially taken on modern day Robin Hood folk hero status.

I didn't feel as though Joey's attorney would have a lot of questions. I was dead wrong. I was on the stand for hours. I never faced such hostility. As I testified and established eye contact with the jury, it was clear they didn't like me. The packed gallery was no different. Even the judge seemed to be in Joey's corner and didn't hesitate to take a shot at me when he saw an opening.

"Speak up, Agent Moran, we can't hear you," he sneered. I was face-to-face with the same citizenry that pelted Santa Claus with snowballs at a legendary Philadelphia Eagles game on national television in December 1968! The jury was out for only a short duration.

"Joey Not Guilty," *The Philadelphia Inquirer* headline read the following day.

A movie starring John Cusack and a book followed. Given Joey's prior history of sub-par negotiating skills with the mob, he probably wasn't living large with these ventures. He had a long struggle with an addiction to methamphetamines and sadly, in 1993, took his own life. Yes, sometimes money is nothing but trouble.

MODEL GARAGE

Investigating stolen merchandise taken from armed hijackings and property thefts was often a long and arduous process.

Enough probable cause had to be established to apply for a search warrant, which often led to days of round-the-clock surveillance at a fixed location.

Very often, there were no bathrooms or decent places to get food for those of us that were fussy eaters.

The most difficult part of any investigation of stolen merchandise as we quickly learned was when we finally moved in, made arrests, and recovered the goods.

A call would be placed to the victim company and often would go something like this:

"Oh, the FBI has recovered our gumball machines. What great news. We'll send out a crew to pick up the recovered items. We can't thank you enough."

Hours later, a tractor trailer would pull up ready to haul the merchandise back to the company and "the crew" usually consisted of a seventy-year-old driver, who upon arrival would say, "I only drive trucks. Nothing else. It's in our contract."

For the next four to five hours, depending on the commodity, five to ten FBI agents could be seen hauling gumball machines, color televisions, tin ingots, liquor, and anything else one could imagine, from a warehouse, or a cumbersome basement and begin loading the goods onto a trailer.

It could often be backbreaking work and in July, August, December, or January, it could also be brutal.

The FBI's administrative division in the New York office had obtained the name of a reliable towing business in the Sunset Park section of Brooklyn, called Model Garage.

The office had been preparing for its move from East 69th Street to the federal building downtown at 26 Federal Plaza in 1978.

Model Garage had been in business since the late 1940s and was operated by Harold and Maxine Pincus and their son, Harvey.

Model's resume included contracts with twenty-six Brooklyn car dealerships and a longtime relationship with Carriage House Motors, a premier motor car dealer in Manhattan, specializing in luxury brands including Rolls-Royce, Ferrari, Aston Martin, Porsche, and Mercedes Benz.

Model Garage was tasked with the movement of cars from several nearby garages the office had leased through the years and had stored all their cars for daily usage by the agents.

"There had been several break-ins at the garages on and near East 69th Street and a number of the cars had their tires stolen and had been vandalized. We managed to get everything out without a hitch and we made a good impression," Harvey Pincus recalled.

"This is stuff we had been doing for years and to us it wasn't a big deal, but the people in the office seemed to like our work and so the relationship began."

The hijacking squad had been asking the administrative folks for years to help us out with a reliable towing service, and nothing ever seemed to work out.

Enter Model Garage.

We had recovered a load of stolen cigarettes and had been told that the office had found a reliable firm to assist us. They reached out to Model, and they responded within the hour.

Harvey Pincus, accompanied by his father, Harold, and four of their employees came on the scene and I will never forget Harvey's words, "Relax guys, we've got this."

And for the reminder of that day, we barely lifted a finger. We had been so used to doing this by ourselves, we all felt obligated to pitch in, which we did, primarily so we could get the hell out of there quicker.

And so, it went from that point forward.

Whether it was the hijacking squad and then in the years that followed with the Joint Auto Larceny Task Force with the NYPD, Model Garage was our 'go to' business to solve any and all of our logistical problems.

As we had more and more dealings with Model, it wasn't uncommon for us to go to their office in Sunset Park.

I will never forget the first time I walked in and saw the condition of the garage. You could literally eat off the floor.

In our experience, towing, collision, or repair shops weren't necessarily the neatest places. It wasn't uncommon in most shops to see a transmission, car doors, or other car parts strewn about and oil and grease stains in abundance.

Not so in Model.

The lady's department at Sak's Fifth Avenue had nothing on Model when it came to organization and fastidiousness.

The office was the domain of Harvey's mother, Maxine.

I don't think I ever walked into the office when Maxine didn't have a telephone in both ears.

"Model, can I help you?" she would belt out.

"Model, please hold."

In another life, Maxine could have fit in perfectly on the old trading floor of the New York Stock Exchange or even as a drill instructor on Parris Island, putting U.S. Marine recruits through their paces.

It seemed the more hectic, the better.

Multi-tasking was Maxine's middle name.

In summary, the place was run like a well-oiled machine.

For once, the New York FBI office had gotten it right.

When I retired from the Bureau in May 2000 and for most of my post FBI career, I worked at the accounting firm, BDO Seidman, now BDO USA. One thing I learned quickly, no matter what the request from a client or potential client, never say no to potential business. There is always a way to figure it out and make it work.

Model Garage and Harvey Pincus followed that tenet.

"I had received a call from an inspector in the NYPD, who asked if I had that ability to remove concrete from the floor of an old auto body shop in Staten Island. The inspector told me that they were trying to solve an old homicide and believed the victim was buried beneath the concrete.

"Naturally, I said, 'Of course,'" Harvey recalled.

Since its inception in the late 1940s, Model had an impeccable reputation and over that time their Rolodex was sizeable. They knew they could pick up the phone and get virtually anything done.

"Our relationships were by handshake, first with my dad and then as he got older, with me. No contracts. We didn't operate that way." Harvey said.

"People knew that our word was all they needed."

Of course, Harvey made everything work in Staten Island. The victim was unearthed and so began Model's reputation as 1-800- "We dig for dead bodies."

"We have done a total of five 'digs,'" Harvey said.

One high profile 'dig' which lasted several weeks was an FBI/NYPD request to search for two high-ranking members of the Bonanno LCN Crime Family.

In May 1981, as depicted in the movie, *Donnie Brasco*, starring Johnny Depp as undercover FBI agent, Joseph Pistone, and Al Pacino as 'Lefty Guns' Ruggiero, three Bonanno LCN Crime Family capos, Alphonse 'Sonny Red' Indelicato, Philip Giaccone, and Dominick 'Big Trin' Trinchera were called to a sit-down in Brooklyn, in an attempt to make peace within the family.

All three were gunned down by the rival faction and their bodies were eventually dumped in a vacant lot in Queens.

It was only a short time after when 'Sonny Red's' body was discovered at the lot.

Acting on the information of Bonanno family members now cooperating with the FBI, in December 2004, Model Garage was called to help the FBI and the NYPD with a 'dig' in the immediate vicinity of where Alphonse Indelicato's body was buried.

"I had to call in a few favors for this one," Harvey Pincus began.

"We needed heavy excavation equipment. We were there for three weeks before we finally uncovered the remains," he added.

At the conclusion of the 'dig,' at what became to be known by investigators as 'The Hole,' the New York Medical Examiner's Office identified the skeletons as those of Philip Giaccone and Dominick Trinchera.

In 2004, an old nemesis of the truck hijacking squad, seventy-one-year-old Burt Kaplan, began cooperating with the government in an effort to reduce his sentence and get released from prison.

Kaplan advised that in the 1980s and 1990s, he had collaborated with Lucchese LCN Crime Family underboss, Anthony 'Gaspipe' Casso, in retaining the services of two corrupt NYPD detectives, Louis Eppolito and Stephen Caracappa, later dubbed the 'Mafia Cops,' to murder at their behest.

One such contract was an Israeli diamond dealer, Israel Greenwald, whom Kaplan feared might be cooperating with the government.

At Kaplan's direction, in February 1986, detectives Eppolito and Caracappa pulled over Mr. Greenwald and took him to an auto repair garage on Flatbush and Nostrand Avenue, in Brooklyn, where he was shot by a mob associate and later buried beneath the concrete floor.

In 2005, following the arrests of detectives Eppolito and Caracappa and with witnesses coming forward, the FBI and NYPD were led to the garage where Mr. Greenwald had been buried some nineteen years prior.

1-800—"We dig for dead bodies," was now on the case.

"We didn't pinpoint the exact location on the large garage floor right away," Harvey recalled.

Anthony "Gaspipe" Casso—Lucchese Family underboss.

"It was either the second or third try and we noticed heavy plastic and thought we might have something. As we continued removing the heavy pieces of concrete, we saw what looked like a body inside the plastic. I will never forget it. It was a man who was wearing a dark suit with a dress shirt. His tie was still perfectly knotted. The tie clasp was in place. The body was virtually entombed and very well preserved. It really looked like he was just sleeping. It was pretty amazing."

Harvey Pincus and FBI agents at the Brooklyn garage where the body of Israel Greenwald was unearthed.

Mr. Greenwald's remains were eventually turned over to his family and he was buried in Israel.

Harvey recalled early on in his relationship with the Bureau having just finished dinner at his Brooklyn home, when the evening switchboard operator from the New York office called.

"Mr. Sheer (Tom Sheer, assistant director in charge of the office) is broken down on the Prospect Expressway in Brooklyn. Can you respond and help him?" the operator asked.

"Of course, I will be there within the hour," was Harvey's reply.

"Hi, are you Harvey?" Tom Sheer asked upon Harvey's arrival.

"Yes, Mr. Sheer. I'll get you out of here in a few minutes and on your way."

As the two sat in the tow truck, Mr. Sheer asked, "So is the office treating you well? Are we paying you on time?"

There was a long pause as Harvey pondered whether he should tell the boss that the office was behind some $91,500 in payments.

"What, you must be kidding—$91,500, that's unacceptable. You must make a living too. I'll get to the bottom of this, I promise."

Two days later, a check for the full amount arrived via Express Mail at Model Garage.

Harvey also recalled another case when he was summoned to the Bronx by the NYPD to remove all the heavy construction equipment at a scrap yard belonging Carmine Agnello, the son-in-law of Gambino LCN Crime Family boss, John Gotti.

Carmine Agnello, married to Gotti's daughter, Victoria, was in the scrap metal business and was being prosecuted by the U.S. Attorney's office in Brooklyn. The government ordered that all his equipment be seized.

Among the functions that Mr. Agnello's operation performed was shredding cars into small metal strips.

Harvey engaged one of Agnello's workers in the upstairs office at New York Shredding, when he observed a 55-gallon, steel drum filled with pennies, nickels, dimes, and quarters.

"I had never seen anything like it," Harvey said.

Naturally curious as to where all the change came from, the worker explained.

"He told me that when the employees would prepare to shred a car, they would normally strip the inside clean, the seats, the glass, the radio, and anything that was removable until there was nothing left but metal. As the car was put on a conveyor belt, which was able to rotate the vehicle in a number of positions, any loose change in the car would drop down to a pan they had rigged up to catch the falling money."

When Harvey asked how much the employee believed was in the drum he said unhesitatingly, "about $75,000."

Hopefully, for Mr. Agnello's sake, there were many 55-gallon drums filled with change.

He was ordered to forfeit $10 million, pay $950,000 in restitution, and $150,000 in back taxes to the Internal Revenue Service.

Next time you're in your car and loose change falls out of your pocket somewhere and it's difficult to reach just think of this story.

Maxine and Harold are now sadly gone. They were wonderful and honest people, not always the case in this line of work. I don't know any agent or detective who ever had a cross word to say about Harvey or his parents.

Through the years, I count myself as one of many FBI agents and NYPD detectives who became personal friends and remain in contact with Harvey and often socialize with him.

Personally, we love going to dinner in Brooklyn with Harvey and his girlfriend, Emily. You always get the best seat in the house, a recommendation for the finest of the menu's 'specials,' and leave being on a first-name basis with the staff.

ITSP

ITSP or Interstate Transportation of Stolen Property is just one of the hundreds of federal statutes for which the FBI has investigative jurisdiction.

It was now 1980. Bob Joyce, Andy Conlin, Jerry Cox, and I had been transferred to Dave Steckler's squad in Queens.

We had all worked on the Lufthansa Robbery investigation since December 1978 and Henry Hill was cooperating and uncovered the Boston College point shaving scandal that rocked the world of collegiate basketball and all collegiate sports.

ITSP is exactly what it says: the transportation of stolen goods across state lines.

As one can imagine, this was quite a common occurrence that kept us busy.

By sheer default, Bob Joyce and I quickly became art specialists in the New York office.

Simply by getting assigned several cases involving stolen art, interviewing victims of the thefts of high value artifacts, and establishing relationships with New York's Metropolitan Museum of Modern Art (MOMA) and the International Association for Art Research (IFAR), we quickly became educated.

Now full disclosure—Bob and I wouldn't be able to discern a Rembrandt from a Renoir or a Michaelangelo sculpture from a Rodin or the Hope Diamond from a cheap imitation but we soon learned that we really didn't have to.

What we learned early on was that the art world is a tight community and people talk to one another, which is good for investigators.

Unlike truck hijackings, where the bad guys stick up a truck and have an unlimited number of buyers for a load of color televisions, it's not that easy to unload a precious and priceless artifact.

Take Leonardo da Vinci's *Mona Lisa,* surely one of the world's most well-known paintings.

In 1911, the *Mona Lisa* was on display in the Louvre Museum, in Paris, France.

In August of that year, Vincenzo Peruggia, an employee, walked out of the museum with the painting stashed under his clothes.

Apparently, Peruggia believed that the *Mona Lisa* had been stolen by Napoleon, and felt it was his responsibility as an Italian to return it to Italy.

Although there are those who questioned Mr. Peruggia's 'patriotic' motives and why he was still in possession of this priceless work two years later, Mr. Peruggia, unable to offload the painting elsewhere, attempted to sell it to a gallery in Florence, Italy, and was arrested.

A prime example of the cooperation we enjoyed was a tip we received through the art community from our Legal Attache in Ottawa, Canada.

The FBI maintains a presence in many cities throughout the world including Paris, London, Tokyo, Tel Aviv, Rome, Mexico City, Beijing, New Delhi, Canberra, and dozens of others.

Attached to the U.S. Embassies in these locales, the FBI coordinates requests from the host country for assistance with investigations in the U.S., as well as our requests for assistance in the host country.

Authorities in Quebec had been provided with information from an art dealer in early 1983 that one Paul Kunkul, a well-known art journalist in the U.S., was in possession of a painting, *Spring in Central Park*. Mr. Kunkul was reported to have stolen the painting from its owner's home in Montreal. It was said to be valued at $200,000.

Bob and I were provided with the name of the individual, and he was believed to be residing in Manhattan.

It took about ten minutes to locate Mr. Kunkul's address on the Upper East Side.

This was what is known in police jargon as a 'slam dunk,'—Name, address, and telephone number of the suspect.

This was hopefully going to be as simple as it appeared. We were even thinking of calling the suspect to bring the painting in and surrender without us even leaving the office, but there was protocol to be followed.

We learned that we would be joined by two Sherbrooke, Quebec, Provincial Police detectives, Jean Charette and Real Chateauneuf.

We picked up the two detectives at their hotel in midtown Manhattan and immediately headed up to Mr. Kunkul's apartment.

A quick chat with the doorman asking if Mr. Kunkul was at home revealed that he was.

A knock on the door and there stood Mr. Kunkul, a bit taken back with four men standing in his doorway.

"Good morning, Mr. Kunkul, my name is Neil Moran. This is Bob Joyce, and we are FBI agents. These gentlemen are with the Quebec Provincial Police. May we come in?" I asked.

"Yes, of course," he said and visibly shaken.

I thought, *this is going to be a slam dunk, this guy is terrified.*

"Mr. Kunkul, do you have any idea why the four of us are here and why we would like to speak with you?" I asked.

"Yes, I do."

"And would that have anything to do with a painting you might have in your possession, *Spring in Central Park*?"

"Yes, sir," he replied.

"And to cut to the chase, do you have that painting in the apartment?"

"No, it's not here. It's in a locker at Grand Central Station," he said.

I advised Mr. Kunkul of his rights, and he promptly provided us with a key to the locker.

Bob Joyce and Detective Charette drove down to Grand Central Station and retrieved the painting, while Detective Chateauneuf and I continued to chat with Mr. Kunkul.

"One of the easier things we've ever done," Bob said.

Very anxious to get this resolved, after my conversation with an assistant United States attorney from the Southern District of New York, they concluded that if Mr. Kunkul agreed to accompany the detectives back to Canada, they would decline any federal prosecution.

Mr. Kunkul readily agreed.

Mr. Kunkul's attorney later claimed he was suffering from psychological problems and suffered from depression.

As a result, the judge in Sherbrooke, Quebec, sentenced Mr. Kunkul to two years' probation, and he was prohibited from ever returning to Canada.

Detective Charette and Detective Chateauneuf were celebrated as heroes at home.

1983 media coverage in Quebec, Canada of recovery of stolen painting in New York City by the FBI and Quebec police.

In 1983, we received word from our office in Charlotte, North Carolina, that eleven Polish-born men and women had been arrested by local authorities. When the trunks of their vehicles were searched, approximately $275,000 worth of jewelry, furs, sterling silver, and other household items were discovered.

An itemized list of the stolen loot revealed that the crew had begun their journey in Texas, and swung right through the south, hitting Louisiana, Mississippi, Alabama, Georgia, South Carolina, and Charlotte, where they were apprehended.

Oddly enough, somehow, they made bail and yes, all eleven people had identified Brooklyn, New York, addresses as their residences.

Often referred to as 'Little Poland,' the Greenpoint section of Brooklyn has historically been known as a working-class neighborhood with predominantly Polish-themed restaurants, butcher shops and businesses.

With the gentrification of many New York neighborhoods today, Greenpoint has changed considerably and is now home to many Gen X and Gen Z'ers.

My past impressions of Greenpoint were that it was one of New York's better-kept neighborhoods with the Polish people taking immense pride in maintaining clean streets and contributing to making it safe for their residents.

Bob was a bit more familiar with the neighborhood as his wife, Kathy, had been raised on North Eighth Street.

The defendants and those like them, commonly known as 'Gypsies,' were another story altogether.

They have a variety of swindles in which they try to gain access to a home to bilk people and make a quick buck.

A group of women and small girls will swarm into a store and attempt to distract security while others are running out with stolen merchandise hidden.

Another popular ruse, and what the FBI learned was most prominent in the seven states they connected to the eleven people arrested, was when a woman and two children would ring the doorbell of an upscale home and begin to engage the homeowner in conversation.

Sometimes, they would attempt to keep the discussion going long enough so other members of the group could ransack the home by gaining entrance to the rear of the house.

Other times, the woman would feign passing out while talking to the homeowner saying that she was overcome by the heat, again while the home is being burglarized.

We were directed to an address on Meserole Street and one on nearby Java Street—locations where all eleven suspects had listed as their apartments.

Armed with mug shots of all eleven, Bob and I sought out the superintendent at the Meserole Street location, who upon seeing the photos flew into a rage.

In heavily accented Polish, I recall him saying, "Those fucking people. They better not ever come back here, or they will be sorry. Come I show you," he yelled angrily.

Here we were, in an upstairs apartment that had been completely cleaned out in the middle of the night.

"Look at this fucking mess," the super continued.

And mess he wasn't kidding—trash everywhere, cigarette butts, empty beer and soda cans, liquor bottles, food scraps, ants and roaches crawling up the walls, and a telephone cord ripped out of the wall with no telephone. They even left their most recent telephone bill behind.

A quick look saw dozens of international calls to the tune of $50 to $60 each. The bill was well over $1,500.

"I was nice to these people. They pleaded for me to let them catch up with rent. They were behind three months. The landlord makes me responsible for collecting the rent and he was getting impatient. Now he is mad with me—all because of these fucking people."

We did feel bad for the guy, but this was the scenario at every stop we made.

Apparently, word had spread amongst the Romani community that the south was easy pickens and we continued to get more cases with addresses in Greenpoint.

Bob and I became obsessed with these investigations and started a bulletin board in the office with dozens of pictures like we were organizing an LCN crime family.

You knew we were really in the thick of things when I received a call from a detective in the 105th Precinct in Queens.

"Hello, agent Moran, I understand you and your partner are the FBI's 'Gypsy' experts."

I burst out laughing,

"Don't laugh," he said.

"I got your name from a detective in Greenpoint who said you and your partner are fixtures in the 94th Precinct. I have some Polish 'Gypsies' who are sweeping through the neighborhood and they're like cockroaches—we can't catch them. Our captain is furious, and he wants these people the hell out of our precinct."

These cases were among the most frustrating we ever worked.

With heat on and outstanding warrants on many of them, in the early 1980s it was a lot easier to get out of the country than today and through Interpol, we believed that a good number of them fled back to eastern Europe and eluded us.

Matty Moran holding Neil Moran and Patricia Murphy in 1951.

PATRICIA

I think about her regularly, especially now since I've gotten older. She was taken much too soon with so much ahead. This wasn't in anyone's plans, least of all Patricia's.

We were the two oldest grandchildren in the family and although we didn't live in the same Bronx neighborhood, our families would regularly meet at Williamsbridge Reservoir Oval Park on Sunday afternoons after Mass and then it was onto Grandma's apartment for dinner.

In the 1950s, it was a scene that probably played out regularly in numerous New York neighborhoods, where Italian, German, Jewish, Irish, and other immigrant groups had settled. Their children were now raising families of their own nearby.

Although only a little less than three years separated us, every eight-millimeter movie or still photo showed Patricia hovering over me, so much so that my regular falls seemed to be triggered by said hovering.

With Irish uncles owning bungalows in Breezy Point and Lavalette, New Jersey, all our vacations made for lasting memories. Patricia was a blessing to the parents, as she would organize games for all the cousins and keep everyone occupied on those occasionally dreadful rainy days.

The Murphy's were the first of the O'Brien and Moran cousins to move from the city and settled in Floral Park. As our family was still living in the Bronx, Patricia now seemed so far away, but I always was invited to spend several weeks on Long Island which was truly the highlight of my summer.

In the blink of an eye, Patricia was in high school attending Mary Louis Academy in Jamaica, Queens. My aunt's house always seemed to be a gathering place for Patricia, and from a grade schooler's perspective, her very glamorous friends.

"This is my cousin, Neil," she would begin, "but we call him Neilly boy," as she always referred to me.

Even though just a few years separated us, Patricia was growing into a young woman, while I was still doing boy stuff with my cousins Brian and Kevin.

While attending St. John's several years later, Patricia and her friends attended a mixer, where cadets from the U.S. Military Academy at West Point were in attendance. It was there, Patricia met the love of her life, Joe.

"Neilly boy, it would make me so happy if you would be in my wedding party," Patricia said following their engagement while they were still in college.

After graduating in 1968, Patricia and Joe were married at the Holy Trinity Chapel at West Point, in a beautiful military ceremony, of which I was proud to be a part.

It was off to Fort Sill, Oklahoma, and then a tour in West Germany. Suddenly, Patricia, who had never been outside of New York, was seeing the country and the world.

It was off to Fort Bragg, North Carolina, and following reassignment to Fort Devens, in Massachusetts, Joe was offered an opportunity to attend law school at nearby Northeastern University.

Patricia and I were both conscientious writers and we regularly exchanged letters that kept me updated on the life of a military wife.

"Why don't you come up for a visit," she wrote, shortly after I graduated from college.

I didn't hesitate. I hopped into my Volkswagen and drove up to Belmont, Massachusetts, for the weekend. It was as if we were children again. I never enjoyed myself so much, but as I left on Sunday, I couldn't help but think that Patricia missed home a bit.

Sometime after receiving his JD from Northeastern, Joe was offered a post to join the faculty and staff at the Judge Advocate General School, attached to the University of Virginia, in Charlottesville.

It was only about a year later, that Joe received word that he was being transferred to South Korea.

Now with two small children, they decided that Patricia and the little ones would remain, while Joe completed his tour, hopefully for only a year or so.

I was now married with two little ones of my own when Patricia called one summer evening, "Neilly boy, would you and Maureen and the girls come down to stay for a week or so? I would love the company, and the children would have so much fun."

We didn't hesitate and drove down to Charlottesville during a very steamy week in July.

Patricia, true to form, couldn't do enough when we arrived. A tour of the UVA campus, including historic Monticello, barbecues, meeting neighbors, and the highlight of the visit, our middle daughter, Colleen, taking her first steps.

"Your cousin is about the sweetest person I've ever met," my wife Maureen said on the car ride home.

About a month or two after our trip, I received a call from my father.

"I just got off the phone with your aunt, Patricia hasn't been feeling well. She's going through some tests to see what's wrong. Seems that she can't stop coughing. They're even talking about Joe possibly coming home and cutting his tour in Korea short."

Then came the news that blindsided the entire family. At thirty-five, Patricia had contracted esophageal cancer.

Where did this come from?

Patricia neither smoked nor drank was very trim and certainly had never done anything to bring this on.

Radiation, chemo, and all that ensues from those often-dreadful treatments, followed.

As Patricia led her life, like the little girl I knew and the gracious and loving woman she became, she didn't change the slightest throughout her illness.

Upbeat and sometimes straining to smile, Patricia was determined to attend every family function, and forever more interested in what you had been doing than talking about or focusing on herself.

Patricia finally lost her struggle on December 4, 1983.

She was buried in a military ceremony at the cemetery in West Point, only steps from where she had exchanged wedding vows only fourteen years earlier.

I visit her grave every December. It's so calm, peaceful, and immaculately maintained, with not a blade of grass askew. Christmas wreaths adorn every plot. Headstones from the 1800s appear as though they were mounted last month.

A fitting resting place for such a beautiful and loving woman.

With no distractions and alone in my thoughts, I keep Patricia updated about my daughters and now grandchildren, who would all have undoubtedly benefited from her character, love and friendship.

THE VOLVO

"There are eight million stories in the naked city; this has been [is] one of them," so goes the quote at the conclusion of the 1948 film set in New York, *The Naked City*.

Through forty-nine years of a blissful marriage, memorable stories are likely to emerge. This is among the best.

It was probably sometime in the early to mid-1980s when our normally reliable 1976 Chevrolet Nova began to experience one mechanical nightmare after another. This workhorse had served us well.

Annual vacation treks to Cape Cod and the infamous trip to Seabrook Island, South Carolina, when our fuel line decided to cease operating on I-95 at 3:00 a.m. I am as sentimental as the next guy, but just like my beloved '69' Volkswagen had eventually met its demise, it was time to move on.

"All my cousins have Volvos, and they swear by them. They're supposed to be a very safe car," as my wife, Maureen, weighed in on her preference.

A *Volvo*, I thought. Pretty damn expensive. My wife was studying for her nursing degree, we had three children in Catholic school all wearing braces and we were paying the bills on a paltry government salary. But as my father once advised, "Sometimes you do things for marital harmony," so I tried to make it work. After all, she wasn't asking for a Bentley or an Aston Martin.

So, as many of us did almost forty years ago, I picked up *Newsday* and began to thumb through the used automobile sales.

"Massapequa—1978 Volvo, 240 DL, Hunter green, beige cloth interior, four-door, sunroof, 56,000 miles, mint condition—a steal at $4,995—call 516-555-1234 and ask for Morty."

Morty from Massapequa, I thought. Sounds like a caller to WFAN radio, the all sports network. At 56,000, it was a little more mileage than I had hoped, but I decided to take a ride to Massapequa and check it out.

Morty sounded like a bit of a character when we spoke, and he certainly didn't disappoint.

As I pulled up in front of his house, I could see him in the picture window on the phone and he gave a quick wave as I began to inspect the car, which sported several bumps and bruises and was far from "mint."

I did notice that the license plates were crooked as though they had just been slapped on and a quick observation of the registration sticker revealed that the plates didn't match.

"Neil?" Morty asked.

"Yes, how's it going? Morty?"

"Yes, nice car, isn't it? You're not going to find many like this around. This baby's in mint condition."

Oh boy, I thought. Morty with his combover should be doing TV commercials for the "Hair Club for Men." I asked all the logical questions and it was no shock that Morty had all the standard stock answers. From the looks of him, in street vernacular, Morty could best be described as a knock around guy, who may have run a regular three-card monte game on Canal Street.

"How come the plates don't match those on the registration?" I asked.

"What are you a cop?" was Morty's quick reply.

"Only a cop would ask a question like that."

If Morty only knew, I thought.

"No, I'm not a cop. I'm just one of those people who notice little things."

When we got past the plate issue and talked about flexibility in price, we agreed that I would bring my wife back that night for a look and a test drive.

So, here we were on Sunrise Highway several hours later, as I prepped Maureen to deal with the likes of Morty from Massapequa.

Even though Maureen was raised on East 99th Street and Lexington Avenue and navigated through the New York City subway system each day in high school, I often wondered if she had grown up in Cedar Rapids, Iowa.

"I can't believe it has a sunroof, Neil," she blurted out excitedly.

"See, this is what I mean. You're already gushing about the damn sunroof. Don't say anything about the car when you get in, I'm begging you. If this guy asks if you like it just be non-committal. Don't volunteer anything. Very low key. If he senses that you're head over heels, he's likely not to budge in price."

"I understand, I got it."

Did she really get it, I thought?

"You must be Mrs. Moran," Morty from Massapequa said as we arrived, exhibiting all the charm as though he was greeting Princess Diana of Wales.

What had I gotten myself into?

"Would you like to get behind the wheel and take her for a drive?" Morty asked.

Suddenly, this seven or eight-year-old car was assigned its own pronoun, "her."

"Oh yes, Morty thanks."

What was she thanking him for, I wondered?

Everything was about to go south, I thought. Nothing good can come of this. Morty would no doubt jack up the asking price after ten minutes with this rube from Cedar Rapids at the helm.

As she pulled away with Morty in the driver's seat and me, now quite anxious in the back, Maureen asked, "Morty could we open the sunroof while I drive?"

"Oh, of course, how could I forget. It's such a nice evening and perfect for driving with the sunroof open."

You would have thought Morty was opening the hatch to a space capsule with the eyes of the nation on him as he very slowly and deliberately reached for the gizmo to open it.

It didn't take long when Maureen's hair, which was shoulder length at the time, began flying around from the soft summer breeze and as she brushed it aside with a smile as wide as the Brooklyn Bridge blurted out, "Oh Morty, I love this car!"

You know the feeling you have when you bump your head badly, and the blood seems to give a rush that makes you lightheaded and you think you might lose consciousness?

I wanted to die right in that back seat. I felt like getting sick to my stomach.

I think we were somewhere in the next town on our way home before I agreed to speak to Maureen.

"How could you?" I asked.

"Everything we spoke about. It's as though we never had that conversation."

"I know but I really do love that car and a sunroof, imagine having a sunroof?"

"No, quite frankly, I haven't been kept awake nights dreaming about a damn sunroof. My big concern is what we will pay for the car."

As it turned out, before we spoke again about a price, Morty and I took the Volvo to my friend Albert's transmission shop in Amityville. It didn't take five minutes for Albert to show me that the car had been in a major accident.

"The chassis is bent like a fucking pretzel Neil," Albert said.

"This guy is trying to run a game on you. Lucky you brought it in," Albert said annoyingly.

"Hey, you, what's your name, Morty? Come over here. What the fuck is this?" as Albert motioned to the car's undercarriage which was on the lift.

"This car has been in a major accident, and I suppose you're going to tell me you had no idea, right?" Morty, not quite as cocky with Albert from Amityville as he was in his brief encounter with Maureen from Cedar Rapids, looked like he had just been fingered in a lineup for a double homicide.

"Don't even say a word. I want you and this fucking car out of my shop, and I mean now."

It goes without saying, we never bought the car from Morty and as luck would have it, a colleague from Garden City had a neighbor who was selling a Volvo station wagon with only 8,000 miles, fully equipped and yes, thankfully with Maureen's beloved sunroof.

AN AFTERNOON SAIL

We had vacationed together in recent years and given the ages of our young families, each summer was more enjoyable than the last.

My wife's cousin, Bryan, was an avid sailor and a U.S. Navy veteran. In the weeks preceding our upcoming trip, he called to say that he had seen a 'For Sale' sign at his local VFW post for a sailboat.

"The owner gave me a good deal, so I bought it."

Bryan, his brother, Michael, and three sisters, Mary, Patricia and Barbara, had been raised in the Inwood section of Manhattan, in the Dyckman Street housing complex before moving to the Jersey shore where he soon found love being on the water.

During the height of the Vietnam War rather than immediately attending college, Bryan decided to join the U.S. Navy Sea, Air, and Land Teams, better known as the Navy SEALs. During training, he discovered that he had an inner ear issue that affected his equilibrium while submerged in deep water. He could not complete SEAL training but was soon reassigned to a nuclear submarine.

As was the case with many of us of Irish heritage sporting freckles and fair complexions, growing up in the 1950s, where sunscreen was non-existent, we didn't realize that prolonged exposure to the sun could be harmful. The prior year, he had been diagnosed with melanoma and had gone through a difficult round of chemotherapy and radiation treatments, resulting in the loss of all his hair.

Now bald as a newborn yet still strikingly handsome, Bryan was not anticipating any movie opportunities and never once considered wearing a toupee. His wife did not agree and for what my father used to refer to as 'marital harmony,' Bryan now wore a hairpiece.

We all settled in at beautiful Charlestown Beach, just over the Connecticut border into Rhode Island, and although weakened considerably by his medical condition, Bryan was determined not to allow anything to interfere with making this another memorable vacation.

As he pulled back the tarp, he was brimming with pride at his recent purchase.

"What do you think, nice huh?" he said.

"Why don't we try it out this afternoon when we return from the beach?"

"Sounds good," I said.

As the oppressive heat of the July day began to wind down and we made our way back to our bungalow, we gathered the children, life preservers, and the necessary gear for our maiden voyage.

Being a true Navy veteran and a stickler for safety, Bryan read off a list of dos and don'ts to the little ones as we strapped their preservers into place. Another thing that we explained to them was the importance of 'coming about,' or ducking down to avoid being hit in the head when the sail's mast and boom switch in a direction more advantageous to the wind.

As I looked at this pristine New England setting called Ninigret Pond, the largest of nine ponds or lagoons as they are also called, in southern Rhode Island, I thought scenes like this were what must have inspired Thoreau in his writings. Lily pads hugged every inch of the shoreline, and the water looked like a gigantic pane of smooth glass. It was as quiet and serene as the inside of a church.

As we slowly moved away from the shore, the children were abuzz with excitement and Bryan, with a wide smile, looked as though he could maneuver the boat while fast asleep. After traveling a considerable distance with the aid of an obliging breeze, we saw another small craft approaching when Bryan announced, "Remember guys, what I said earlier, when we need to change direction and 'come about?'" to which everyone nodded.

"So, when I give the signal, everyone is going to duck down, so they won't get hit by the boom, right?" and again, everyone concurred.

"Here we go, coming about," and with that the sail and boom suddenly swiveled around quickly whipping toward us as I shielded several of the children to ensure they wouldn't get hit. As I glanced upward, I saw the boom graze the back of Bryan's hat, which flew off his head and with it his hairpiece, as both plunged into the water.

As I saw the toupee sinking fast, I looked squarely at Bryan who was laughing hysterically as the children, all open-mouthed, stared at our now hairless ship's captain. When Bryan had recently confided in me his reluctance to wear the wig, I was shocked to learn the cost, which was quite considerable. With that conversation in mind, I said without hesitation, "Bryan, I am going in," and I dove into the water.

As I cupped both hands while submerged, I frantically searched where the hat and wig had landed and suddenly grabbed what felt like the missing rug. I triumphantly emerged with my hand thrust in the air, holding up the soaked hairpiece as if it was an Olympic medal.

With the children still shrieking with the sight of me in the water and Bryan laughing loudly, he successfully maneuvered the boat alongside where I was treading water and eventually, I struggled to get on board. We never stopped talking and laughing about the afternoon's events for the remainder of our stay.

It was only a few months later when I went to see Bryan at Memorial Sloan Kettering as the cancer had spread and ravaged his strapping 36-year-old body. Heavily sedated at this stage, I sat alone for a good while trying to make sense of it before he finally opened his eyes.

"Neil, thanks for coming," and almost without hesitation he said, "You know what I've been thinking about? The wig flying off my head into Ninigret Pond. Wasn't that the funniest?"

I was taken back. On the way over to the hospital with Bryan's bleak prognosis, I struggled with what I would say and how I would say it. Now suddenly we recounted every detail of that afternoon, talked about the vacation, all the fun and laughs we had, and how lucky he felt to have done something he truly enjoyed with his children before he could no longer do so.

Bryan passed away a short time after, but we continued the summer vacation tradition for the years that followed with his wife, Patty, and their children, Colleen and Brendan, and they never tired of recounting that memorable sail on Ninigret Pond.

Bryan McDermott

Bryan McDermott pictured with his daughter, Colleen at Ninigret Pond, Rhode Island, 1983.

THE CAPE

It was Labor Day weekend, sometime in the mid-1980s, as we wound down our annual trip to Cape Cod. Never allowing inclement weather to discourage us from enjoying the beauty New England has to offer, we piled our daughters in the car and headed to Provincetown. As we traveled up Route 6 and saw signs for Eastham, my wife, Maureen, suggested that we turn off and do some exploring. Winding through the streets and admiring the lovely homes and impeccably kept properties, the distinct smell of salty air was evident as we neared Cape Cod Bay.

Much like today, it wasn't uncommon to see people running on the roads thirty-five years ago, so it wasn't out of the ordinary when we saw a man in the distance approaching us. A person's running style is akin to his or her thumbprint, no two are the same. As the figure grew closer, I said to my wife, "This guy has a gait exactly like Frank Shorter."

On September 5, 1972, terrorists belonging to the group called Black September, murdered eleven Israeli athletes at the Munich Olympics. After deciding not to cancel the remainder of the Games, five days later, Frank Shorter won a gold medal in the Olympic Marathon, becoming the first American to do so since 1908. As a result of that victory, he is often credited with igniting the running boom in the U.S.

As both Maureen and I were avid runners and followed the sport closely, she knew that Shorter resided in Boulder, Colorado, where he operated several highly successful running shops.

"What would Frank Shorter be doing in Eastham, Massachusetts?" Maureen asked.

"I don't know," I said, "But look at this guy, he's really moving. If that's not him, it's his twin brother."

Before we knew it, the mystery man was steps away and as we slowed to get a good look, he did as well. Now one thing one runner would never want to do is startle another or interfere with his or her workout and the fact that we were in a car, I suddenly felt like we were stalkers and thought I should speed up. As we passed one another, we exchanged glances and continued on.

"Do you think that was him?" Maureen wondered.

"I guess we'll never know," I replied.

Several hours later I was bored out of my mind as my wife and daughters dragged me through shops with the largest selections of junk one could fathom. As I attempted to busy myself, searching for some small item that I would find appealing, my daughter, Meghan, now out of breath, startled me when she blurted out, "Daddy come quick; mommy's talking to Frank Shorter and his wife. That was him we saw running. He wants to meet you."

Everyone recalls times in their lives when suddenly the heartbeat grows faster, and things don't seem all that clear. As my daughter led me by the hand through the shop, this was quickly becoming one of those occasions.

As we grew closer, I saw Maureen and our other daughters smiling and laughing with a couple, as though they were former neighbors, and yes, I now realized I was standing alongside the 'Father of the Running Boom.'

"Hi, Frank Shorter," he said, extending his hand. As I exchanged greetings with one of the world's most highly decorated, influential, and successful track and field athletes, I'm sure that I must have looked excited yet confused, that this could actually be happening.

"We were chatting with your wife, and I told her that I was a little nervous when I saw the Dodge Caravan with the New York plates slowing down when I was running, but then when I passed and saw the children in the car, I was somewhat relieved. Your wife told us that you knew it was me even from a distance."

It's not often that any of us meet famous people and somehow throughout my lifetime, I've always wondered if they're that much different than ourselves. I don't remember too much of what I initially said to the 'Father of the Running Boom,' but as we stood there in the crowded shop, after a minute or two, I felt like I was trading cross-country and track stories with an old friend. He truly could not have been more unpretentious, and it was a September afternoon that I often look back upon fondly.

THE SWAT TEAM

About a year or so after the office opened in February 1978, in order to augment the SWAT Team in the main office in Manhattan, the offices in New Rochelle and Brooklyn Queens formed their own teams.

The Queens team is what I would call an 'All-Star' lineup if there ever was one.

Joe Klonowski, John Cable, Phil Hayden, David Carman, Al MacDonald, John Keenan, Billy Lynch, Ralph Ianuzzi, Tom Lenehan, George Hanna, and me were the original members.

George and I were the only team members that had not served in the armed forces.

The U.S. Marine Corps, the U.S. Army, and the U.S. Air Force were the three branches represented. The honors and decorations bestowed on these brave combat veterans and received in the Vietnam War are too numerous to list.

I was very proud to be a part of this elite group of FBI agents.

We trained once each month at Camp Smith, a military installation in Cortlandt Manor, New York,

Execution of search warrant and arrests of Hells Angels in lower Manhattan by the New York Office SWAT teams. Top photo shows John Cable atop the stairs carrying an MP-5. Neil Moran pictured below with a crowbar over the shoulder; Bottom photo shows Al MacDonald holding an M-16. The women pictured lower left were girlfriends of Hells Angels' members.

about thirty miles north of the city. The base is affiliated with the New York Army National Guard.

In addition to regular firearms training, we were schooled in utilizing specialized weapons and equipment not normally issued to regular FBI agents. These included automatic handguns (we all had been issued revolvers in Quantico, which was the standard issue), sniper rifles, M-16s, stun grenades, body armor, night-vision glasses and others.

Room clearing, close-quarters combat, door breaching, and rappelling out of helicopters were also things in which we were trained.

The primary use of SWAT was in high-risk situations where there was a likelihood of encountering problems.

The first high profile case that I can recall began on a Saturday evening, December 1, 1979.

SWAT Training Camp Smith, Peekskill, New York—Neil Moran learning to rappel out of a helicopter with Ed Guevara standing at right.

The Shah of Iran, Mohammad Reza Shah Pahlavi, was certainly a controversial figure to say the least.

A ruling monarch from 1941 through early 1979, with Iran in complete upheaval, he was overthrown and sought refuge in several countries until President Jimmy Carter reluctantly granted him entry into the U.S., on October 22, 1979.

The controversy surrounding the Shah led to the seizure of the U.S. Embassy in Iran being taken over and American hostages being held until they were released on January 20, 1981.

The Shah had been ill with cancer for some time. Once in the U.S., he was treated at New York's Weill Cornell Medical Center.

With pressure on the Carter administration to find a country that would welcome him, the U.S. rumors swirled as to where he might land.

The media was camped outside the hospital 24-7 as they sensed something would happen.

It was a Saturday and my wife and I were expecting company that evening, when the office called.

"Pack a bag for several days. I am not at liberty to say anything else, but you will not be coming home tonight," the operator said.

What the hell could this be? I wondered.

The first thing out of my wife Maureen's mouth was, "I bet it's the Shah."

Our SWAT team was short of manpower. Four of them were at the FBI Academy receiving training, but we would be joined for this operation by the Manhattan and New Rochelle teams.

It seemed like we were in the office forever and it was sometime well after midnight that we learned that instead of taking the Shah to Egypt, which is what we were initially told and was rumored to be a country that was likely to welcome him, we would be flying, via Air Force II, to Lackland Air Force Base, in Texas.

The plan was for the Manhattan SWAT team to personally accompany the Shah out of Weill Cornell Hospital and the New Rochelle and Brooklyn Queens teams would provide security as he was transported to nearby LaGuardia Airport.

December 2-3, 1979 media coverage of the the FBI's New York SWAT teams moving the Shah of Iran from New York City to Lackland AFB, San Antonio, Texas.

I was shocked to learn, given the short notice, that the best we could do in the way of transportation was the surveillance van used by the truck hijacking squad, an old beat-up Ford Econoline that had seen its best days long ago.

Certainly not what this man of vast wealth was accustomed.

I can recall being stationed in the vicinity of where it was determined the van would travel on its way to the entrance to the FDR Drive, where we would eventually enter onto the Triboro Bridge.

The Manhattan team had signaled over the air that the package had been secured and was now moving.

The press sensed something and began to give chase.

Suddenly, it was onto the FDR Drive at a high rate of speed. I was in one of the cars near the van as the media grew closer. I even recall seeing a flashbulb pop as I drove.

As I saw what I believed to be a press vehicle pull up alongside the van containing the Shah, suddenly a shotgun pointed out the window of the van and the press car immediately retreated.

As all the security cars were now in place, we were able to ward off the press vehicles and before I knew it, we were on the Grand Central Parkway, approaching the exit for LaGuardia.

I observed the van carrying the Shah stop at the entrance where the Port Authority Police were stationed and the van and all of us were waved through.

In later conversation with the Manhattan SWAT guys, we learned that the Shah was seated in an office swivel chair with rollers on the bottom. The SWAT team had all they could do to keep the Shah from toppling over as the van reached high speeds trying to distance itself from the press.

The Shah, likely was used to more comfortable traveling accommodations, had to stand in our shoes for a short time.

Once through security, we all boarded Air Force II, the plane used at that time by Vice President Walter Mondale.

As I entered, not knowing what to expect, I envisioned the front portion, as was the case on most commercial flights, to be first class.

As I looked to my left, the only person seated was the Shah. He had a magazine in his hand which was opened, and I noticed that his picture was on the cover.

He lowered that magazine, looked at me as I passed, gave a faint smile, and nodded as I made my way to the rear to join my teammates.

In several hours we touched down at Lackland Air Force Base and none of us knew what to expect.

The Shah and his aides were first to deplane and we followed.

Several hundred Air Force officers and enlisted men and women stood and saluted as we walked off the plane.

A sight I won't soon forget.

I think the collective feeling was that we were excited and happy for the FBI, the New York office and ourselves that everything went off without a hitch.

This was international news, and we were smack in the middle and gave a pretty good account of ourselves without any problems.

You would never know by what transpired next.

We were transported to a local hotel where breakfast had been arranged by the Dallas FBI office. The Special Agent in Charge or SAC of the office was on hand and we all saw him conferring with our SWAT coordinator, Dan Bertrand, a veteran New York office supervisor.

Our SWAT leader, Dave Carman, walked over and said, "Can you believe it, the SAC says we have to get back on an afternoon commercial flight to New York." Apparently, all the arrangements had been made.

Dan Bertrand was having none of it.

I'm not sure of the exact exchange but basically, Dan informed the SAC with both voices elevated, that his men had been up since early Saturday morning and it was now Sunday afternoon.

The New York office SWAT teams had just orchestrated the high-profile movement of a noteworthy international figure halfway across the country in exemplary fashion and there was no way in hell we were getting back on a plane that afternoon.

The SAC, who I'm sure was not used to being challenged in that fashion, was visibly not happy.

And you know what? We all got rooms, went to bed for a few hours and got to tour and enjoy dinner at San Antonio, Texas' charming and beautiful River Walk.

The next day, we took a commercial flight with hardly a passenger on the plane. The flight attendants got wind of who we were, and we were treated like the royal family.

EDDIE JOSEPH

On October 20, 1981, members of the Black Liberation Army, an outgrowth of the Black Panther Party and the 1960s/1970s radical group, Weather Underground, joined forces and robbed a Brink's Armored truck containing $1.6 million in cash as it made its pickup at the Nanuet Mall, in suburban Rockland County.

A Brink's guard was shot and killed, and two others were wounded in the process as the gang made its way from Nanuet to the sleepy village of Nyack, where they hoped to make their escape via the New York State Thruway and cross the Tappan Zee Bridge into Westchester County.

At the Thruway entrance, the gang was met by members of the Nyack Police Department and a shootout ensued. Two police officers were killed, and one was wounded. Many of the gang members were arrested at the scene but several escaped and were captured in the days that followed.

As the FBI's Manhattan office began to conduct its investigation, additional suspects began to develop and were identified. As evidence unfolded, many of the participants of the group involved in the events of October 20 were found to have participated in several other armored car robberies and also were reported to have aided in the daring prison escape of Black Liberation Army leader Joanne Chesimard. Two such suspects were Cecil Ferguson and Edward Joseph.

In late March 1982, the Queens office SWAT team leader Dave Carman and assistant team leader, John Keenan were summoned to a meeting at 26 Federal Plaza, at the FBI's Manhattan office to participate in discussions regarding the arrests of Mr. Ferguson and Mr. Joseph. Given the violent nature of the Brink's robbery and its use of automatic weapons, it was determined that this was a "high risk" arrest situation, thereby necessitating the use of the New York SWAT teams.

Dave Carman, a very laid-back native of Iowa, a highly decorated U.S. Army Ranger and John Keenan, a Queens, New York native and also a much-decorated combat wounded infantry officer of the U.S. Marine Corps, were both veterans of the Vietnam War and attended the meeting representing our team.

With Dave and John, we always knew we were in the very capable hands of two men that would make sound decisions and above all else, keep us safe.

The meeting was led by then New York Assistant Director in Charge, Kenneth P. Walton.

ADIC Walton was a bit of a character and certainly not in the mold of the older J. Edgar Hoover era bosses. In his obituary in *The New York Times*, on June 16, 2016, he was identified as the "Caped Crusader," who could often be seen walking the streets of lower Manhattan with his overcoat thrown over his shoulders. He was further described in the obit: "Mr. Walton mixed the panache of a central-casting G-man with an audacity to defy rigid protocol, a combination that defined him inside the F.B.I. as an 'agent's agent' and allowed for unusual joint operations between the bureau and its frequent rival, the New York Police Department."

John Keenan recalled discussions at the meeting.

"The plan as it was laid out was for the three SWAT teams, Manhattan, New Rochelle and Queens to hit three separate locations simultaneously in the early morning hours of March 26, 1982. At about 5:00 a.m. or thereabouts, members of the squad handling the investigation would make three telephone calls from 26 Federal Plaza, one to each location and strongly encourage anyone answering the phone to surrender to FBI agents who were currently at their respective locations.

"Dave and I weren't crazy about the plan," John added. "We would be completely losing the element of surprise. Given the events that had occurred and the violent criminal backgrounds of these people, no one was interested in shooting it out with them and potentially getting someone seriously hurt or even killed.

"We went back to the Queens office and discussed it with our boss, Assistant Special Agent in Charge, Jim Murphy."

Jim Murphy was one of the great bosses with whom we all had the privilege of serving, and at a relatively young age he had a wealth of experience. Jim began his career in the NYPD as a member of the Tactical Patrol Force, an elite unit often called upon in highly stressful situations like riot control and fighting the most violent of street crimes. From there, Jim joined the FBI and was a longtime member of the Bank Robbery squad and later became its supervisor. Jim was largely responsible for foiling a potentially deadly situation in the bank robbery/hostage events of August 22, 1972, when he shot and killed one of the two subjects at JFK Airport, as depicted in the Hollywood film *Dog Day Afternoon.*

"We were anxious to see what Murph had to say," John Keenan continued, "and as it turned out, he didn't like the plan either. There was some back and forth with ADIC Walton but ultimately, we were told to stick with his directive."

The Queens team was assigned to arrest Eddie Joseph, who was believed to be living at an address in Manhattan. The other two teams were hitting separate locations also in Manhattan.

"Several minutes before 5:00 a.m. we stood outside the ground-floor apartment and waited for the phone to ring. We had two people, Michael 'Hulk Hogan' Oristano and George 'Arnold Schwarzenegger' Hanna manning the battering ram. At exactly 5:00 a.m. we heard the faint sound of a telephone ringing and in the moments that followed some shuffling inside the apartment. Then, to probably no one's surprise, we heard the racking of an automatic weapon. Dave Carman gave Mike and George a nod and BOOM, in an instant the door came completely off its hinges on top of Eddie Joesph who was found to be armed with a fully-loaded .380 automatic. The door came off with such force that, for a moment, Mike Oristano was knocked to the ground as we wrested the gun away from a struggling Eddie Joseph and took him into custody."

As John, Mike, George and others defused the situation at the front door, other members of the team and I were led by Dave Carman to secure the rest of the apartment not knowing if anyone else posed a danger. As we entered a bedroom, we observed a woman and yelled "FBI, don't move." With that, the woman threw off the covers and reached for a nearby pillow. Dave leaped on top of the now screaming woman as we wrested a gun away from her which was hiding under the pillow. In addition to the weapons, there were also approximately 100 rounds of ammunition recovered in the apartment.

All went well at the other locations without incident and Cecil Ferguson was taken into custody.

Many of the Nyack Robbery defendants served long prison terms, with several having recently been paroled—others have died. Messrs. Ferguson and Joseph got off easily compared to many and received sentences of twelve and a half years each.

STORIES

Media coverage following the March 26, 1982 SWAT Team arrests of Brink's Armored Car Robbery suspects, Cecil Ferguson and Edward Joseph.

Wanted flyer issued by the FBI on November 23, 1981, shortly after the Brink's armored truck robbery on October 20, 1981 for four suspects in the robbery; Flyer also identifies Joanne Chesimard, a close associate of the suspects and an escaped prisoner, while serving time for killing a New Jersey state trooper.

OPERATION WINGED FOOT

Ever wonder what goes into the code names for major cases undertaken by the FBI?

Lots of them have followed very simple logic.

The first major investigation of which I was a part was the December 29, 1975, bombing at the TWA baggage terminal at LaGuardia Airport where eleven people were killed. That investigation was deemed 'LagBomb.'

The May 15, 1972, attempted assassination of then Governor of Alabama and presidential candidate, George Wallace, was called 'WallShot.'

Ted Kaczynski had initially targeted airlines and universities in his bombing campaign which was dubbed, 'The Unabomber Investigation.'

There was no such ingenuity in naming an undercover operation targeting reported widespread automobile insurance fraud in New York, when, in 1983, the NYPD and the FBI established a joint undercover operation entitled, 'Operation Winged Foot.'

Winged Foot Golf Club is located in a tony, New York suburb, Mamaroneck, in Westchester County. Home to a number of golf's 'Major' championships, it was established in 1921 and is among the most prestigious golf venues in the U.S. It was also a favorite of our supervisor, Steve Carbone, a low handicap golfer in his own right. So, our undercover operation, named after one of our boss's favorite golf haunts, had an official title.

Several years prior, the FBI's New York boss, Ken Walton, joined forces with the NYPD and established the Joint Terrorist Task Force and the Joint Bank Robbery Task Force. These joint ventures paired NYPD detectives and FBI agents, who worked out of the Bureau's New York headquarters at 26 Federal Plaza.

This brainchild broke down a lot of barriers that had always existed between the FBI and local law enforcement throughout the country. The FBI had a culture that it was willing to take information, but very unwilling to share any. Understandably, that rubbed police departments the wrong way.

There was also the ingrained perception from the FBI's hierarchy that local police were not to be trusted. Not the best foundation to foster cooperation with the cops.

Bob Joyce, Neil Moran, Steve Carbone, George Hanna—December 1984 "Operation Winged Foot."

STORIES

The creation of these task forces was a big step forward. That's not to say that issues didn't arise where disagreements occurred, but few marriages are ideal.

So, in 1982, the Joint Auto Larceny Task Force (JALTF) was formed, in the Brooklyn-Queens Metropolitan Agency (BQMRA). This was comprised of NYPD detectives from the Special Operations Division's Auto Crime Unit and agents from the BQMRA.

Some of the original members from the NYPD included Danny Pisculli, George Terra, Jimmy Eagan, Don Gallagher, and Larry Andrews. The NYPD supervisor was Sgt. Jim Torrens. The FBI side included Donald Winters, George Hanna, Richie Mika, Gerry Fornino and Warren Flagg. The FBI supervisor was Steve Carbone.

The squad targeted major car theft rings, which, given all of New York's crime problems, sometimes tended to be overlooked and of which the bad guys were well aware.

Props used at press conference—"Operation Winged Foot."

It's kind of a well-kept secret that there is profitability in cars and car parts. Start breaking down all the items including doors, fenders, bumpers, radios, glass, transmissions, etc., and sometimes the parts can have a value higher than the car itself.

Detective George Terra had been directed to a confidential source that was a part owner of a truck repair shop in Richmond Hill, Queens. He shared the business with two partners.

"When I sat down with him, he told me that he was good for six or seven 'IJs,' or insurance jobs. I thought to myself, *six or seven. What was that each month? That's nothing to write home about.*"

"No, six or seven per week," the source said.

"*Wow*, I thought, *maybe we have something here.*"

The source also owned a junkyard in Brooklyn's East New York, home of the NYPD's 75th Precinct, historically one of the highest crime areas in the five boroughs of New York.

The informant told us that he was being strong-armed by members of organized crime. "Made guys" and associates would routinely drop off their cars at the shop and expect him and his partners to fix them for free. He had had enough and wanted out of New York.

"I can introduce somebody to my customers with the story that he is going to eventually take over my operation. It might take time, but I think it will work," he told Detective Terra.

George Hanna stepped forward as the undercover agent. He was a perfect fit. Born and raised in Brooklyn and an antique car collector, George would be able to talk shop much the same as Marissa Tomei's Mona Lisa Vito in the movie *My Cousin Vinny* when asked what she did in her father's garage: "Tune ups, oil changes, brake re-linings, engine rebuilds, rebuild some trannies . . ."

Much like Ms. Vito, George would be able to go toe to toe with the best of them.

George had barely gotten started when our cooperator recommended taking over his junkyard in East New York. It was actually a great idea.

It had lots of props including fenders, doors, windshields, radios, seats, and all sorts of engine parts. In addition, there was a trailer where business could be conducted. This was quickly taking on the tone of a larger operation than initially imagined. Steve Carbone and Sgt. Torrens felt George needed a partner.

There were really no takers for the role. Bob Joyce and I had been transferred to the squad only months earlier. Steve and Jim Torrens were actively interviewing agents from squads in Manhattan in an effort to get George another undercover. I had never done any undercover work, and it never even crossed my mind to throw my name in the hat.

George Hanna recalled, "When the activity began to increase, I told Steve Carbone that I could really use another person with me to run our 'chop shop'. Steve said he had been speaking with Neil Moran who had shown some interest."

"Even though Neil wasn't a 'car guy' *per se*, I thought he would be great. Neil has a magnetic nice-guy personality, and I knew these street guys, the source, and his partners, who spend the entire day working on and talking about tractors and heavy equipment might not be comfortable and somewhat hesitant to view Neil as one of them.

"The confidential source and his two partners were not easy guys to warm up to and not overly friendly. They were all about cars, trucks, heavy equipment repairs, and mechanical work.

"To these three imposing figures, size matters in men, equipment, and vehicles.

"All three had a combined weight of close to 1,000 pounds. I was accepted fairly quickly because of my mechanical knowledge, and I was 6'3" and a muscular 240 pounds.

"So, the day came when I introduced Neil into the operation.

"Neil was about six feet, weighing at best 150 pounds, in very good shape but mind you, far from an imposing figure in their eyes.

"For the first few days, we would stop at the truck repair shop for coffee from the 'roach coach' as they called the coffee truck that stopped each morning.

"The three of them, despite the early hour, would eat anything that wasn't nailed down: doughnuts, muffins, Twinkies, Ring Dings, Yoo-Hoo, and bagels.

"Neil, on the other hand, would order a coffee and a poppy seed bagel with no butter!

"Every day began with conversations about engines, flatbed trucks, and cutting up cars. I had noticed that Neil didn't contribute much to the conversation which he confided to me was of concern.

"One day the subject of old movies came up. One of the source's partners loved old gangster movies and, in particular, James Cagney.

"That was Neil's intro. A Cagney devotee growing up, knowing every movie and famous line by heart, he immediately launched into his outstanding impression.

"They all loved it! For the next hour and several times a week, they begged Neil to do another Cagney impersonation. From that point on they couldn't get enough. His engaging personality kicked in and we never experienced any problems in being accepted for the duration of the undercover operation."

Operation Winged Foot now had an undercover team dubbed G & N Storage, complete with business cards with our address, at the corner of Liberty Avenue and Montauk Street in East New York.

Our tech people installed audio and a video camera in the trailer so we could capture any visitors on tape. We obtained an old NYPD tow truck with the decals scraped off the side, which definitely raised some eyebrows out there the first few weeks, but we soon began to blend in.

Once again, the target of this operation was the alleged widespread insurance fraud.

Our source advised that amongst the auto-related businesses: repair, body, and transmission shops, used car dealers, towing businesses, even neighborhood gas stations, were normal outlets for people to have their cars 'disappear.'

A typical car owner, who for one reason or another wants to arrange to have his or her car stolen, seeks out the neighborhood repair shop guy, who is known as a 'middleman.'

That 'middleman' then contacts someone else (in this case the FBI), who will come to get the car and tow it away.

Presumably, the recipients of the car, George and me, are taking the car to our yard, stripping it down and selling the parts. The proper parlance describing us was, 'itinerant vehicle dismantlers.'

Now the actual mechanics of a transaction are fairly simple: the owner contacts the middleman, who charges the owner several hundred dollars for the service.

The owner provides the middleman with the keys and registration and is told not to file a theft report until the middleman returns both items.

The middleman then reaches out to his contact (George and me) and we pay him anywhere between $200-$300 for each car, so the middleman makes out quite well.

Obviously, George and I were not dismantling each car. What the NYPD and the FBI arranged was for us to bring all the cars to an old airplane hangar at Brooklyn's Floyd Bennett Field. Once there, we were met by members of our squad who inventoried each vehicle. They then made a duplicate set of the keys and registration and created a folder for all information related to that car.

In a few days, we would return the keys and registration to the middleman, informing him that the car was "gone."

The middleman would then reach out to the owner, return the keys and registration and tell him or her that they could now report the car stolen. Bear in mind, when the owner files a police report indicating that his or her car was parked at the mall and when they returned it was gone, the FBI and NYPD already had possession of that car for several days.

Additionally, when the owner filed a theft report with the police and his or her insurance carrier utilizing the U. S. Postal Service, they were in violation of federal mail fraud statutes.

It wasn't more than a month that went by when our trailer, with no heat or bathroom facilities, was burglarized. Thank goodness none of the technical equipment was disturbed. The few tools we had accumulated were stolen. Given the high crime nature of the area, it was most likely junkies looking for anything they could sell.

It didn't take all that long before our beepers (no cell phones in 1984) were ringing 24-7.

"Bobby Bandwagon," "Joey International" (he drove an International tractor), "Sally D," "Ralphie Parts," "Fat Tommy" (every bit of 375 lbs.), "Mikey Glasses" (he wore thick glasses) and "Shakey" (the guy was a nervous wreck) were some of our new friends.

At the outset, George and I were both a bit unsure of ourselves. I recall being anxious the first time I had to hook up a car onto our tow truck. Any hesitancy, uneasiness or a hint that I had no idea what I was doing in front of guys that made their living this way could have signaled the end of the operation.

On April 15, 1984, several months into the operation, the city was rocked by the sudden murder of ten people, which given the day, was dubbed, the Palm Sunday Massacre.

Two women in their twenties and children ranging from three to fourteen years of age were all shot in the head at close range.

This occurred at 1080 Liberty Avenue, exactly one block from our junkyard.

This horrendous mass killing made national headlines and upon learning that two undercover agents were operating a short distance away, FBI Headquarters expressed concern and ordered the site to be taken down and moved elsewhere.

In the dead of night, our technical people arrived at the yard and removed all the audio and visual equipment and now we were hunting for new space.

As luck would have it, we secured a much nicer spot in the mostly industrial section of Richmond Hill, Queens—a short distance from our source's truck repair shop.

STORIES

December 1984 media coverage of joint NYPD/FBI
undercover "sting" dubbed "Operation Winged Foot."

COCK-EYED ANTHONY AND ENZO "THE BAKER"

At the outset, our steadiest customers were an uncle and nephew duo in Brooklyn, "Cock-eyed" Anthony (One eye was askew) and his nephew, Enzo "The Baker," so nicknamed "The Baker," following the 1972 movie classic, *The Godfather*.

The unforgettable scene unfolds when Michael Corleone, played by Al Pacino, visits his father in the hospital following an attempt on his father's life. While attempting to move him to another room a man suddenly appears in the hallway startling Michael who asks, "Who are you?" to which the mystery man replies, "I am Enzo the Baker. You remember me?"

These guys were good for two to three 'give ups' each week and wow could they talk.

"Can yous do me a favor and cut this car in half?"

Cock-eyed Anthony asked on one occasion.

"Then deliver me the rear portion and I'll have it welded onto a legit car. Yous do that kind of work, no?" Cock-eyed Anthony asked on one occasion.

"Sure, we do," George replied.

"Neil does all the cutting. He has the hands of a surgeon, steadier than Ben Casey," a reference to the 1960s television series *Ben Casey* starring Vince Edwards as Dr. Ben Casey, the hospital's chief neurosurgeon.

I thought I would collapse right on the spot as Anthony looked at me (or at least one eye did) with newfound respect.

Although we began to settle in and became more comfortable with steady customers like Anthony and The Baker, there was aways the unexpected.

As I stood on our now rented flatbed after discarding our NYPD tow truck after hooking up a car one morning, George engaged Enzo in conversation and suddenly began glaring at me—his eyes got wider and directed me toward my boots.

As I glanced down, I saw the wire from the tape recorder tucked inside my boot had become disconnected and was dangling on my shoelaces. I felt like all the blood had rushed out of me. I knelt, as if tying my laces, and tucked the wire back into my sock.

A few weeks later, George and I met Enzo for dinner at Gargiulo's Restaurant in Coney Island. As we were seated and ordering, with The Baker sitting next to me and George directly opposite us, I saw a guy approaching the table and bend down to get a better look at George.

"Jesus Christ, Georgie, how the hell are you? I haven't seen you in years."

My heart began racing as I wondered how this would play out.

George calmly got up, looked at us and said, "I'll be right back."

He put his arm around the guy walking away and said, "How are you Vinny, you look great."

As the operation began to wind down after a year, and obtaining over 150 'give ups,' and turning down dozens, simply because we couldn't manage any more, the U.S. Attorney's office became concerned that several of our regular customers were providing us with "too many" cars.

"It will look to a jury like you were targeting them," Cecilia Gardner, the prosecutor, told us.

"Stop taking cars from Cock-eyed Anthony and Enzo the Baker, like now."

Over the course of a year, we had built up credibility in the street we argued. Guys that hung out at the source's shop had even asked us to participate in the burglary of a construction site.

What will it look like if we stop taking cars, which is how we were supposedly earning our keep?

Then came the perfect story.

It was a good two to three weeks of our beepers going off all day and night when we decided to return a call from Enzo.

"Where the fuck have you guys been?" Enzo asked angrily.

"You didn't hear?" George shot back.

"Neil got arrested in Canada by the Royal Canadian Mounted Police trying to cross the border into Vermont with 20,000 Quaalude tablets. He tried to outrun the Mounties on their horses, but they nabbed him. I had to drive up there and post his bail. He resisted arrest which didn't help."

The extended pause on the phone signaled that The Baker was completely thrown for a loop.

"Are you kidding me? The fuckin Neilster's a pill head, a fucking drug kingpin and he fights with cops?"

"Oh yeah," George replied.

"He's got the biggest pill operation in the Bronx. He just does the car stuff with me as a cover like he's semi legit. And he has no love for cops. That wasn't the first time he took a swing at one, believe me."

Thank goodness that the operation lasted only several more weeks as once the word of my arrest hit the street, I now was inundated with requests for large orders of Quaaludes, and every pill imaginable, including Cock-eyed Anthony and Enzo the Baker, who now treated me like I was Pablo Escobar.

FRANK "FRANKIE CADILLAC" BARONE

At the outset of "Operation Winged Foot," the plan was for George Hanna to be on his own with the informant. A neighborhood guy named Frank "Frankie Cadillac" Barone, so named because of his obsession with Cadillacs, was known to the source to deal in insurance jobs, stolen cars and "swag" or stolen property.

The source had learned that Barone had come into a trailer load of stolen air conditioners and was interested in a buyer. What an opportunity for George to begin the operation.

Cadillac agreed to meet the informant and George at one of the cargo terminals at John F. Kennedy International Airport in Jamaica, Queens. George was to bring a $500 downpayment as a show of good faith. He could then bargain with Cadillac on the price for the entire load.

Frankie, coming from a restricted area with apparent access, met George and our source, chatted for about five minutes, and disappeared back into the restricted space and never returned.

The word quickly got out that Cadillac had stiffed George and to keep up appearances, George let it be known that should anyone see him, they should beep him (George) right away.

As I came into the case as the second undercover, Frankie Cadillac was often the topic of discussion, especially with the informant and his two business partners. George would play it up big.

"He'll be sorry if he shows his face around here. Nobody fucks me like that and gets away with it."

"He reminds me of a Vegas lounge singer," the source said.

It's like everyone hoped that Frankie would unexpectedly show up while we were there to watch George smack him around or perhaps dish out something a bit harsher.

It was a Friday evening on what had been a hot, August day. George had just dropped me off and I was looking forward to the night and a relaxing evening when he phoned.

"Get dressed, Frankie Cadillac is at the shop (the informant's place of business) and they're stalling him for us. I'll be over in five minutes to pick you up."

Friday evenings in the summer are not a fun time to be on the road in New York. People are anxious to get away for the weekend and all the highways are jammed. We were surprised that the Belt Parkway wasn't that bad going into Queens, but the Van Wyck Expressway leading from JFK Airport was another story.

As we finally got off the exit at Jamaica Avenue, George reached into the glove compartment and retrieved a pair of black leather gloves. Given the ninety plus degree temperatures, I was a bit taken back.

"Expecting a cold front to sweep down on us?" I asked.

With that, George fumbled while he was driving as he put on both gloves.

"George, what the hell are you doing?" I continued.

"Neil, we've got to do something with this guy. We can't just ask, 'Where's our money?'"

"And you think the gloves will help?" I shot back.

"We'll just rough him up a bit—nothing bad. These guys are thinking we're going to really teach him a lesson. There's a reason we were asked to go in on that burglary with them. They really trust us. Whatever we do here is going to go a long way."

Not to be dramatic but admittedly I was nervous. Suppose Cadillac had three guys with him? What would we do then? Suppose he had a pistol? The informant and the guys that frequented the truck repair shop painted Cadillac as "all talk," but who was to say?

We pulled up to the shop and immediately inside the open rolltop door were about five to six guys and our man, Frankie Cadillac. He wore an open collar black shirt with a fair bit of gold, dark slacks, and thick wraparound sunglasses. It was fair to say that Cadillac had never done a day's honest work in his life.

George shot out of the truck, black leather gloves and all and slammed the driver's door. Frankie was genuinely taken back and blurted out, "George, good to see you."

"I'll bet you are. Look I don't settle my problems in front of a crowd, let's go to the back and hash this out."

"Sure, sure George, anything you say."

Cadillac was understandably nervous, in fact, very nervous.

As much as he tried to crack a smile, he had no idea what was about to happen—and a funny thing, neither did we.

We walked to a storage area of sorts, in the back of the shop, where we wouldn't be interrupted. With everyone trailing behind, they were anxious to see Frankie get what was coming to him. I turned and said "Guys, back off, we'll manage this."

Meanwhile George had Frankie by the arm, guiding him toward the door to the room.

"George, we don't have to go back here. We can settle this outside," Frankie said, now in a much higher pitched voice.

With that, George flung open the door and tossed Cadillac to the ground like he was a 'Cabbage Patch' doll.

"George no, no please," Cadillac screamed.

The scream was so loud, it was as if we had cut off his fingers.

"Please, you don't understand, I was gonna get back to you, but no one knew how to reach you. I'll pay you, I promise. Please don't hurt me."

"You fuckin' liar. Everyone knows how to get a hold of us. You thought you could steal from me?" George yelled.

With that George grabbed Frankie by the legs and turned him over on his stomach. Cadillac was now struggling to get free, and George motioned for me to hold him down. I grabbed hold of his pants, and he was squirming so violently his pants started to come off.

At that point, George began to give him 'nuggies' in his calves with Cadillac screaming loudly.

"No George, pleeeeeaaase, I'll do anything, pleeeeeaaase, don't hurt me."

At this point, he had only been the recipient of 'nuggies' to his calves. Had George wanted, one solid punch would have knocked out Cadillac for a month.

All I could think of was the scene from *The Wizard of Oz*, when Judy Garland's Dorothy confronts the cowardly lion, who is whimpering from her slap on his nose, when she says, "My what a fuss you're making."

By now, somehow the pants were completely off, and there sat Frankie, clad only in his boxer shorts, knee high black nylon socks and Italian loafers.

"This doesn't end it. I want my money, Frankie," George said.

I delved into Cadillac's pants pockets, which contained car keys and about $50 cash.

"Guess what Frankie? We're taking your fucking Cadillac as a downpayment on the $500, which has now jumped to $750 for the fuckin' aggravation you caused us. We don't need this, you understand me? Now get out of here," as George pushed him out the door.

"What about my pants?" Frankie asked.

"We're keeping them too. Keep moving."

We guided Frankie Cadillac out the front door onto Atlantic Avenue, clad in only a torn shirt, boxer shorts, nylon socks and his black, Italian loafers. The traffic was bumper to bumper waiting to get onto the Van Wyck Expressway and drivers were stunned as Frankie ambled down the block still whimpering in his underwear.

Ultimately, Cadillac walked away without a mark on him. With the screams overheard by the group at the shop, they probably envisioned that we had given him what he deserved, but had probably gone somewhat easy, but seeing him walk away half-dressed and humiliated, as far as our 'street cred' was concerned, we hit the lottery.

Frankie Cadillac apparently had gotten the message. We were never to see him again until he was arrested several months later.

FAT TOMMY

Tomasso "Fat Tommy" Stabile and his brother, Anthony, were reportedly affiliated with the Paul Vario faction of the Lucchese LCN Crime Family, depicted in *Goodfellas*. Other members of the crew included James "Jimmy the

Gent" Burke, Angelo Sepe, Henry Hill, and Tommy DeSimone, all of Lufthansa Robbery fame.

Our informant advised that Tommy ran a used car operation operating out of a trailer on Rockaway Boulevard in Ozone Park and was the neighborhood 'go to' guy for give-ups or insurance jobs.

It didn't take all that long following our initial introduction to Tommy that he became one of our steadiest customers.

As a way to immediately enhance our credibility, the informant suggested that George and I take over his 'vig' payments on a loan Tommy had extended to him.

Tommy was known as a shylock in Ozone Park and the source had borrowed $3,000 from him. He was slowly paying Tommy back at an

exorbitant rate, and we agreed to take over those payments which we continued each month in addition to our regular business.

An old school guy, Tommy was in his early to mid-forties and had to weigh 350 to 375 pounds. According to our information, Tommy had done a stint in prison in the 1960s for armed robbery. We also believed he was a very worthwhile target because of his alleged connection with the crew responsible for the Lufthansa Robbery. This was someone who "knew where the bodies were buried."

Our informant warned that Tommy was a dangerous guy who was not to be trifled with.

As was the case with all our subjects or 'middlemen' as we called them, Tommy would beep George and I and we would find the nearest phone booth and arrange to come and meet him at his trailer.

As we took more and more insurance jobs from him, he seemed to take more of a liking to us.

"I don't know what yous are doing with these cars, and I don't want to know, but nothing ever shows up. They vanish into thin air. My customers are all getting checks from the insurance companies right away. You guys are good for business. I was giving these cars to neighborhood kids, and they wound up torching them on the Belt Parkway or on Fountain Avenue. When the cars are burned and recovered, there's an investigation which holds up the payment. It's a real pain in the ass. Keep doing what you're doing."

George and I were somewhat taken back when Tommy had asked us one day early on if we had seen the news where a reputed organized crime figure had been discovered shot through the head in the trunk of a car at the long-term parking area at JFK Airport and the discussion that followed.

"Yous can't be too careful out there. Watch yourselves. Always watch your backs, there are a lot of treacherous fucks out there when it comes to this business—be careful."

Imagine that, I thought, *Tommy Stabile looking out for the welfare of two FBI agents.*

Tommy continued, "Yeah they killed my brother about a year ago. Gunned him down with a few other guys on Cross Bay Boulevard," as he motioned in that general direction. Fucking shame—be careful, you hear?"

As was reported in *The New York Times* on May 9, 1982:

> *Three Queens men were slain and a Long Island man was critically wounded early yesterday in a fusillade of shotgun blasts and pistol fire that erupted on a street near Kennedy International Airport in Queens, the police said. Several assailants, who the police said may have been organized crime gunmen, escaped in one or more cars. The motive for the attack was not immediately known, though robbery and drugs were apparently not involved, detectives said.*
>
> *The victims, a father, his son and two other men, apparently were lured to the scene of the shootings, on 156th Avenue near Cross Bay Boulevard in Howard Beach, about a half mile west of the airport and the grounds of Aqueduct Race Track.*
>
> *An unfired .38 caliber pistol was found on one of the bodies, and three cars, all believed driven by the victims, were found near the spot where the four were felled.*
>
> *Those killed were identified as Anthony Stabile, 36 years old, of 114-14 149th Avenue, South Ozone Park, and Nicholas Gregoris, 57, and his son, Ralph, 26, both of 160-04 92d Street, Howard Beach.*
>
> *The wounded man, Adrian Persico, 27, of 149 West Sherman Avenue, Freeport, L.I., was listed in critical condition at Jamaica Hospital, where the police said he had been placed under around-the clock guard. He was the only known witness, the police said.*

George and I were truly shocked. It wasn't often that a guy like Fat Tommy would discuss matters like this with people he barely knew. We felt good that we could rest a bit easy as far as Tommy was concerned. He believed we were legit.

It was a Monday in June when we met Tommy at the trailer in response to his page.

"How yous doing?" he always asked, as he greeted us at the door of the trailer.

Considering his sizeable girth, Tommy always was pulling up his pants as if they were a size or two larger than he needed. There was little doubt that Tommy had seen "XXX" eons ago.

He pulled out a copy of the *Daily News* which reported on the world lightweight boxing match over the weekend between Livingston Bramble and the champion, Ray "Boom Boom" Mancini. Bramble took away Mancini's title in a bloody slugfest.

"Did you guys see this fight? Fuckin' awful. Imagine, this black guy beating an Italian. I almost threw my bowling ball through the fuckin' television."

Despite Mancini's title changing hands, as was the usual case, Tommy was in an upbeat mood.

"Did yous see this shit?" Tommy remarked and then proceeded to pull out the most recent edition of *Penthouse* magazine.

This edition had created a firestorm, as it featured the reigning Miss America, Vanessa Williams, in a series of explicitly nude photos with another woman. As Tommy turned one page after another, with the tape recorder tucked in my boot and running, Tommy began to describe, in painstaking detail, each and every photo.

I happened to be seated closest to him while George remained safely out of direct eyeshot.

"Look at this shit, Neil, look. Can you believe it?" he asked.

A quick glance to my pal, George, revealed a grin that said, "How are you gonna wiggle out of this one; you have to say something?"

The most I could muster were some "Oohs" and "Aahs" and maybe one "Oh my God," with a "Wow," thrown in for good measure.

Maybe a year later, when the case had wound down and George and I became fixtures at the Brooklyn federal courthouse, the word had spread amongst the assistant United States attorneys of the tape's existence. On more than one occasion, assistants with whom we were friendly, would greet me with an "Ooh" and "Aah," and even a "Wow."

But now it was time to get down to business, and Tommy asked his niece, who managed the paperwork, to make a call.

"Rose, call that guy will ya," he said.

"I got him, Tommy," Rose said as she handed her uncle the phone.

Now remember, Tommy was old school and one of the tenets of the old school guys was, "Be careful whenever you're on the phone. Just assume the feds are listening."

Tommy followed that principle to the letter.

"How ya doin?" Tommy began in a gruff tone.

"You know that thing we were talkin' about? Well, I got those people here. I want to do it now."

The recipient of the call was obviously now replying and Tommy's eyes immediately widened.

"Didn't anybody ever teach you not to talk on the phone you fuckin' idiot? Shut the fuck up and don't say another word. Don't move."

With that Tommy furiously slammed down the phone, looked squarely at us and said, "Let's take a ride."

Let's take a ride, I thought, as the three of us, including the normally unflappable George, who shot me a side glance showing concern, left the trailer.

"Let's take your truck," Tommy ordered.

Now this was a sight to behold. This was a flatbed truck, not a minivan with rear seating. One front seat and that was it. I climbed up the passenger side and sat in the middle with George driving and Tommy squeezing, and I do mean squeezing, into the passenger side. I had one leg draped alongside George's and my other along Tommy's. In between, both legs rested the stick for the manual transmission. At 150 pounds, I was sandwiched in between some 600 to 700 pounds of humanity. I prayed we weren't traveling to Manhattan.

Of major concern for me was the tape recorder. A mini-cassette, I always tucked it into my sock with the wire running up my leg, through my underwear, and taped to the inside of the waist of my pants.

Suppose the damn thing falls out. Thinking maybe that I should keep Tommy talking so he wouldn't be distracted and begin looking around, I never got a chance to open my mouth.

"This mother fucker is an ex-correction officer. You would think that this stupid bastard has got enough fuckin' sense not to talk on the mother fuckin' phone. He thinks he's got a license to say anything he wants when he's talking to me. I'm gonna teach this fuck a lesson."

A lesson.

What the hell does that mean?

What are we going to be a party to here?

With a series of left and right turns at Tommy's direction, we were in the City Line neighborhood, bordering Brooklyn's East New York, in just a short time.

"Pull over here," Tommy ordered.

It was early afternoon and there were people everywhere, so in my mind I'm thinking, *how bad could this be?*

Even with his considerable size, Tommy flew out of the truck and slammed the door so hard I thought it would come off the hinges.

"Yous wait here, I'll take care of this."

Now, with the tape running, George and I couldn't say anything to each other, so I announced, "This is Special Agent Neil Moran. I'm here with Special Agent George Hanna and Tommy Stabile has just left the truck and is speaking with a woman in her early to mid-thirties on the sidewalk."

A terrified young woman with a baby carriage was getting an earful from Tommy. With arms flailing, pointing his finger, and yelling at her, this was definitely a side of Tommy we had not seen. About five minutes elapsed when Tommy got back in the truck and announced, "Back to my trailer. Shithead drove over there after I told him not to move."

As we approached Rockaway Boulevard, I could see a man in his thirties pacing back and forth in front of the trailer.

"Look at this stupid fuck," Tommy said.

"Let's straighten this out."

"You stupid mother fucker," Tommy began, and as was always the case, pulling up his pants as he exited the flatbed.

"How many times have I told you to be careful when you're on the phone with me?" as Tommy gave him a whack across his head so hard I thought he would knock him out.

As he lay on the ground begging not to be hit again, Tommy said, "I'm not one of your correction officer friends. I always got people looking at me. I don't need some shithead like you giving the law a reason to lock me up. I can do that myself."

"These are my friends I was telling you about," Tommy said.

"Now give me the keys to your car. They're gonna put it on the flatbed and take it away. They'll let me know when it's chopped up and when you can report it stolen. Then they'll bring back the keys and I'll give them back to you."

The guy was holding the side of his head, still reeling from the blow inflicted by an angry Tommy.

"I was wondering, Tommy, can I have the car radio and the windshield?" he asked.

Whack—this time, Tommy, with an open fist cracked him across the face so hard, I'm sure it was heard in Howard Beach.

"What's the matter with you? These are businessmen, they make their money by taking these fuckin' cars apart and selling the glass, the radio, the tires, and everything else. What, you don't want them to get their cut?"

This poor soul didn't have the sense to come in out of the rain.

After getting smacked twice, you would have thought he would have cut his losses and called it a day.

I thought Tommy had finally gotten through to him when he said, "Okay, Tommy, here are the keys and the registration, but how am I gonna get home from here?"

With that, Tommy kicked the guy so hard, if he was a football, it would have cleared the uprights from forty yards.

"Get home, what? What do you think I'm running, a fucking car service? Get the fuck out of here, now and don't come back and don't fuckin call me again."

"Imagine this guy," Tommy said, as he looked disgustedly at George and me.

I did feel bad for the guy. He was clearly out of his league with Tommy and although it was hard to imagine him mixing it up with inmates at one of the many tough NYC prisons, he was essentially kind of a 'zhlub', (A Yiddish term meaning a dumb or clumsy person).

"We'll give you a ride home," I said innocently.

Tommy looked like he wanted to strangle me.

"Fuck no, he's walking," and with that, Tommy whacked him in back of the head and gave him another kick in the ass. He was last seen walking down Rockaway Boulevard and probably had a few bruises from the short encounter.

Professionally speaking, I suppose the best compliment Tommy could have paid us was on the morning FBI agents and NYPD detectives fanned out across the five boroughs to arrest the twenty-six middlemen in the case in December 1984.

According to members of our squad, Tommy had come along peacefully and as they were pulling away from his south Ozone Park home, he asked, "What's the charge?"

"Mail and insurance fraud," was the response.

Tommy appeared puzzled when an agent John Cable asked, "Do you know two guys named George and Neil?"

"Never heard of them," was Tommy's reply.

The first time George and I had set foot in the office in a year was the morning of the arrests, December 17, 1984.

The plan was as the defendants were brought in that we would sit with them and try to see if there was anything they might have to offer to make their legal troubles less problematic—we were looking for cooperation.

Make no mistake about it, this was an emotional day for the two of us. There were very few of the middlemen, in some small way, that we weren't fond of.

One of the informant's partners was visibly shaken.

"Neil, they told me you're an FBI agent and I don't believe them. It's not true is it, Neil? Please tell me it's not true."

"Can I see your id, Neil? I don't believe you're an FBI agent."

I pulled out my credentials and allowed him to hold them. He took his index finger and scratched at my photo thinking that perhaps it had been pasted on, and this was just a big ruse.

"Can you recommend a lawyer to me, Neil? I really trust you," he said as tears streamed down the face of this 325-pound behemoth.

Yes, this was highly emotional for the two of us.

Now it was time to pitch Tommy.

To reiterate, this was someone who knew where the bodies were buried and if we could gain his cooperation he would solve a lot of past crimes and perhaps prevent some future ones.

"Oh, they got yous, too, I see," Tommy said, as we entered the conference room.

"Tommy, it's George and Neil but actually it's *agents* George and Neil," George said.

This is a guy that didn't rattle that easily and from our experiences with him, he liked to be in control and call all the shots.

There was a long pause before Tommy said, "Not bad, not bad at all. I guess yous got me."

There was some back and forth and although I wouldn't say we were going to be receiving Christmas cards from him in the upcoming weeks, he didn't seem to harbor any ill feelings.

"Yous was just doing your jobs and I ain't got nothing against that. It's the other guy (the informant) I'm pissed off at. You have to take shots in life. Sometimes things work out and sometimes they don't."

"Tommy," George began. "You aren't getting any younger and I'm sure you don't want to go back to jail. We have a good case against you and you're looking at five years. You know you can make this easier on yourself."

Suddenly, Tommy cut George off.

"Are you guys asking me to cooperate, become a snitch like that motherfucker (the informant)? Let me tell you something. I could get sentenced to a thousand fuckin' years, but I ain't gonna tell on nobody, so don't waste your time."

All totaled, the case netted the arrests of 122 people, which included car owners and the "middlemen" like Fat Tommy Stabile. The car owners included a doctor, a lawyer, an accountant, a NYC fireman, several police officers, and the "Catholic Woman of the Year."

The value of the 150 vehicles recovered exceeded $1,000,000. The case was heralded in the media as the most successful to date in the effort to combat automobile insurance fraud.

At every subsequent court appearance, when we encountered Tommy, he smiled broadly and shook our hands. Ultimately, he pleaded guilty and was sentenced to five years in federal prison.

It was several years down the road and George and I were still working together. We had learned that Tommy had been released from prison and was back in the used car business on Atlantic Avenue, in Ozone Park. We were in the neighborhood and thought we would check out his new operation from afar.

Lo and behold, it's like we were going back in time as Tommy was holding court out front with two guys, who no doubt were welcoming him home. He must have hiked up his pants six times in the ten minutes we sat there.

"Let's go talk to him when these guys leave," George said.

"Oh George, I don't know. We took five years off this guy's life. Why don't we just leave him be," I replied.

Within minutes, the duo left, and George started to drive toward the trailer. Once again, old school Tommy didn't miss a trick and always seemed to be highly cognizant of what was going on around him. He seemed to be looking squarely at us as we got closer. As I leaned my arm out the window and he lowered his head to see who was driving, he uttered, "Jesus Christ, I can't believe it. Pull over."

We must have talked for fifteen to twenty minutes about a wide range of topics including life in prison and the new LCN regime of

John Gotti. We were quite surprised how candid Tommy was, and we left off with handshakes and a goodbye.

Sometime after, Tommy had relocated to Florida, and we received a call from the federal parole officer who was assigned to monitor him for the remainder of his parole.

Tommy was just one of those guys who was destined to always find trouble.

The October 29, 1994, edition of the *South Florida Sun Sentinel* reported:

> *An alleged criminal associate of the New York City-based Lucchese organized crime family was sentenced to 14 years in prison on Friday for his role in a conspiracy to distribute 100 kilograms of cocaine in South Florida. Thomas "Fat Tommy" Stabile, 54, of Hollywood, was also sentenced to five years probation by U.S. District Judge..."*

Tommy Stabile passed away in March 2017.

Tomasso "Tommy" Stabile

Ellen Moran compiled this graphic when "Operation Winged Foot" concluded.

Neil Moran (L) and George Hanna (R) undercover role in "Operation Winged Foot"—December 1984.

Neil Moran at Floyd Bennett Field, Brooklyn, where all vehicles were stored in "Operation Winged Foot." This is the original NYPD tow truck used before the undercover agents leased a flatbed.

Some of the 142 cars obtained by George Hanna and Neil Moran during "Operation Winged Foot" stored at Floyd Bennett Field, Brooklyn.

Confidential source's business, Atlantic Ave., Richmond Hill, Queens—"Operation Winged Foot."

STORIES

U.S. Department of Justice

Federal Bureau of Investigation

Office of the Director

Washington, D.C. 20535

March 12, 1985

PERSONAL

Mr. Neil F. Moran
Federal Bureau of Investigation
New York, New York

Dear Mr. Moran:

    I would like to take this opportunity to commend your exceptional efforts in "Operation Winged Foot," an undercover investigation into the large-scale perpetration of automobile insurance fraud. As a token of my appreciation for your accomplishments, I have approved the enclosed check, which represents a well-deserved incentive award.

    You worked on a daily basis to establish credibility to your undercover role as a partner in a salvage business. Through your totally convincing role, you were eventually able to obtain a number of vehicles from a variety of outlets, which were eventually reported stolen to insurance companies by the individual owners. Your willingness to sacrifice your personal time and effort and, at the same time, sustain a selfless and tenacious attitude toward your work were of significant impact upon the overall success ultimately realized in this exhaustive investigation into automobile insurance fraud. The very fine job that you did for the FBI regarding this matter is something in which you may take a great amount of pride.

Sincerely yours,

William H. Webster
Director

Enclosure

March 12, 1985 letter from FBI Director William H. Webster on "Operation Winged Foot."

WINGED FOOT'S IMPACT

The day the case came down, December 17, 1984, George and I set foot in the office for the first time in over year. For security reasons, we had been completely separated from contact with everyone except for our supervisor, Steve Carbone, and the case agent, Bob Joyce. The only occasion we would see anyone else was when several agents and detectives would meet us at the airplane hangar at Floyd Bennett Field, where we would store all the cars.

One by one, as the defendants were led into the office in handcuffs this was an emotional time for us both. Of course, these were people who broke the law and contributed heavily to ever increasing insurance rates.

Many of them had checkered pasts that included armed robbery, burglary, vehicular homicide, and assault with a deadly weapon.

The plain simple fact of the matter is that to make this case work, all George and I had to do was be ourselves. We are both conversationalists who can talk with anyone, generally about anything.

Over the course of a year of dealing with people who were now defendants in a major federal case, we got to know almost each and every one of them, without having to reveal anything about ourselves. We attributed that to our personalities and our ability to be liked.

Some forty-one years later, I can't explain how I felt at that moment. It still sends a chill through me.

One defendant, who had left the NYPD after about ten years, told us, "How stupid am I," he began.

"As I look back, I should have known. You guys were too legit. You always showed up exactly when you said you would. You always brought money as you promised. If you said you were bringing back the keys and registration for the owner on Wednesday, you would come on Wednesday. Most guys I deal with don't do any of those things. I should have known."

One of the defendants, Frank Riccio, upon being introduced by our source to George and me, at the outset of the case looked uncomfortable. As he laid out what he could do for us and what his expectations were, pointing his finger into George's chest he said, "I don't care how fucking big you are, if yous turn out to be cops or feds, I'll kill yous both."

At the time, it sent a chill through George and me, and we immediately reported it to Bob Joyce and Steve Carbone.

On the morning of the arrests, the team for Frank Riccio included John Bowe, who had left the NYPD and joined the FBI. John was at least 6'4", a very lean 240 pounds and quite an imposing presence.

The word got back to George and me that while transporting Riccio to the office, he received an explicit message from John that should anything happen to George Hanna and Neil Moran, the consequences would be dire.

John had assured us that the message was indeed received.

And that was that.

The press conference that afternoon was a media circus.

United States Attorney for the Eastern District of New York, Raymond Dearie, NYPD Police Commissioner Benjamin Ward, and our Special Agent in Charge, Lee Laster, took to the podium.

"We have a doctor, we have a lawyer," U.S. Attorney Dearie began.

"We have an accountant, we have police officers, we have a firefighter. We have people from every profession imaginable. We have every day people from whom you would not ever expect this type of behavior."

The case was the first on all the local evening news programs and even made all the national news broadcasts.

The following day's New York news dailies all carried extensive coverage of the case.

It was a great success and a group effort by our entire squad.

Bob Joyce commented on the success of Operation Winged Foot and its impact.

"Virtually each agent and detective on the squad was assigned to assist with this year and one-half long investigation. Sgt. Jim Torrens and Steve Carbone did a masterful job doling out assignments each day. There was a voluminous amount of information and documentation being received from George Hanna and Neil Moran daily. The most important detail on a case of this size was to not get behind on paperwork, and administrative duties related to the investigation. The squad worked as a team to ensure that all assignments were completed in a timely fashion so that when the covert phase of the investigation ended, the prosecutive phase was ready to go. During the entire operation, the squad worked very closely with the U.S. Attorney's Office for the Eastern District of New York.

"As a major undercover operation, it had to meet with the approval of U. S. Attorney Raymond Dearie, indicating that he approved of the case and was willing to prosecute the offenders.

"The success of this investigation helped enhance the investigative reputation of our squad, the NYPD, and the U.S. Attorney's Office."

STORIES

Media coverage of the prosecution and conviction of Anthony Harper.

ANTHONY HARPER

In 1985, some six months after 'Operation Winged Foot,' began to wind down, once again, George Hanna and I began to get regular cases assigned as members of the NYPD/Joint Auto Larceny Task Force.

For many years, the New York office maintained a 'Fugitive Squad,' that exclusively handled nothing but chasing down people on the run.

Unlawful Flight to Avoid Prosecution or in Bureau parlance, 'UFAP,' was probably the most popular, with Bond Default and Unlawful Flight to Avoid Confinement or 'UFAC' rounding out the bulk of the rest.

How the FBI winds up with these cases is pretty straightforward.

A local police department investigates a case and develops a suspect. If the police have reason to believe that the suspect has fled the jurisdiction, they seek an Unlawful Flight warrant in U.S. District Court, after providing evidence to support their claim. The FBI office where the warrant was obtained will then contact the office or offices where the suspect is believed to have fled, and a case will be opened in that or those locales.

The fugitive squad, at least in the New York office, was comprised of older and highly experienced agents who were generally 'big guys.' It was rare that any fugitive case was not assigned to this squad and how this one fell through the cracks I'll never know, but one afternoon, Steve Carbone called George and I into his office and asked us to handle a UFAP matter.

The Albany Police Department had been investigating an incident surrounding the August 24th murder of a forty-seven-year-old night watchman, Cyril Marshall, a native of Guyana, at the Albany Dodge car dealership.

The suspect that developed, Anthony Harper, was alleged to have bludgeoned Mr. Marshall to death, stole a car in the process and fled. Further information led the Albany Police to believe that Mr. Harper, had a girlfriend in the Bronx, and we were provided with that information.

We located the girlfriend in a large New York City Housing Authority apartment complex on Webster Avenue, close to where I grew up. In addition to George and me, we were joined by fellow agent John Cable and Detective Danny Pisculli of the NYPD, both members of our squad's task force.

I'm sure that when country western legend Merle Haggard wrote "Okie from Muskogee," he had John Cable, actually a native of Muskogee, Oklahoma, in mind. John had worked in New York for many years and Danny was a Brooklyn native and one of the senior members on the NYPD side of our squad. Both veterans, John an Army Ranger and Danny, a former Marine, were highly capable and seasoned investigators.

After knocking at the apartment door on one of the upper floors, I wouldn't exactly say we were *welcomed* but the girlfriend's mother said we could come in. In addition to the mother, also present were Harper's girlfriend and her sister.

I was anointed to carry the ball to see if we could get anywhere.

The girlfriend was very pregnant and appeared reserved as opposed to her mother and sister, who knew exactly why we were there. The girlfriend had yet to utter a word but before I could even get going, the mother began to scream:

"Don't say anything to these cops, honey. You know what these cops do—they all lie. That's what they are, no good liars. Don't say anything. You don't have to say a word."

Admittedly, I was a bit taken back. Why had the mother let us come in at all?

She could have easily never opened the door. It wouldn't have been the first or the last time someone refused to cooperate and denied us entry simply because we were the police.

The girlfriend showed no hostility at all, and I figured that the best approach was to don my Roman collar a la Bing Crosby's Father O'Malley in one of my favorite films, *Going My Way*.

"Is this Anthony's baby?" I began.

She nodded that it was.

"When are you due?"

"Next month is my due date," she replied.

"How is your pregnancy going?"

She simply smiled and nodded in the affirmative.

"You know this is a bad way to start out for you and your baby. Anthony is believed to have murdered a father with young children. He is in serious trouble. Don't you want the best for you and your baby? Let me ask you, do you know where Anthony is?"

Before she could say anything, the mother exploded, screaming at her daughter not to answer me.

"You don't have to talk to this fuckin' cop. Don't say nothing, nothing, you hear me? He's trying to trick you. Don't say a word."

The screaming continued with the sister adding her occasional two cents and as George, John, and Danny tried to lower the temperature, the two were yelling so much that they momentarily took their eyes off the girlfriend.

She calmly jotted down something on a small piece of paper, which turned out to be an address, complete with apartment number, on nearby University Avenue. I discreetly covered it and swept it off the table into my lap and then my pants pocket.

For appearances, I continued with a few more pleas, then announced, "Okay guys, I can see we aren't getting anywhere here, we might as well go."

With that, the mother added a parting shot, "I hope you're all happy. See what you've done to my daughter, you upset her."

I looked over and she gave me a tiny smile. *Always better to use the soft approach*, I thought.

We all hopped over to the address on University Avenue and spoke with the superintendent in his basement apartment. We showed him a photograph of Anthony Harper and asked if he had seen him in recent days. He said he had not.

We also asked who lived in the apartment in question. It turned out that his sister had resided there for several years. The super then provided us with a complete description of the apartment layout and we proceeded upstairs.

Moments later, we knocked on the door and after a short time, during which we could hear some commotion inside, a woman asked, "Whooooo?" which is a common response to a hard knock on the door of many a NYC apartment.

"FBI and the police," George yelled.

"Please open the door."

We could hear the peephole sliding back from inside as Danny held out his gold detective shield, so it was visible.

With that, moments later she unlocked the door and let us in.

"Ms. Harper, is your brother here?" George asked.

"No, he's not," she said.

"Well, we have a warrant for his arrest and we're going to have to look around."

With that, George and Danny proceeded to the back bedroom and John and I trailed behind.

Danny and George had gone past a closet in order to get to the back as quickly as possible to search the rear rooms, and John now nodded to me that we would search inside.

With our guns drawn, John flung open the closet door, which contained some clothes, and a large cardboard box covered with a blanket. John then kicked the box hard and with that we heard, "Ugh."

I then put my hand on the blanket and felt the outline of what seemed to be someone's head. John kicked the box and announced, in his best Oklahoma twang, "FBI, come out slowly with your hands above your head or you'll be really sorry."

Following John's directive to the tee, a man slowly came to his feet as I tore the blanket off.

John had one of those Clint Eastwood's Dirty Harry handguns, which looked to have a three-foot long barrel, and uttered, "Well, well, well, look at what we have here. Thought you could hide from us in a box, huh. Don't make any sudden moves you hear me?"

I yelled to George and Danny that we had him and George ran out and asked, "Are you Anthony Harper?"

"Yes," he replied. George then cuffed him, and we took him away.

At that point in our careers, a significant number of the people with whom we came in contact and prosecuted were affiliated with organized crime and it was rare that anyone cooperated. So, we were all quite taken back when once we were in the office, Anthony Harper provided a complete handwritten confession.

He had gone to the car dealership in Albany with the intention of stealing a car to travel to the Bronx to visit his pregnant girlfriend. When confronted by the nightwatchman, he repeatedly hit him in the head with a brick, killing him in the process. He then fled in one of the dealership's new cars and drove to the Bronx.

Having been extradited back to Albany, it was a short time after that when George and I heard from one of the senior members of the Albany District Attorney's Office, Dan Dwyer, who would be prosecuting Mr. Harper.

Danny, George and I drove up to Albany for our appearances before the grand jury to explain what had transpired in the Bronx, some months before. I don't think we realized what a big deal this had been up there and the widespread publicity the case had received. ADA Dwyer was joined by some senior members of the Albany PD and the three of us were treated like Hollywood royalty.

Months later, even though he had fully confessed to murder, Mr. Harper decided to put his fate in the hands of an Albany jury. George and I were the main witnesses, and the local media was reporting on the trial's daily progress.

On the first evening following the first day of testimony, ADA Dwyer and the Albany PD reps took George and I to dinner at what was then an Albany landmark Italian restaurant, Lombardo's.

This was something right out of "Louie's Restaurant in the Bronx," of *Godfather* fame, red and white checkered tablecloths and the like.

"Mr. Lombardo, please say hello to George Hanna and Neil Moran from the FBI in New York. They were responsible for arresting Anthony Harper," Dan Dwyer said.

As George and I stood to exchange handshakes, Mr. Lombardo said, "These gentlemen don't need any introduction. I know who they are. The whole city is appreciative. Nice work boys."

As other customers dropped by to exchange greetings with Mr. Lombardo, who was now seated with us and the Albany police officers and ADA Dwyer, we must have been introduced to twenty people during the course of the evening.

It was as though we had found a cure for cancer.

Days later, after deliberating only a short time, a jury found Anthony Harper guilty of second-degree murder and a host of other charges. He was sentenced to twenty-eight and a third years to life in prison.

Chief Assistant District Attorney Daniel S. Dwyer told an Albany court at Mr. Harper's sentencing that this was "not a case of a simple assault with the motive of robbery, but an intentional murder because Marshall recognized Harper, himself a former security guard at the dealership."

He went on to say that the tragedy broke the dreams of Marshall for a good life in America and destroyed the dreams of his wife and children, who had come to this country only a month before the slaying.

NEIL MORAN

SOL GREENBERG
DISTRICT ATTORNEY
DANIEL S. DWYER
CHIEF ASSISTANT DISTRICT ATTORNEY

COUNTY OF ALBANY
OFFICE OF THE DISTRICT ATTORNEY
COUNTY COURT HOUSE
ALBANY, NEW YORK 12207
(518) 445-7555

April 4, 1986

Mr. William H. Webster, Director
U.S. Department of Justice
Federal Bureau of Investigation
Washington, D.C. 20535

Re: George Hanna and Neil Moran
Joint Auto Larceny Task Force

Dear Mr. Webster:

The above named Special Agents, under a warrant for the theft of an automobile in the County of Albany, arrested one Anthony "Tony" Harper. These Agents in furtherance of this investigation developed evidence against Mr. Harper for the murder of one Cyril Marshall here in the County of Albany, a night watchman in a Dodge dealership. Your Agents, once this information was made available to them, proceeded to take oral and written statements from the defendant which ultimately led to the indictment of Harper on State charges for felony murder, robbery, burglary and larceny.

The case against Anthony "Tony" Harper was tried in the Albany County Court in February resulting in a conviction of the defendant for the crime of felony murder and other charges. This defendant was subsequently sentenced to life imprisonment with a minimum of 30 years.

During the course of this proceeding your Agents worked closely with this Office and me personally and I wish to acknowledge to you their professionalism as Police Officers, as witnesses and as men of high esteem. Their testimony at trial and their demeanor was a true asset to the prosecution and to the ultimate verdict rendered by the jury.

April 4, 1986

Thank you for the cooperation of your Agency and the excellent cooperation and rapport extended by these two outstanding men. This cooperation certainly indicates the Criminal Justice System is viable, alive and successful.

Very truly yours,

Daniel S. Dwyer
Chief Assistant District Attorney

DSD/ltc

April 4, 1986, letter to FBI Director William H. Webster from Albany Chief Assistant District Attorney Daniel Dwyer, citing efforts of George Hanna and Neil Moran leading to the conviction of Anthony Harper.

STORIES

U.S. Department of Justice

Federal Bureau of Investigation

Office of the Director

Washington, D.C. 20535

March 4, 1986

PERSONAL

Mr. Neil F. Moran
Federal Bureau of Investigation
New York, New York

Dear Mr. Moran:

     I have learned of your superior efforts in connection with the investigation involving fugitive Anthony P. Harper, and I am pleased to take this time to commend you.

     You and Special Agent Hanna played a vital role in the eventual success achieved in this matter. Not only did you convince the subject's uncooperative girl friend to reveal his location, but you also arranged for his arrest, which was accomplished without injury to Harper, the arresting Agents, or innocent bystanders. I am aware of the highly professional services and significant interviewing ability which this task required, and I want you to know that your worthwhile efforts in this matter have not gone unnoticed.

Sincerely yours,

William H. Webster
Director

March 4, 1986, letter from FBI Director William H. Webster concerning the arrest and prosecution of Anthony Harper.

HANDSOME TOMMY

The Genovese Family capo had reportedly been responsible for ordering or carrying out several murders of individuals who were suspected of cooperating with authorities. And there were those who borrowed money through his prolific loansharking business and soon realized after plunging deeper in debt, that they'd never be able to pay the high "vig" or interest charged and suffered brutal beatings and sometimes violent death.

We were gathered outside the palatial Bay Ridge home of Thomas "Handsome Tommy" Fontana at about 5:00 a.m. Mr. Fontana was on parole for serving time after engineering a failed bank burglary. Tommy and his crew, anticipating a sizeable payday, lowered themselves into a Staten Island bank over the President's Day weekend into the waiting arms of FBI agents and NYPD detectives. He had been accused of recently consorting with other known members of organized crime, a violation of his parole. A federal judge issued a warrant and ordered the U.S. Marshal Service to bring Mr. Fontana before the court. The marshals allowed the FBI to participate in the execution of the warrant to get Mr. Fontana to cooperate. George Hanna and I were selected to join the arrest team, given our successful track record in eliciting the cooperation of various organized crime figures.

As we quietly exited our vehicles, the marshals opened their trunk and removed a battering ram, which bore a striking likeness to the menacing siege weapon often seen in epic movies, where angry mobs storm twenty-foot high and three-foot thick doors guarding a massive medieval fortress.

"Is this necessary, guys? I asked. "Are we breaking this door down without trying any other options?"

"Depends. When we announce U.S. Marshal Service, if we don't hear anything from inside quickly, and I do mean quickly, the door comes down."

I looked at George as he rolled his eyes, which after working with him for years told me, "It's not our warrant; not a whole lot we can do here." *Not the ideal scenario for ingratiating ourselves and extracting cooperation*, I thought.

As we stood outside, the spotlights illuminated the cathedral style archway, surrounded by Picasso Italian stone, which encircled a stunningly charming, lightly colored mahogany door.

"U.S. Marshals, we have a warrant for your arrest," followed a loud bang on the door.

Not a peep from inside as I heard one of the marshal's cadences: "One Mississippi, two Mississippi, three Mississippi."

Boom! A stick of dynamite could not have dealt as vicious a blow, as the door cascaded backward and collapsed to the floor in one piece with a thunderous wallop. At the top of the staircase with hands on hips and attempting to open his eyes, stood a clearly startled, and at that instant, a not so 'Handsome Tommy.' At the early hour, clad in oversized boxer shorts and a what's known as a "wife-beater," which should have been oversized but wasn't, and only accentuated his considerable girth, Tommy was not happy.

"What the fuck, guys," was the gorgeous one's initial remark. "I hope this is serious. You just broke down an $11,000 Italian hand-crafted door."

"Yes, it's serious, Tommy, we have a warrant for violation of your parole. We'll take care of the cost of the door. Get dressed and move," one of the marshals said.

Tommy quickly threw on a pair of trousers and a sweater, which also was several sizes too small and true to his nickname he asked if he could comb his hair in the bathroom. "Sure, knock yourself out," the marshal obliged. "Just make it quick."

In his early to mid-60s, our prisoner had a full head of platinum blond hair. A significant showing of black and gray was creeping in at the roots and various locations. He clearly had not recently visited his hairdresser. In retrospect, an apt comparison would be strikingly like the style and color of our current commander-in-chief. *His nickname was "Handsome Tommy?"* I thought.

For the next minute or two, Tommy proceeded to comb his tresses with the precision of a Swiss watchmaker. I thought I was watching John Travolta in *Saturday Night Fever*. Each section received the same meticulous attention. After he put on the finishing touches with a nasty smelling hair spray, as he brought the comb to his eyebrows, the marshal shouted, "Tommy, enough, let's go."

As we placed him in handcuffs and threw his coat over his shoulders, one of the marshals announced, "These two gentlemen are FBI agents and they'll be taking you back to their office for processing."

"Oh, the FBI's here too? Wow, I'm honored, guys. Looks like I got everyone out of bed early."

Following our brief introductions and the recital of his Miranda warnings, we proceeded eastbound on the Belt Parkway. At the early hour, we had no problem navigating our way to Cross Bay Boulevard in what seemed like a matter of minutes.

George was driving, and I was seated with our passenger in the back. He stood about 5'8" and was a corpulent 260 lbs. He had asked me to remove his coat and his snug sweater emphasized his sizeable arms and shoulders, leading me to conclude that at one time he probably was a body builder.

"Tommy, you want coffee and a bagel?" George asked as we pulled up outside Cross Bay Bagels.

"Wow the FBI's springing for breakfast? Absolutely, coffee, half-and-half, four sugars and an everything with extra cream cheese, please."

"I'll have a tea—milk, no sugar, and a dry plain bagel," I announced.

Tommy, who was handcuffed with his hands behind his back was clearly taken back and suddenly shifted and spun around to get a better look at me.

"No sugar in your coffee and no butter on your bagel, you work out, don't you? You look like you take care of yourself. You don't have an ounce of fat on you."

"Yeah, I work out and I suppose I'm pretty careful about what I eat. Watching my figure, you know."

"Yeah right," Tommy said slowly, as he continued to eyeball his new nutritional counselor.

"Hey buddy, cancel that cream cheese and skip the half-and-half. I'll have low-fat milk and no sugar in my coffee," Tommy announced. "I'm turning over a new fuckin' leaf. I want to look like this guy. I'm a mess and I'm sick of this gut."

For the remainder of the trip to our office and before we got down to the subject of beatings and murder, Tommy was like a skilled defense attorney quizzing me on my fitness regimen and quirky dietary habits. Schooling Tommy on HDL cholesterol v. LDL cholesterol while on Cross Bay Boulevard, he even challenged me to a push-up contest in the interview room when we arrived at the office, but when George warned him, "Tommy, I saw him do sixty-three pushups and barely take a breath in between, so unless you think you have that in you, I'd give it a second thought." Tommy's eyes lit up and he backed away.

Tommy was "old school" and never did cooperate. He later died in prison, but as was my experience with many like him, although we got off to a rocky start when we crashed through that front door, when you treated people like Tommy the way in which you would like to be treated, it never failed to make for some memorable and entertaining theater.

GOING TO THE MET GAME

We had hoped the information was solid. An informant acted as a middleman in providing weapons to a gang from South Brooklyn who were planning the armed robbery of a jewelry store.

With experienced criminals like these, information is not shared outside a normally airtight inner circle but thanks to our source, we knew the event would occur on a Friday morning and we were also privy to the identities of the participants.

After conducting the appropriate research, which included retrieving known photos of the gang, as well as identifying their vehicles, our squad, consisting of NYPD detectives and FBI agents, began familiarizing themselves with each subject's residence. Fortunately, we found that everyone lived in the same Red Hook, Brooklyn, neighborhood.

Next, were meetings with senior management of the NYPD and the FBI, as well as federal and state prosecutors.

Would this eventually be a local prosecution or was the robbery going to occur in New Jersey or Connecticut, at which time the federal government might take the lead?

What was the danger to the public?

At what point in the robbery would we intervene?

The feeling of some was to execute a car stop and arrest the crew for gun possession. We could never allow armed participants to enter a retail establishment and risk that an employee, customer or bystander would be injured or killed.

Ultimately, the decision was reached that to charge the participants with conspiracy to commit armed robbery, they would have to be in the immediate vicinity or be observed about to enter the premises. This was no easy task and would require split-second decision making on our part.

At 5:00 a.m. the first Friday morning we convened, the teams met on Bay Street in the vicinity of Brooklyn's Red Hook Park. Given its proximity to the water, a cold, late, winter mist hung over the grounds, which would soon burn off at sunrise.

What were the chances the crew would pull this off this morning? All we knew was that the plan was for a Friday.

Would it be today, next week or a month from now?

Unlike television or a movie, these are how these scenarios normally play out and all we could do was to set up, be patient and wait.

Almost like this was scripted for the big screen, at about 9:00 a.m., one of the subjects entered what we later learned was a stolen vehicle and proceeded to pick up three additional participants in the neighborhood.

Onto the Brooklyn-Queens Expressway and stuck in late rush hour traffic, which was to our advantage, making them easy to surveil, the gang eventually wound their way through Queens and across the Throggs Neck Bridge into the Bronx and onto the New England Thruway.

Were they going to Connecticut?

Perhaps upscale Greenwich?

Main Street in Greenwich has some nice jewelry shops I recalled, which are only a stone's throw away from I-95 and would make for a quick getaway.

Suddenly, they took the exit for Rye Playland, a longstanding amusement park, where as children, our parents took us on many occasions.

These guys are probably going to wind up going on the roller coaster and then head back to Brooklyn, we thought.

Now in suburban Westchester, without the city congestion, we had to hang back a bit or risk being made by the crew. As they zig-zagged through local streets, suddenly they pulled into the Rye Ridge Shopping Center, where among the many stores was R&S Jewelry.

The communications on our car and hand-held radios were now at a minimum realizing that in minutes we could be confronting four heavily armed men in a suburban setting.

"All units standby," the command went out.

The vehicle literally crawled through the lot and was now passing in front of the jewelry shop. All the units were now in position to effect the arrests as we awaited their next move.

Once again, they circled slowly.

Had we been spotted?

As they began to come around a third time, they slowly pulled out of the lot and drove away.

It was now close to noontime, and we were back in Red Hook having followed the car on its journey to Brooklyn.

Did they think it was too risky and decide to abort?

Did they make the surveillance?

We now hoped our source could learn some small bit of information which would direct our plan.

"It was a dry run," our informant reported.

The crew had simply wanted to ensure that they weren't being followed, of which we were quite pleased, and that the jewelry store was an easy target. It sounded like it was a go.

The following Friday, once again we took our positions in Red Hook on a cold and rainy morning and to no one's surprise, given the weather, nothing happened. Even bad guys don't like to get out of bed in the rain.

It was now the following Friday, the same four men left South Brooklyn, drove onto the BQE and about an hour later were getting off the Rye Playland exit.

As they pulled into the Rye Ridge Shopping Center, over the radio we heard, "This looks like it could be it. Let's remember our plans. Everyone be patient."

This time, there was no drive-by, as what we learned later was a stolen car, gently pulled into a spot outside the store.

"Easy everyone," the command began, "Let's wait till they make their move."

All eyes were transfixed on the car as we waited for the doors to open. Our timing had to be precise to charge the crew with the more serious offense, we couldn't move too early.

Both rear doors suddenly opened together as two men slowly began to walk with heads down toward the store. The car's front doors opened moments later as the two remaining occupants looked around as they exited to ensure they had not been followed and then fell in behind the other two.

As they moved forward, I noticed several women with strollers talking with older men standing on the sidewalk in immediate proximity to our subjects.

"All units move in," the command went out over the air.

We all flew out of our vehicles and raced toward the jewelry store.

"FBI, police," we shouted.

"Don't move, hands in the air."

"Get down," I began to yell at the pedestrians who were completely oblivious to the small legion of detectives and agents suddenly descending on the would-be robbers.

"Get down folks, get down," I screamed again as everyone stood motionless and glared open-mouthed as though waiting for Martin Scorsese to appear and yell, "Cut."

No one budged an inch.

As we disarmed the quartet and placed them in handcuffs, the pedestrians were ushered a short distance away. As I looked around, there were dozens of people apparently not the least bit shaken and completely oblivious to the sight of men and women walking through the shopping center at 11:00 a.m. carrying automatic weapons and bearing NYPD and FBI jackets.

Bob Joyce and I had been riding together on these surveillances, and we took one of the defendants, Michael "Big Mike" Fabriano into custody.

With Bob at the wheel, I read "Big Mike" his Miranda warnings and asked him if he was willing to speak with us without an attorney present.

"Yeah, why not," he said.

After obtaining his pedigree information, I began to ask him his whereabouts the past few Fridays, wondering if he had ever been to this area on prior occasions.

He had conflicting and evasive answers to almost every question.

Bob and I were quite surprised when I asked, "Mike, when you left Brooklyn this morning with a gun and traveled to the shopping center with your companions, who were also all armed, where did you think you were going and what did you think you were going to do?"

"Let's put it this way pal," he began.

"I knew we wasn't going to the fucking Met game."

It was about a week after the arrests, I was called to testify at the Westchester County grand jury.

We didn't often present evidence in settings other than the five boroughs of New York City. Whenever you ventured outside the city, there was a totally different vibe. All eyes were riveted on you. Most of these people probably had never seen an FBI agent before, other than watching television. You had their complete and undivided attention.

The assistant district attorney ran through the entire few weeks leading up to the day of the arrests, the apprehension of the suspects and my discussion with Big Mike in the car.

During the questioning, the assistant district attorney asked me if Big Mike made any statements when asked where he was going that morning, and I answered:

"Yes, he said, 'Let's put it this way, pal, I knew we wasn't going to the fucking Met game.'"

The entire grand jury broke out in hysterical laughter, so much so that the ADA had to ask them to calm themselves.

Eventually, all four men pleaded guilty and received hefty prison terms.

Westchester is not New York City.

PHILLY

The January 19, 1973, *New York Times* headline read in part:

> **3 Held in Brooklyn Church—Jewel Theft**
> *Three persons were arrested yesterday in the theft of jewels insured for $100,000 from the Basilica of Regina Pacis, in Brooklyn, on Jan. 10. Arrested were Frank Morici and Phillip Paradiso. The two suspects live near the church, which is on 65th Street. Paradiso has 16 previous arrests and Morici has 9. Paradiso was sentenced to spend five years at a narcotics center in Staten Island last September, but he escaped, in November. Both men listed their occupations as unemployed construction workers. It was suspected that Gambino Crime Family boss Carlo Gambino had intervened on the church's behalf.*

It was August 1986 when George Hanna and I got a strange telephone call from Phillip "Philly" Paradiso. Philly advised that he had some information of value and would like to meet with us.

A career criminal, Philly had been in and out of some of New York's toughest and most notorious prisons including Attica, Clinton, and Greenhaven, doing stints for burglary, armed robbery, assault, and drug

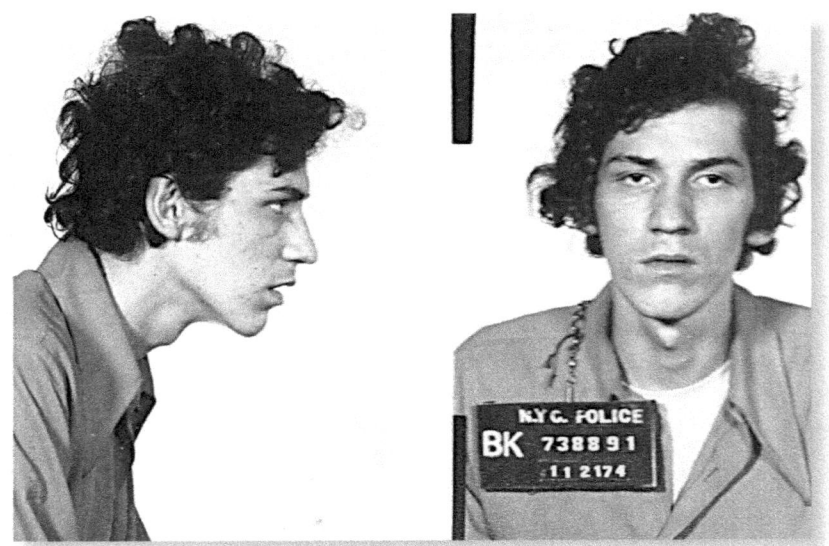

Phillip "Philly" Paradiso

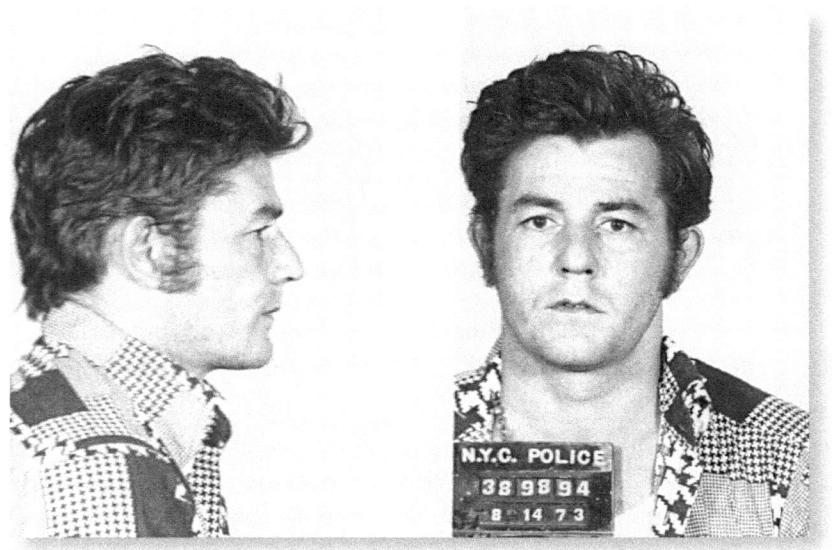

Michael "Mickey Boy" Paradiso

possession. We were more than a bit curious as to what he would have to say.

We arranged to meet him on the boardwalk at Coney Island, adjacent to the handball courts, which, given the warm weather, were packed with men in their 60s, 70s and even 80s, still dedicated to this once popular New York pastime.

Standing next to a park bench and staring out at the Atlantic Ocean, Philly was immediately recognizable, standing 6'4," weighing about 240 pounds, and dressed in what we would learn was his trademark Tony Soprano-type navy blue track suit and snow-white Air Jordans.

As we approached, he walked toward us with an unmistakable limp, courtesy of a swan dive from the second story of a home he was burglarizing as a seventeen-year-old in attempting to flee the police.

"You guys know Jimmy Hydell, right?" Philly began.

Hydell was alleged to be an associate of the Gambino LCN Crime Family and was believed to have carried out several 'hits,' on their behalf.

Philly had learned that following a violent argument between Hydell and his longtime girlfriend, Annette Di Biasi, Ms. DiBiasi, who was badly battered, testified in the grand jury against Hydell. When Hydell learned of her testimony, he murdered her.

At this initial meeting, Philly also revealed that his brother, Michael "Mickey Boy" Paradiso, a reputed member of the Gambino LCN Crime Family, had been responsible for the murder of Frank Morici, who, even though he was a colleague at one time, had Philly arrested after he burglarized his Bensonhurst, Brooklyn home.

Philly said that he was willing to work with us on these and other crimes of which he was aware, and so our relationship began.

Since the crimes outlined at our initial meeting with Philly appeared to be state charges, George Hanna, Detective George Terra, and I met with the people at the Brooklyn District Attorney's Office Rackets Bureau.

George Terra was an original member of our task force and had been George Hanna's partner. He had taken a transfer to work in the prestigious Brooklyn District Attorney's Squad and now George Hanna and I were reunited with him.

George Terra was Brooklyn born and raised.

"My father wanted me to be a 'G-Man,' George began, the acronym made famous by George "Machine Gun" Kelly. At the time of his arrest in the 1930s by Bureau of Investigation agents, Kelly was to have said, "Don't shoot G-Men," meaning government men.

My father actually wanted me to follow in his footsteps—'G-Man' to him meant, 'Garbage Man.' George's father worked for the NYC Department of Sanitation.

As many of our parents did at that time, they felt civil service was a logical path to security.

After spending two years in the U.S. Army, George, who had taken tests for the Sanitation Department, the Fire Department and the NYPD, opted for the Police Department, in June 1969.

After spending several years working in uniform, George and his sometimes radio car partner, Danny Pisculli, took a transfer to the newly formed Auto Crime Unit, which was created to combat the ever-growing auto theft problem in New York.

In 1982, when the JALTF was formed, he and Danny Pisculli transferred to work with the FBI.

Under the supervision of Rackets Bureau Chief, Laura Drager, we sat with Assistant District Attorneys Eric Seidel and Eric Kraus. We outlined what we had learned from Philly and indicated that we would begin by having him wear a body recorder and meet Jimmy Hydell.

It was only about a month later, when Philly met with Hydell and began to probe the disappearance of Ms. DiBasi. It didn't take too much probing before Hydell admitted to kidnapping and murdering Ms. DiBiasi with a former NYPD officer, Robert Bering.

As Philly continued meeting with Hydell, he also spoke freely about the August 11, 1986, murder of Giacomo "Jack" D'Angelo, who had been an unindicted co-conspirator in a heroin conspiracy case. D'Angelo had been an inmate at Lewisburg Federal Correctional Institute at the same time as Philly's brother, Michael "Mickey Boy" Paradiso.

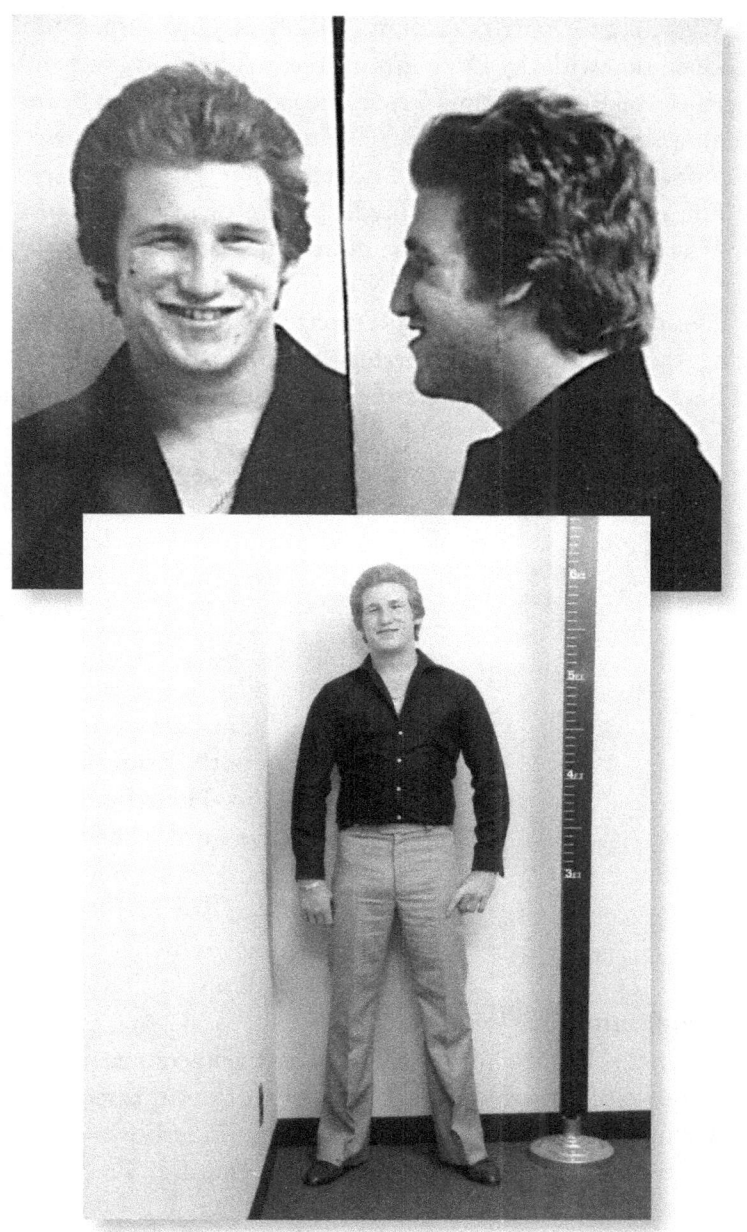

Jimmy Hydell

According to Hydell's account, Mickey Boy had suspected D'Angelo of cooperating with the Drug Enforcement Administration and enlisted Hydell to "take care of him." Hydell boasted that he and Robert Bering and an associate Nicholas "Nicky" Guido, gunned D'Angelo down in the doorway of his Staten Island home.

The next hit that Jimmy Hydell spoke of in a series of recorded conversations with Philly was the murder of Joseph Trinetto, reputed to be an associate of the Lucchese LCN Crime Family.

Investigation revealed that Trinetto had been living with Helen Bering, the ex-wife of Robert Bering. At Robert Bering's request, Hydell and his brother Francis "Frankie" Hydell had carried out the hit when Bering learned that his ex-wife and Trinetto had attempted to defraud him out of monies they derived in a business venture.

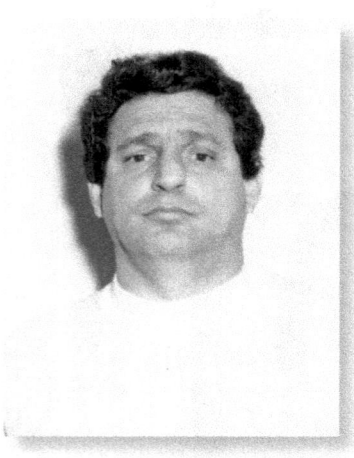

Frankie DeCicco

What proved to lead to Jimmy Hydell's eventual demise was a conversation with Philly where he detailed his failed attempted hit on Anthony "Gaspipe" Casso, the underboss of the Lucchese LCN Crime Family.

Along with Robert Bering and Nicky Guido, Hydell claimed that he was acting on orders of the Gambino Crime Family, who believed that in June 1986, Casso had engineered the car bombing, which killed Gambino underboss Frankie DeCicco, but was intended for the boss, John Gotti.

In just a short few months, Philly had delivered as promised with admissions by Jimmy Hydell in his participation in three murders and the attempted 'hit' on an organized crime underboss. Given Philly's addiction problems, and often unreliable nature, we had hoped to introduce an undercover agent or detective so when it came time for the prosecution, the undercover would be able to give testimony as opposed to Philly.

During the week of October 12, 1986, Philly agreed to introduce me to Jimmy Hydell as the undercover. We agreed to meet him outside O'Sullivan's Bar & Grill on 89th Street and Third Avenue, in Bay Ridge, Brooklyn.

With George Hanna and George Terra looking on from a block or so away, the entrée we had devised was that I was a "car guy" with great contacts at the New York State Department of Motor Vehicles ("DMV"). I could handle "straight steals," "insurance jobs," and "tagged cars" or those with bogus vehicle identification numbers ("VINs"). Tag jobs involved taking a stolen car and altering the Vins with a legitimate number. With my extensive contacts at DMV, who were on my payroll, I boasted to Jimmy, "I can get a donkey cart registered, complete with plates and registration." We agreed to meet again soon and begin to do business.

Philly "vouched" for me, which in street parlance meant that if Neil turned out to be a snitch or a cop, Jimmy would hold Philly responsible. Given Hydell's track record of which we were all aware, it would spell trouble for Philly.

That was the last time any of us would see Jimmy Hydell.

At the conclusion of *The Godfather*, Michael Corleone, played by Al Pacino, is seen speaking to his brother-in-law, Carlo: "You have to answer for Santino, Carlo." Michael had suspected Carlo of setting up the murder of his brother, Santino Corleone, played by James Caan and judgment day had arrived.

In our case, Jimmy Hydell had to answer for the failed attempt on the life of Anthony "Gaspipe" Casso.

Casso had put the word out that he wanted Hydell tracked down and delivered to him.

That very Saturday, October 18, 1986, Jimmy was summoned to a meeting at a popular hot dog stand in the vicinity of Brooklyn's Bay 8th Street. Philly learned about the meeting too late and by the time George

Terra and George Hanna were notified, they couldn't get there to cover it. Given the fact that I had recently met with Jimmy in an undercover capacity, there was no way I could be involved.

Detectives Stephen Caracappa and Louis Eppolito were NYPD detectives and on the payroll of the Lucchese LCN Crime Family. They became known in the media as the "Mafia Cops."

On orders from Anthony Casso, Eppolito and Caracappa kidnapped Jimmy Hydell in the vicinity of a popular mob social club near the hotdog stand on October 18th and delivered him to Casso.

According to testimony at the Mafia Cops trial in April 2006, Hydell was tortured and gave up the names of his accomplices, Robert Bering and Nicky Guido, who had joined him in the attempted hit on Casso in 1986. Jimmy Hydell's body was never recovered.

Robert Bering

In an airing of the news program *60 Minutes* in April 2005, Anthony Casso described his relationship with Louis Eppolito and Stephen Caracappa and how Jimmy Hydell met his demise.

"I had law enforcement on my payroll, certainly. I had them looking after me," Casso began.

"Louis and Steve went by a club where the kid (Hydell) was staying, making believe they were going to arrest him. They put him in the car. I used to have cars for them. I gave them a car. Like a police car. An unmarked car. I gave them a car. They put him in the car," Casso continued.

"The kid thought they were taking him to the station house. But they took him to a garage. When they got to the garage, they laid him on the floor. They tied his feet, his hands cuffed, put him in the trunk of the car. The police car comes in, the guy's kicking in the trunk. He's making noise. I took him to a place that I have pre-arranged. You know, somebody's house that I could use.... Sat him down. I wanted to know why I was shot, and who else was involved. And who, you know, gave the orders to shoot me."

Casso then described how he killed Hydell.

"I didn't shoot him in the head. That was somebody's house. You make a mess," Casso said.

"No, I shot him a couple of times. I didn't torture the kid. I didn't do anything like that."

"What's a couple?" asked CBS correspondent Ed Bradley.

"More than a couple. Really, I don't know the exact amount. Maybe I shot him 10 times, 12 times," says Casso.

"At that time, I gave Louis and Steve, I think, $45,000 for delivering him to me."

Within days of his disappearance, Philly had arranged for me to meet Jimmy's brother, Frankie Hydell.

My entrée to Frankie was much the same as when I met Jimmy. I was a "car guy" with DMV people on my payroll. I was in the market for insurance jobs and straight steals which I would be able convert into a legit car by altering the VIN.

Operating and keeping tabs on Philly certainly had its challenges. This was a guy who was a career criminal. He once told the two Georges and me, "While you guys were busy being altar boys growing up, I was breaking into houses and robbing people."

On another occasion, Philly spoke about his time in prison, which never included turning over a "new leaf."

"All we thought about in prison were new ways to scam and get over on people."

We had set up Philly with a rented car, a brand-new white Buick Regal. Within a week, he called us and said the car was hit while unattended.

"How bad is the damage?" I asked.

"The side is bashed in a little," was his reply.

When we arrived at Philly's apartment in Coney Island, the car was totaled. When we cleaned out the glove compartment, we found evidence that Philly had been running a private car service with the Regal, transporting dialysis patients from a nearby clinic to Coney Island Hospital.

And then there was "Eewee."

I had accompanied Philly to Frankie Hydell's home in Staten Island and because of the nature of the conversation, it would have struck Frankie as odd that I would be present, so I equipped Philly with the body recorder and a transmitter and parked nearby.

Back in the 1980s, we often struggled with the quality of the equipment, so I couldn't really make out the gist of the conversation between the two. It was a chilly day and Philly had worn a heavy overcoat.

"How did it go in there?" I asked, as Philly got into the car.

"Okay, no big deal," he said.

The next day, as I listened to the tape recording of the meeting, I thought I heard Frankie talking about a sawed-off shotgun and it sounded like he asked Philly to hide it for him.

I grabbed Bob Joyce, who was sitting nearby, and asked him to listen to see if I was hearing things.

"Yeah, it sounds like he gave it to Philly alright. And you mean Philly didn't say anything?"

"Huh, fat chance," I replied.

"Great," Bob said. "Now we have Philly wandering round Brooklyn with a sawed-off shotgun—we're all going to get fired."

I immediately beeped Philly and about ten minutes later he phoned.

"Philly, are you fuckin' kidding me?" I began.

"You had a sawed-off shotgun under your coat yesterday in the car and said nothing to me?"

"Neil, let me explain," he said.

"Never mind, don't go anywhere, George and I are coming out."

About an hour later, we got the shock of our lives when Philly calmly told us, "I don't have it. I gave it to Eewee."

"Who in the hell is Eewee, Philly?" I asked.

"He's a drug dealer from the projects on 28th Street."

"So, let me get this straight, you're telling us that you gave a sawed-off shotgun, that very possibly may have been used in a homicide, to a known drug dealer, whose name you don't know other than Eewee, and somehow you think that's okay?"

"Neil, calm down, I never saw you this mad."

It was true. It definitely ranked up there on the "being mad" scale for me.

"Well, Philly, I have a tendency to get a bit out of sorts when I have to go home and tell my wife and daughters that I no longer have a job and may be facing criminal charges. It does tend to rub me the wrong way, Phillip."

This was probably the only time I ever called Philly by his given name—I was steaming.

"I'll get it back, don't worry," Philly told us.

The two Georges and I seemed to be on some sort of a random "Who should I call next?" process with Philly. It depended on what mood he was in, when he decided which one of us to call in the middle of the night.

This night it was George Terra who got a call.

"George, come quick. Someone just shot through my door," Philly said when George answered the phone at 2:00 a.m.

"When I got to Philly's apartment, I saw a huge gaping hole in the door," George began.

"Someone had unloaded a few shotgun rounds. The door was blown to bits. Philly had heard some commotion and took a mattress and stood it up against the door to try to absorb the shots and prevent anyone from coming in. The mattress was also in shambles. It was a real mess. Philly wanted to stay but I hustled him out of there in case they were coming back."

We had learned, during the time of the missing shotgun, Philly and Ewee may have teamed up to rob some neighborhood drug dealers. This attempted hit on Philly may have been as a result of our suspicions.

George Terra continued, "About an hour or so later, Philly asked me to bring him back to the apartment so he could get some belongings to bring to a motel where we were going to put him. When we arrived, the fire department was there fighting a raging blaze. We later learned from the firemen that several Molotov cocktails were used to set the fire."

Except for Bob Joyce, George Terra, George Hanna and me, we kept all this strictly to ourselves. We dared not share this with anyone.

For days, George and I knocked on every door and sat on every known drug location we could come up with in an effort to locate the now legendary Eewee.

It was about a week later when Philly reached out to us and said that Eewee was getting so much heat that he gave Philly back the shotgun and now it was finally safe in our hands.

With Anthony Casso beginning to extract his revenge for the attempted hit on his life, on Christmas morning, 1986, Nicky Guido was gunned down in a hail of bullets in front of his south Brooklyn home. George Hanna called me and said that he had just heard from George Terra, who was on his way to the 76th Precinct.

George Terra learned from the squad detectives that the deceased was an employee of what was known back in the day as the "Phone Company" or New York Telephone.

"I knew that our Nicky Guido didn't work for the phone company, and I am thinking that they just shot the wrong Nicky Guido. I told the detectives, who knew nothing about our case, that this might be a case of mistaken identity, and they looked at me like I was nuts," George said.

According to testimony in the Mafia Cops trial, Detectives Caracappa and Eppolito had provided the incorrect address for a Nicholas Guido, who lived in proximity to the deceased and Anthony Casso directed the hit team to the wrong address.

Only a month later, apparently reeling from the disappearance of Jimmy Hydell and the murder of the wrong Nicky Guido, Robert Bering began cooperating with George Terra and George Hanna.

He directed them to a shallow grave on Staten Island where he and Jimmy Hydell had buried the body of Annette DiBiasi.

On February 24, 1987, Ms. DiBiasi's remains were unearthed. Bering would ultimately plead guilty to the murders of Ms. DiBiasi, Jack D'Angelo and Joseph Trinetto. He was sentenced to terms of fifteen years to life and eight and a third to twenty-five years.

In July 1987, Frankie Hydell was arrested and charged with the murder of Joesph Trinetto, narcotics charges as a result of selling me cocaine and criminal possession of stolen property resulting from stolen cars, he had also sold to me.

After his eventual release from prison, Frankie Hydell was murdered outside a Staten Island nightclub, on April 28, 1998, by members of the Gambino LCN Crime Family, who suspected him of cooperating with the government.

In June 1987, Philly bought one-eighth of a kilo of .88 percent pure heroin from Anthony "Tony Roach" Rampino. The two had served time in prison together. Rampino was a longtime Gambino associate who could never achieve "made guy" status due to his drug history.

He was one of the prime suspects in the December 16, 1985, murder of Gambino Boss "Big Paul" Castellano as he entered Spark's Steakhouse, in midtown Manhattan during the Christmastime evening rush hour.

On the edge of cooperating with George Hanna during his interview,

Anthony "Tony Roach" Rampino

he decided to go to trial. The prosecution was led by ADA Eric Seidel and Rampino was convicted and sentenced to twenty-five years to life.

In January 1988, Michael "Mickey Boy" Paradiso was indicted by a Brooklyn grand jury for the murder of Frank Morici.

In April 1989, Philly was the star witness at his brother's trial.

Under fierce questioning from Mickey Boy's lawyer, Philly reluctantly admitted to his long and colorful criminal past.

Defense counsel asked, "Mr. Paradiso, is it true that you've been a heroin addict with a twenty-year habit, a thief who stole $250,000 worth of religious artifacts from Regina Pacis Church and a common thief who broke into more apartments than we can count to feed your drug habit and stole drugs and money from Colombian drug dealers at gunpoint?"

"Yeah, it's all true," Philly replied.

"I ain't proud of none of that but working with the agents has turned my life around."

"Brother Against Brother—He's a Rat and a Liar," page three of the *New York Post* read the next day, citing comments from Mickey Boy's wife and daughters, who attended the trial and were not shy in sharing their thoughts on Philly's testimony.

"He's the lowest form of scum ever," Mickey Boy's daughter, Michele, was quoted.

"It's the agents. They've been after my father for years and got him (Philly) to say these things."

The remainder of his time on the stand did not go well or win Philly any favors with the jury. As anyone with his checkered background, although forewarned by ADA Eric Kraus presenting the case not to be combative with defense counsel, he got into several heated shouting matches and at times, had difficulty controlling his temper. He had played right into their hands.

In the end, Mickey Boy was acquitted of the murder charges and Philly reunited with his wife and children from whom he had been estranged.

As our time with Philly had run its course, he pondered whether he should enter the Witness Security Program, commonly known as Witness Protection.

As these discussions continued, for his safety, we transported him to Ocean City, Maryland.

With the assistance of a local FBI agent, Robert Twig, from the Wilmington, Delaware office, we put Philly up in a beautiful high-rise hotel overlooking the Atlantic Ocean. The hotel had all the amenities, an indoor swimming pool, spa, sauna, and even an ice-skating rink, although we didn't feel Philly would be lacing up anytime soon.

Philly was dyed-in-the-wool Brooklynite. He was raised in Bensonhurst, which claimed one of the highest concentrations of Italian Americans in New York's five boroughs. This was a guy who was used to people with ethnic sounding surnames. For some odd reason, he was utterly fascinated with the name Robert Twig.

"Who has a name like that?" he asked George and me.

"I love that guy's name."

We called Philly every day, sometimes two or three times. Past history had taught us that this is a guy, given too much time on his hands, will go out of his way to find trouble.

It was about three or four days when we got a telephone call from Bob Twig.

"Your guy checked out of the hotel. I had left instructions that if he left for any reason, they were to call me. I have no idea where he is. Oh, and something else, he racked up a bunch of charges while he was here and for some reason signed my name on all of them. I'm looking at a bar bill here from last night for $65 and it's signed 'Bob Twig.'"

Will our lives ever get back to normal? I wondered.

"How the hell do we get a hold of this clown, George?" I asked.

Fortuitously, about fifteen minutes later we heard from Philly, aka Bob Twig.

"I got tired of that fuckin' hotel. I found a better place down by the amusement park. I took a room above a bar."

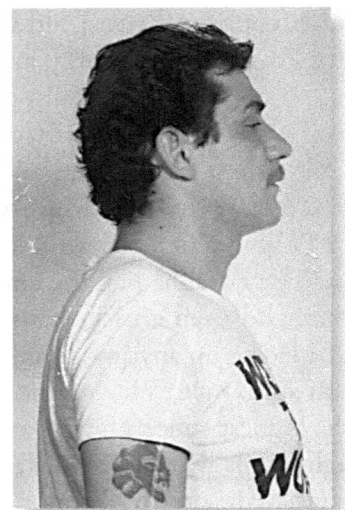

Phillip "Philly" Paradiso

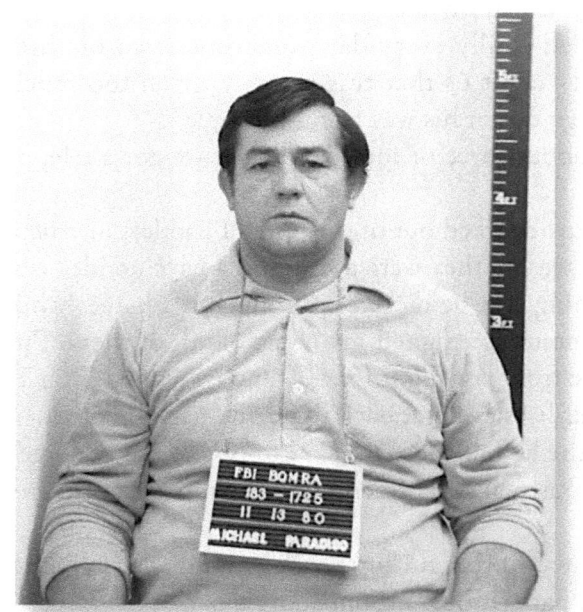

Michael "Mickey Boy" Paradiso

"Philly, we can't have this. You are driving us crazy. You can't just pack up and leave on your own," I said, with George listening on the extension.

"Neil's right, Philly, we just want you to be safe. You know that. And Philly, what's with signing the agent's name to charges at the hotel? He's pretty upset."

"Tell him to relax. I just love that guy's name."

We figured it probably wasn't the best thing to have the real Bob Twig track down Philly, so George and I made plans to drive back to Ocean City. Philly had given us the name of the bar and told us that he didn't want to use his real name, so he decided to check in as, yes you guessed it, Bob Twig.

"Just ask the barmaid for Bob," he said.

We arrived the next day in the early afternoon and leave it to Philly to pick the only dodgy area in all of Ocean City. There were five or six motorcycles parked out front as we pulled up. Yes, Philly was living at a biker bar.

As George and I walked in, trying my best not to show how upset I was, I asked the barmaid, complete with a cigarette dangling from her mouth, "Is Bob here?"

"Bob who?" she asked with a real snippy attitude.

I glanced at George and felt like grabbing the cigarette out of this chick's mouth and wanted to ask, "Well how many fuckin' Bob's to you have here honey?" but I bit my tongue.

"Twig, Bob Twig is who we're looking for," George said.

"Oh, Bob, sure, hang on," she said.

"Bob, you got two angry looking guys down here better come down."

"Tell them to hang on one second, I'll be right down."

With that, Philly ambled down the stairs, and I couldn't resist saying sarcastically, "Hope we didn't wake you, Bob."

It's probably fair to say, following this brief but memorable episode, that the other agents in the Wilmington FBI office had probably been forewarned by the real Bob Twig, "If anyone from the New York office calls, hang up."

Weeks later, Philly and his wife and children made plans to enter the Witness Security Program and George and I were to pick him up on a Saturday morning as he was now back in New York.

I put him in one of the hotels near LaGuardia Airport and left him strict instructions.

"Philly, I need you to stay in your room—you have to promise me you won't go anywhere."

"You worry too much, Neil. I'm a big boy. I can take care of myself."

"I will call you after my wife and I watch *Dallas* which ends at about 10:00 p.m.," I told him.

"Alright, alright, Mr. Worry Wart, I'll be there. I ain't going nowhere."

It was 10:00 o'clock on the button and I asked to be connected to Philly's room.

"Hello," the unmistaken sultry voice of a woman answering.

"Hello," I began again. "Is this room _____?" asking if I had the correct room.

"Yes, it is, who's this calling?"

"Never mind who this is," I exploded.

"Who the hell are you and what are you doing there?" I demanded.

"Is Philly there?" I asked.

"Phil, there's a very angry gentleman on the phone. I think you better take this."

"Hello," Philly began.

"Never mind, hello, Philly. Can you tell me what in the ever-living hell you're doing? What do you have a death wish or something?"

"Who the hell is the woman?" I continued.

"I think she's an airline pilot. She has wings on the collar of her uniform. I gotta have some fun, don't I?" he shot back.

"Do I have to come in there and move you to another hotel? Honestly, Philly, you're going to give me a heart attack."

"No, don't come in. Please don't. She's harmless, I promise. I went out to the bar to get a drink to bring back to the room and I just bumped into her. Neil, she's gorgeous," he said with his hand covering the phone in a low voice.

The next morning, George and I listened to blow by blow of the marathon escapade of Philly and the Kim Basinger look-alike airline pilot as we drove to lower Manhattan to drop Philly at the U.S. Marshal's office.

"You guys wouldn't deny a guy a little fun on his last night, would you?" Philly asked.

"Philly, it's not like you're going to the gas chamber," I replied

Taken from the script of the movie, *My Blue Heaven* with Steve Martin, Philly and his family wound up in a small community where he became a Little League baseball coach and even joined the local Baptist church.

Former ADA Eric Seidel, whose last assignment was Chief of the Rackets Bureau and Counsel to the Investigation Division of the prestigious Manhattan District Attorney's Office weighed in on our case with Philly.

"Philly Boy Paradiso was a difficult cooperator. He suffered from several addictions. We strongly suspected him of committing crimes while working for us. His undercover work could be emotionally demanding and challenging. It included surreptitiously recording his brother, an alleged Gambino LCN Crime Family member, and a vicious crew of associates about murders, kidnapping, and heroin dealing.

"Neil Moran, his partner George Hanna, and George Terra, an NYPD detective assigned to the Brooklyn DA's office, were the perfect trio to handle this problematic yet extremely productive cooperator. Managing and directing Philly Boy required street smarts, a willingness to work 24/7, and, perhaps most importantly, sensitivity and empathy.

"All three possessed that. They were able to forge a personal bond of trust with Philly Boy so that when the inevitable crises arose, and they frequently did, they could get Philly Boy and the investigation back on track. That was a rare skill that most agents and detectives don't possess, but Neil and both Georges did, in spades.

"The trio was critical to the success of this case which resulted in, among other things, locating the body of Annette DiBiasi, who was kidnapped and murdered, indictments for several other murders, an additional attempted murder, and the conviction of a close associate of former Gambino boss John Gotti, a back-up shooter in the Paul Castellano murder, for heroin trafficking. The Brooklyn DA's Office couldn't have made these cases without these three outstanding investigators."

Former ADA Eric M. Kraus, now in private practice, recalled working on this case almost forty years ago.

"Working with Neil Moran and his partner, George Hanna, along with their colleague from the NYC Police Department, Detective George Terra, proved to be one of the great experiences of my legal career. This was a truly dynamic trio: smart, thoughtful and strategic in their tireless efforts to investigate and make cases against really bad guys.

"Their focus when we worked together was a crew of homicidal maniacs and members of a violent organized crime family. Whether it was figuring out how to wire up a meeting in a high security federal prison with an imprisoned Mafia captain, or arranging drug buys from one of the participants in the well-known Mafia execution that elevated John Gotti to the head of the Gambino crime family, doing things the 'right way' and making sure their cases were impeccably put together, was always their focus.

"But their commitment to their work only captured part of what made working with them so rewarding. I saw that their individual personalities and collective charm was part of how they were able to gain the trust of everyone around them, including prosecutors, informants, and often, some bad guys who would then become cooperating witnesses. Perhaps above all else, they became my friends—friendships that have lasted throughout the decades since we worked together."

Despite the heartburn and angina Philly caused George Hanna, George Terra and me, in a series of cards and letters that he wrote to us, he expressed his profound thanks.

He didn't forget that we had all brought him and his children Christmas gifts one year.

He also didn't forget the many times he phoned us at 3:00 a.m. when he was blind drunk or high, lying in the street somewhere, and we hopped in the car to take him home.

Philly told us he knew that we genuinely cared about him as a person, sadly, something that he had not felt others in his life had shown, and he had trusted that we knew that he felt the same about us.

Left to right are retired Detective George Terra, former Brooklyn ADAs, Eric Kraus and Eric Seidel, George Hanna and Neil Moran at Eric Seidel's class at Fordham Law School, in Manhattan, November 2024. They were reunited 38 years after working together on the case involving Philly Paradiso.

STORIES

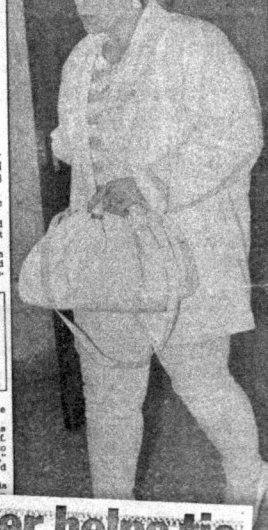

April 1989 media coverage of murder trial of Michael "Mickey Boy" Paradiso, in Brooklyn, New York

Media coverage of crime spree involving the defendants
in the case working with Philly Paradiso.

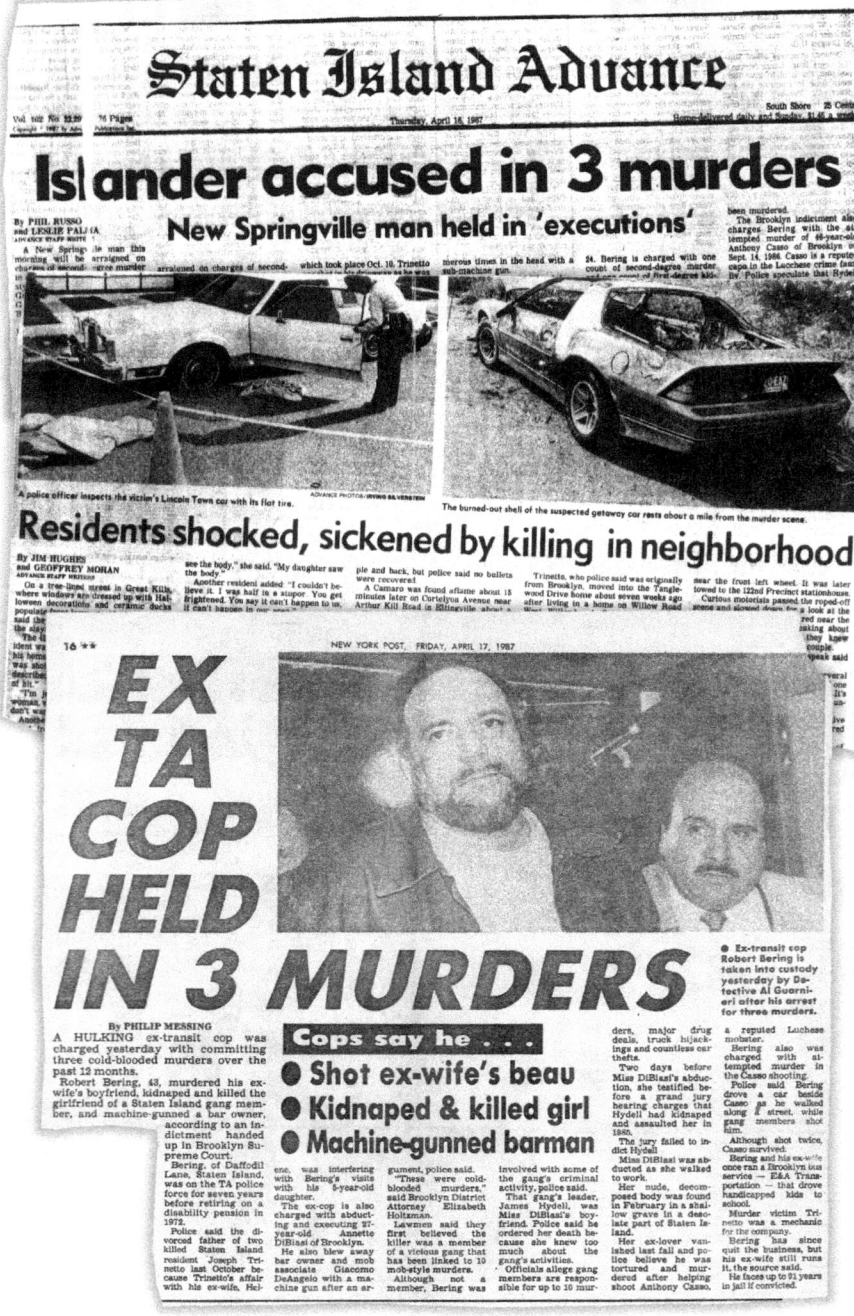

Media coverage of crime spree involving the defendants in the case working with Philly Paradiso.

Media coverage of crime spree involving the defendants
in the case working with Philly Paradiso.

STORIES

DISTRICT ATTORNEY OF KINGS COUNTY
MUNICIPAL BUILDING
BROOKLYN, N.Y. 11201
(718) 802-2000

ELIZABETH HOLTZMAN
DISTRICT ATTORNEY

May 13, 1988

The Honorable William S. Sessions
Director
Federal Bureau of Investigation
J. Edgar Hoover Building
Washington, D.C. 20535

Dear Mr. Sessions,

    I am writing to commend the outstanding work of two of your agents, George Hanna and Neil Moran, both assigned to the Joint Auto Larceny Task Force of the Brooklyn/Queens New York F.B.I. office. In a case involving major organized crime figures and criminality ranging from murder to narcotics trafficking, weapons possession to stolen cars, these two agents displayed an unparalleled professionalism and dedication to their work.

    A stolen car ring first attracted the attention of agents Hanna and Moran. From this modest beginning the agents began to focus on a number of violent and ruthless individuals acting on their own or as part of a "crew" primarily associated with the Gambino Crime family who were responsible for a crime spree in 1986 including the kidnapping and murder of Annette DiBiasi in April, the machine gun killing of Giacomo D'Angelo in August, the gangland style "hit" on Joseph Trinetto in September, and the attempted murder of reputed Lucchese Crime family caporegime Anthony "Gaspipe" Casso in October. Through the use of an informant, through clever investigative strategies and through agent Moran's undercover work, admissions to these and other crimes were obtained from several persons responsible for these crimes including Robert Bering, James Hydell, Frank Hydell and Nicholas Guido.

Honorable Wiliam S. Sessions
May 13, 1988

    As this letter undoubtedly reveals, I have come to think of agents Hanna and Moran as friends as well as collegues in law enforcement. It has been a privilege to work with them and it is a pleasure to bring their accomplishments to your attention.

Sincerely,

Eric M. Kraus
Deputy Chief, Rackets Bureau

May 13, 1988 letter from Rackets Bureau Deputy Chief ADA Eric M. Kraus to FBI Director William S. Sessions concerning the Philly Paradiso case.

MICKEY SALTER

On May 24, 1988, 441 Carrier air conditioners were stolen from a warehouse in Edison, New Jersey. Only days later, a confidential source advised that the stolen air conditioners had been offered to him and could be found at a warehouse called Top Lot Trading, in College Point, Queens. Andy Conlin, who had obtained the information, asked me to join him and check out the information.

Andy came from a police family. His father was a retired NYPD lieutenant and his brother an NYPD detective. Following in their footsteps, Andy had joined the NYPD, only to leave after a few years and join the FBI. His first assignment following his training at the FBI Academy was the Minneapolis office, where he spent several years and where he met his future wife.

It wasn't long before Andy opted back home and was assigned to New York.

Andy was one of the senior members of our squad and had worked truck hijackings for years. His track record spoke for itself with many successful prosecutions.

As we pulled up to Top Lot, we observed a van containing several cardboard boxes with the word, 'Carrier' on the outside.

At that moment, we were greeted by one Michael "Mickey" Salter, who said he was the president of Top Lot. We informed him of the nature of our visit, and he indicated that he wished to cooperate fully.

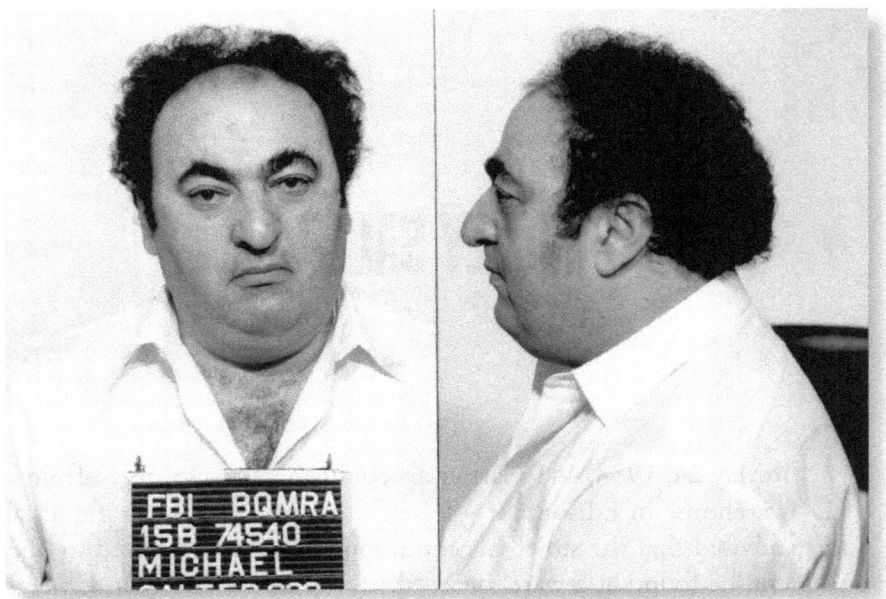

Michael "Mickey" Salter

We gave him his Miranda warnings and asked if he would allow us to search the warehouse. He agreed to a consent search of the premises and again pledged his cooperation.

As we made our way through the warehouse, in plain view, we observed what amounted to 334 Carrier air conditioners. After checking various markings on the packaging, we informed Mr. Salter that he was in possession of the stolen property.

He went on to tell us a rather tall tale of receiving a call out of the blue, a day or so prior, from an unknown male with a Hispanic accent. The individual asked if he could store some merchandise for $500. Later that day, a tractor-trailer arrived and unloaded the merchandise, and the driver paid Mr. Salter the $500.

When asked if he was furnished with any paperwork, such as a bill of lading, which is standard practice, from the driver, he said he was not.

Amazingly, after approximately two hours, when Andy and I were waiting for the original owners to arrive and pick up the stolen air conditioners, Mr. Salter said he had been mistaken earlier, and he had located a bill of lading.

In fact, he was not in possession of a bill of lading, but what appeared to be a hastily put together receipt stating that the merchandise was being stored for $500. The date on his 'bill of lading' was from a week ago and he was clearly even confusing himself. Mr. Salter was arrested and charged.

Sometime thereafter, Assistant United States Attorney (AUSA) Beryl Howell was assigned to the case. I believe she was fairly new and never had heard that she had handled any cases from our squad. I soon met with her and laid out the circumstances and our investigation to date.

AUSA Howell had asked me about my gut feeling and I told her that confidential source information revealed that Mr. Salter had dealt in stolen property in the past and his evasive answers and production of a bogus bill of lading were not the actions of an innocent man.

AUSA Howell then prepared a 'Proffer Letter,' also known as a 'Queen for a Day' letter to Mr. Salter's attorney, which would afford him the opportunity to sit with us and bare his soul. Should he show that he is willing to cooperate fully, leniency may be a consideration.

Weeks later, Mr. Salter and his attorney sat in AUSA Howell's office and basically, he continued with the nonsense he spewed when Andy Conlin and I met him at his warehouse. At several points during our discussion, Salter broke down crying or should I say, 'howling.'

He was hyperventilating uncontrollably.

This was indeed an Oscar-worthy performance, as AUSA Howell offered Mr. Salter a tissue and appeared to be swaying toward being sympathetic.

After listening to this rubbish for about an hour, how Salter was the victim and telling us that the FBI needed to focus on looking for the real culprit, the unknown Hispanic male, much like O.J. Simpson's suggestion that LAPD needed to search for the 'real killers,' I had had enough.

AUSA Howell thanked them for coming and we sat down to talk.

"I have a tendency to believe him, Neil. What do you think?"

I went on for about fifteen straight minutes stating my case, but she felt he had a believable story and was leaning toward dismissing the charges.

I wasn't happy.

"Just an FYI," I began. "I have never done this but if my boss agrees, I plan on pleading my case to Peter Norling (AUSA Peter Norling who was, I believe at that time, deputy chief of the criminal division in Brooklyn) to seek his opinion."

It was days later as I sat with AUSA Peter Norling. As a young assistant, he handled a number of cases from our squad and was very familiar with our collective reputations.

After laying out all the details, including Mr. Salter's sobbing, he said, "I don't take this lightly, but you have never come here with any complaints or a request for a change in AUSAs, so with some reservations, I will assign someone else to the case."

In May 1991, Michael Salter stood trial in Brooklyn federal court before one of my favorite judges, a soft-spoken and very competent jurist, USDJ Eugene Nickerson. AUSA Leonard Lato had been reassigned and felt as though we had a good case.

I will never know whose decision it was for Mr. Salter to take the stand but, much like he had done when Andy Conlin and I questioned him and during his proffer, he couldn't keep his story straight. I observed the judge and jury members rolling their eyes more than once.

I also took the stand and made it clear that Mr. Salter changed his story so many times that even *he* often appeared confused.

On May 21, 1991, Michael Salter was found guilty and released on $50,000 bond pending sentencing. He was ordered by the judge to surrender his passport, as he was an Israeli citizen.

At the urging of ADA Eric Seidel, with whom we had worked on our case involving Philly Paradiso, and was following this case, he recommended contacting the Israeli Mission to the United Nations, in Manhattan, and request that we be notified should Salter apply for a visa.

I received an odd telephone call from Mr. Salter's wife the next day, who indicated that her husband could not locate his passport but was making every effort to find it.

I then received a call from a woman at the Israeli Mission who stated that Mr. Salter was, at that moment, seeking a visa and gave the reason that he had been invited by the Soviet Union's Ministry of Oil and Gas to attend a meeting on a proposed joint venture.

That's all Judge Nickerson had to hear, when I immediately called his chambers, related the facts and will always recall him saying, "Go get him agent Moran."

We arrested Mr. Salter later that day.

At a bail revocation hearing, Mr. Salter testified and related an account of his actions since being convicted at trial days earlier and Judge Nickerson found Mr. Salter's testimony, "blatant perjury," and ordered him remanded.

Mr. Salter subsequently received a three-year sentence.

During the course of the trials, many of the AUSAs often pop in and out of the gallery to observe the testimony and proceedings. Although this was only a two-day trial, I did notice Beryl Howell sitting in the rear of the courtroom at brief intervals.

After the verdict was heard and AUSA Lato and I gathered up the trial exhibits, I was approached by a very gracious Beryl Howell.

"Congratulations to you both. Neil, I watched your testimony. You did an excellent job. Looking back, my recommendation to dismiss the charges wasn't the best decision."

"Not a problem, Beryl," I began.

"You went with your gut feeling and there's certainly nothing wrong with that. Thanks for the kind words."

AUSA Howel rose up the ranks of the Eastern District, eventually becoming chief of narcotics and had a very distinguished legal career.

Judge Beryl Howell was appointed to the federal judiciary by President Barrack Obama in 2009 and served as the chief judge for the District of Columbia from 2016 to 2023. Judge Howell has ruled in some very noteworthy decisions. She has now achieved senior judge status in Washington, DC.

And just think, I knew her when she was proffering the Michael Salters of the world.

JUDGE JOHN R. BARTELS

U.S. District Court Judge John R. Bartels was appointed to the federal bench in 1959 by then President Dwight D. Eisenhower. I was ten years old.

Judge Bartels caught many of our truck hijacking cases, and our squad believed him to be a very fair and able jurist.

My first experience with him was a case that I was assigned, in 1978, involving the theft of 746 Perego Super Bye-Bye Baby Strollers. At that time, Perego's were billed as the Cadillac's of baby strollers.

The confidential source information revealed that Joseph Massino, aka Joey Messina, was in control of the load. Massino, who was reported to be a 'made guy' in the Bonanno LCN Crime Family, would eventually take over the family. Massino enlisted an associate, Tommy Kurz, to hide the load in a small storage facility in Maspeth, Queens.

It was a Wednesday afternoon, the day before Thanksgiving, and I had been at the U.S. Attorney's office a good bit of the day, working with an AUSA preparing an affidavit for the search warrant to recover the strollers.

I probably didn't return to Maspeth, where six or eight of our squad members were anxiously waiting until mid-to-late afternoon. It was Thanksgiving eve, and no one wanted to get stuck working late.

Upon my arrival with warrant in hand, we broke open the roll top gates and recovered the baby strollers.

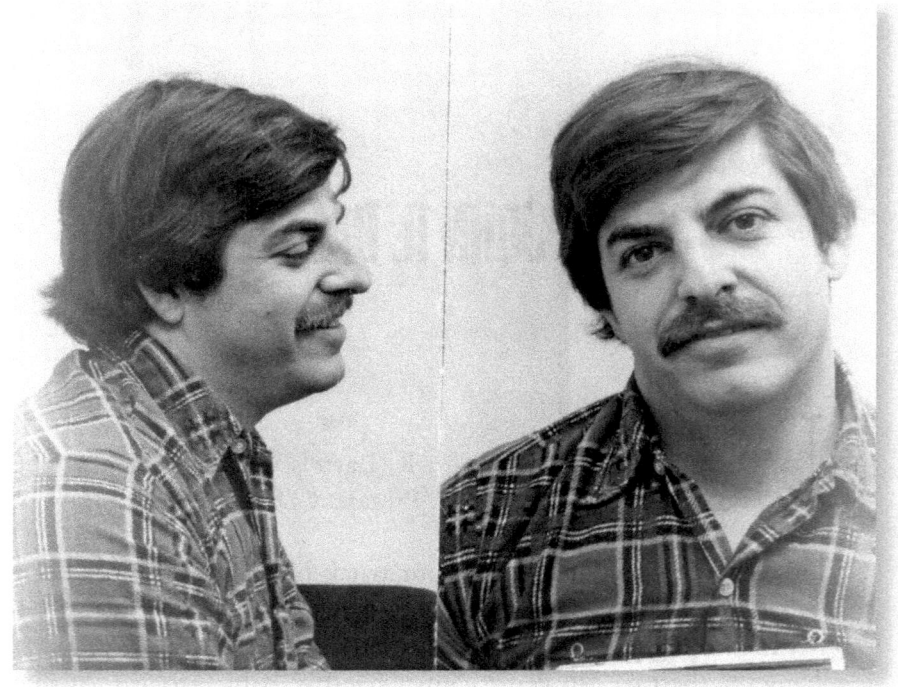

Tommy Kurz

Now was always the difficult part—waiting for the company to come to retrieve them.

Hours went by and a tractor-trailer finally pulled up and the squad began to load them into the trailer. As was the usual practice, $100 worth of merchandise was maintained for evidence and then we began the count. I had a clipboard and a pen and counted each of the strollers as the agents loaded. Three hundred and sixty, 489, 554, etc. and so the count went.

It was somewhere in the six hundreds when we all became distracted by several FDNY fire engines passing by with sirens and air horns blaring.

"Was that 643 or 644?" I asked.

"Are you kidding me, Neil," Andy Conlin asked.

"Tell me you lost count. We can't do this all over. We'll be here all night."

I felt awful. We all wanted to get out of there. We all had things to do. Tomorrow was a major holiday, and it was now dark. We decided to move forward, and I would note that there was a miscount, and we weren't exactly sure how many strollers we recovered. We couldn't rely on the company to inform us of the exact number. That was the purpose of having FBI agents on the scene. It would be our responsibility to testify. This would come back to haunt us.

I swore out an arrest warrant for Tommy Kurz and there was no way he was going to cooperate.

About a year later, his trial began before Judge Bartels. One of our favorite AUSAs, Diane Giacalone, who loved working with our squad, was the prosecutor.

Jerome J. "Jerry" Cox was the first FBI agent to testify. Mr. Kurz's attorney was Marion Seltzer, who we had butted heads with on prior occasions. She did not appear to be a fan of the FBI.

Getting back to the baby stroller count on Thanksgiving eve, I had prepared an FD-302, which is the FBI's reporting form, on that very topic. In it, I detailed exactly what occurred, but the bottom line was that the count didn't match up to what the company said we recovered so it could have appeared that we took one or more of the strollers for ourselves.

In the process known as 'discovery,' defense counsel was entitled to all of our FD-302s and this one, undoubtedly piqued Ms. Seltzer's interest.

"Agent Cox, I draw your attention to . . ." as she went on to point out the miscount.

"Agent Cox, do any of the members of the squad have young children?" she asked.

"Objection," Ms. Giacalone yelled as she exploded out of her chair.

"Your honor, this is highly inappropriate of Ms. Seltzer and the government strongly objects to the implication that the agents acted inappropriately."

"Yes, Ms. Giacalone, I would tend to agree. We'll have none of that Ms. Seltzer, is that clear?" Judge Bartels said.

"Yes, your honor."

Bob Joyce was the next agent to testify, and everyone was taken back when Marion Seltzer calmly asked, "Agent Joyce, do you have any children?"

Before Diane Giacalone could utter a word, Judge Bartels, angrily yelled, "Sidebar," which meant that he wished to speak to Ms. Seltzer and AUSA Giacalone at the bench. Normally, judges do manage to speak in muffled tones without revealing to the courtroom what they are saying, but it was clear that Judge Bartels was not happy.

"Ladies and gentlemen of the jury, please ignore Ms. Seltzer's last question. It has been stricken from the record. You should not give it any weight or consideration as we move forward," Judge Bartels announced.

In summation, all the agents were quite taken back when Marion Seltzer apologized for implying that members of our squad may have stolen baby strollers. It wasn't a half-hearted apology, but very sincere. I recall looking at the jurors when she explained that sometimes in the heat of the moment, things are said that are later regretted and this was one of those occasions.

Tommy Kurz was convicted on all counts and sentenced to four years in prison.

On a summer evening in August 1989, two men from Lawrence, Long Island, traveled by boat to the South Street Seaport Marina, where they docked the vessel, a Progression 29' cherry red, some call a 'cigarette boat.'

After walking around the Seaport for about an hour, the two returned to the boat and now felt that it was too dark and potentially dangerous to make the trip back to Long Island.

The two secured the boat and left it tied to the dock with the intention of returning the next day. They then hailed a cab and went home.

The next morning when they returned, they alleged that the boat was missing.

In addition to filing a police report, they contacted the boat's insurance carrier and filed a claim for $134,000.

Bob Joyce and I conducted the investigation, which included tracking down other boat owners who had docked at the South Street Seaport Marina that evening and no one recalled seeing or hearing the boat. The boat's engine noise bordered on deafening and would have been difficult to miss.

The two men were indicted and stood trial before Judge Bartels in 1991.

Many of the boat owners testified as to their recollection of that evening and their failure to recall observing or hearing the vessel in question.

Now, it was time for me to testify. It was early afternoon, and we had just returned from lunch. I had taken the stand at about 11:00 a.m. and around noon, Judge Bartels said that agent Moran would resume his testimony following the noon break.

At the time of trial, Judge Bartels was ninety-four and it wasn't a well-kept secret that in the afternoons he sometimes appeared to nod off at a variety of intervals. He was in such close proximity that I could hear him breathing deeply and knew he had closed his eyes.

As I was testifying, like he was shot out of a cannon, the judge rose to his feet and blurted out, "Agent Moran what about that clock? Tell us about the clock. I want to hear about the clock again."

Looking directly at me, Judge Bartels waited for an answer that was never coming.

I had not testified about anything concerning a clock.

As I stared into the courtroom and glanced at the jury, everyone, including the judge's court clerk and the court stenographer, were snickering with hands covering mouths. I then glared at the AUSA, Bob Feinberg, who also was smiling and widened my eyes in a cry for help.

"Your honor, if it pleases the court, I don't believe that agent Moran furnished any testimony concerning a clock. We can certainly have a readback of his testimony if your honor would prefer, but I think defense counsel will agree, there was no such testimony regarding a clock."

"Are you quite sure, Mr. Feinberg?"

"Yes, your honor."

Defense counsel agreed.

"Alright then, agent Moran you may proceed and accept my apologies. Apparently, I was in error," the judge said.

There were a number of AUSAs in the gallery observing the proceedings and this episode reverberated throughout the courthouse. Former AUSAs with whom I have remained friendly throughout the years will to this day ask, "Neil did you ever locate that clock?"

JUNE 5, 1992

I had now been working truck hijackings off and on since 1978.

George Hanna, Bob Joyce, and I were still working together in the Queens office. We were now reunited with Steve Carbone, who had been transferred to Manhattan.

With Andy Conlin having taken a transfer to the New Haven office and Jerry Cox to Detroit, we were now considered the 'old guard.'

We had been joined by a group of younger agents including George Wright, Steve Shiner, Eileen O'Rourke, Dawn Smallwood, and Jason Randazzo, a former NYPD officer. Steve Braus, a veteran agent in New York, had also joined our squad.

In 1992, the Major Case Squad of the NYPD and our unit conducted a series of debriefings of a confidential source, who advised that he knew of a gang of seven to ten individuals that had been responsible for fifteen armed hijackings in the last year.

In many of those instances, drivers were kidnapped, beaten, and in several instances shot. The group targeted high value merchandise, including televisions, VCRs, stereo equipment, and expensive furs. Subsequent investigation confirmed that the crew was responsible for stealing $2.5 million worth of merchandise in 1992, alone.

Four leaders of the gang were identified, and we learned that they had previous convictions for armed robbery, drug and weapons possession, kidnapping, and murder.

During a joint FBI/NYPD surveillance in the Bronx of the reported leader of the crew, Joesph Peterson, and another gang member, a shot was fired from inside the vehicle at two detectives.

On June 1, 1992, following this incident, federal arrest warrants were obtained at Brooklyn federal court, charging Peterson and Tyronne Carter with violation of the Hobbs Act ("Actual or attempted robbery or extortion that affects interstate or foreign commerce, as well as conspiracies to do so").

Attempts to locate Carter and Peterson in the next few days were unsuccessful.

However, on June 1 and June 3, two armed hijackings occurred by individuals fitting the description of the gang. On the June 3 hijacking, the victim driver was abducted, brutally beaten, and released some twelve hours later.

In the early morning hours of June 5, FBI agents and Major Case Squad detectives met at the 42nd Precinct in the Bronx, to discuss last-minute changes to our plan, which was to arrest crew members as they approached their vehicles in a nearby lot where they were stored.

Corner of East Tremont Avenue and Crotona Avenue, Bronx, New York, where on June 5, 1992, NYPD's Major Case Squad and the FBI arrested Joseph Peterson and Donald Elder.

A white Nissan Maxima, known to be driven by our main subject, Joseph Peterson, was eventually observed by George Wright and Detective Kevin Butt traveling on East Tremont Avenue, who then pulled the vehicle over.

As the other agents and detectives converged on the location, I was alone in my vehicle and due to heavy rush hour traffic, I could only position myself on the opposite side of the street.

I exited the car and drew my weapon.

Dawn Smallwood, Steve Braus, and Steve Shiner all arrived and positioned themselves in front of the Maxima.

The car being driven by Peterson, and containing another occupant, was now boxed in. I observed agents and detectives exiting their vehicles with weapons, including shotguns, all drawn. I could hear one of the agents yell, "FBI, don't move," and with that Peterson gunned the accelerator in reverse smashing into the car driven by George Wright and Kevin Butt. The tires were spinning so fast that, as the rubber burned, heavy smoke became visible.

The Maxima now had wiggle room and as it began to lunge forward, with Steve Braus in its immediate path, he began to fire at Peterson, as did Steve Shiner and Dawn Smallwood. Peterson successfully escaped the box and with tires still spinning out of control he began to make a U-turn.

As I was positioned across the intersection, catty-corner to where the Maxima had been pulled over, I was unable to get across due to heavy pedestrian and vehicular traffic. Firing my weapon was not an option.

A stray bullet could have wounded or even killed one of the agents, detectives, or one of the many schoolchildren in the immediate vicinity. I hopped back into my car and was now positioned to stop or at least slow up the getaway vehicle.

Instinctively, I drove right into the path of the Maxima as it sped forward and *BANG*, it plowed right into me and pushed the car back, nearly catapulting it onto the sidewalk.

With the Maxima still careening out of control and now somewhat slowed, the next time I remember looking up, it was speeding down Crotona Parkway, into the waiting arms of several NYPD marked vehicles who had responded following the calling of a '10-13' "officer needs assistance."

Joesph Peterson and Donald Elder were taken into custody. A loaded handgun was recovered from inside the vehicle.

It was a chaotic scene to say the least, at 8:00 a.m., on a warm June morning, people were on their way to work, and school was still in session.

NYC Emergency Medical Service arrived, and the agents and detectives directed them to my car. I was still a bit dazed from the force of the Maxima plowing into me.

The EMS folks immediately immobilized my neck as a precautionary measure and placed me on a stretcher. They transported me to nearby Jacobi Hospital. As I was wheeled into the emergency room, apparently, the staff had received word that an NYPD detective had been shot.

"Detective, where were you shot," an RN asked as I looked up from the gurney.

"Shot, I don't think I was shot, I hope you don't see blood anywhere," I said.

A cursory once over and the RN yelled, "This guy wasn't shot; what the hell is going on here? We've gotten bad information."

All the nurses and the ER physician on duty couldn't have been nicer.

Believe me, this hospital had seen more on a daily basis than an FBI agent who got plowed into by the bad guys.

I went through X-rays and MRI and was eventually treated and released. The ER physician said I should follow up with an orthopedic, as there appeared to be potential problems with my cervical and lumbar discs.

No question, this definitely shook me up, but given the circumstances, it could have been much worse.

Further examination revealed that I had a cervical fracture, which severely herniated two discs, one which was resting, but thankfully, not impinging my spinal cord. Physical therapy three times a week was ordered to see if my condition would improve.

Steve Carbone had directed members of our squad to come to my home and transport me for my therapy sessions. We weren't among the highest paid civil servants, but at times like this, the camaraderie and caring are like no other.

In October, my doctor felt that I had reached maximum improvement and opined that the best option was removal of the discs, fusion of my cervical vertebrae and a bone graft from my hip, to be implanted in place of the discs that were removed.

I awoke from surgery with a Philadelphia collar, which was in place to restrict unnecessary neck movement and allow the area to heal. I would wear that for three months, even when I slept.

Post operative physical therapy was prescribed and our squad, once again, showed up for every session.

In February 1993, my wife, Maureen, and I met with my surgeon.

"I think it might be time to find a new line of work, Neil," Dr. Thomas Lansen began.

"You have suffered a traumatic spinal injury. The surgery appears to have been successful, and your progress is good but, in all likelihood, we will see you again. In your line of work, should you experience another similar episode or become engaged in a struggle with a suspect, you could suffer permanent paralysis. I'm sorry."

I was stunned and my eyes began to fill up, as did my wife's. I was forty-three, with three young daughters.

What would I do if I could no longer continue with the Bureau? This is really all I knew.

It was a long ride home as Maureen and I talked. This is where it helps to have an understanding partner to lean on. At the bleakest of times, Maureen never gives up and always feels that the ship will right itself. I truly don't know what I would do without her.

My first call upon arriving home was Steve Carbone. He had been great throughout the ordeal.

"Steve, I'm wondering if you could take a ride out here. I have something important I need to discuss. I would really appreciate it if you could come today, if at all possible. And Steve, please, discuss this with no one."

"Of course, Neil, I am on my way," not even pressing the issue.

Less than a minute later, the phone rang. It was George Hanna.

"Neil, everything okay?" he asked.

I was in no laughing mood, but I had to chuckle to myself.

I suppose "discuss this with no one" means no one except for George Hanna. Among close friends and colleagues who care, there are no secrets. Apparently, there was no code of *Omerta* on our squad.

As Joe Pesci's character, Tommy DeVito, said in *Goodfellas*, as he spoke to Ray Liotta's Henry Hill (in this instance Steve Carbone), "I wonder about you sometimes, Henry, you may fold under questioning."

"Yeah, George, you can come with Steve," I said without him even asking.

About an hour later, George and Steve arrived at my home, and now I was glad to have them both there.

The look of concern on both their faces as they walked into our home was something I won't forget.

"We just came from the doctor. He is suggesting I retire or find some other line of work," I began.

"I'm not kidding guys. He's not ruling out further serious injury or possible paralysis if I get into a similar situation. I can't risk that. Who's going to take care of our family?"

I believe Steve spoke first.

"Neil, we can use you in the office. You can help me out, be a relief supervisor. Fill in for me when I'm not here. It's not like there wouldn't be anything for you to do. I would keep you very busy."

"And am I supposed to do that for the rest of my career, stay in the office while everyone is out working?" I shot back.

"How do you think that would make me feel? What about new people that come onto the squad and see that I never leave the office and don't carry my weight like everyone else?

"Who is this guy and how come he never leaves the office?" they would ask.

"I would be a glorified support employee."

George supported Steve's position, basically saying not to worry about what people think.

"We will always have your back," he said.

We went round and round for a while and left off that no decision needed to be reached immediately. Steve promised he would investigate what the FBI had to offer in the way of disability retirement.

When I was informed by FBIHQ that my retirement disability would amount to $29,000 per year, all of which would be fully taxable, that was completely out of the question. I had to come up with a 'Plan B.'

Enter Kevin Meenan.

Kevin, Colleen, Tara, Maura, Peggy, and Michael are my wife's cousins with whom she is quite close.

A Fordham University alum, Kevin, began his successful Wall Street career at Solomon Brothers, then onto Citibank and now had his own business.

I can best describe Kevin as my brother from another mother and count him among the people that have touched my life that give unabashedly, and don't ask, nor expect anything in return.

Through the years, Kevin has been a confidant of sorts regarding all things professional and financial and has always gone out of his way to be a dear friend to the Moran's.

The word about my plight had filtered down to Kevin through the Meenan family pipeline and he took a ride out to see me.

"Neil, you can come to work with me. You'll love it. You will make more money than you ever dreamed of," he began.

"Kevin, I'm not a Wall Street guy. I have no business background. All I know is how to be an FBI agent," I replied.

"We can teach you. Neil, it's not brain surgery, I'm telling you, really," he added.

Thinking this over, as Kevin laid out an overview of what his firm did, I would have to simply resign and not take any pension. After twenty-two years, counting my clerical time, it would be as if I never worked at the FBI, save for several thousand dollars I contributed toward my retirement.

What a mess.

A number of sleepless nights and after endless conversations with Maureen, I received a call from Steve Carbone.

Our bosses, who were aware of my situation, told him that if I chose to come back to work, they would attempt to place me with the Undercover and Sensitive Operations Unit, also known as 'USOU.' This group, headed by Jim Abbott, supported the efforts of undercover personnel and their operations throughout the country.

"If you want to come back to the squad for a while, they said they will make every effort to accommodate you and find a spot at USOU," Steve said.

Despite Kevin Meenan's generous and thoughtful offer, I truly didn't want to leave the FBI.

Nobody comes into law enforcement with the idea of becoming rich, and chances are that if I did go with Kevin, it might have worked out fine, but I was one of those fortunate people who couldn't wait to get out of bed every day and go to work. I loved the FBI, and all the people with whom I worked. I was truly blessed with my choice of profession and wasn't ready to let go.

So, after nearly a year, I returned to work in Queens, in April 1993.

It was the second or third day after settling in, when Steve Carbone asked me to collect the beepers from everyone. As part of our renewed contract with the company, a representative would be stopping by the office mid-morning to issue new pagers and collect the old ones.

It was about 11:00 a.m., when a young man arrived with a box containing the new beepers. As he ticked off the names of each of the agents, he came to George Hanna.

"Can I ask agent Moran, is agent Hanna here today?"

"He was earlier, but he's out of the office. Why do you ask?"

"I was looking forward to meeting him. We keep running statistics as to the number of pages per day and each month attributed to each unit. We have contracts with other law enforcement agencies and many private companies, and no one ever recalls seeing the number of pages as those recorded on agent Hanna's beeper. The number of pages he receives compares with people who we suspect must be involved in drug trafficking."

I couldn't contain myself. Why wasn't there anyone nearby with whom I could share this juicy tidbit?

"Agent Hanna must be one busy guy," the young man gushed.

Now, anyone who knew George at that time was fully aware there was a better than average chance that out of, let's say, fifty pages per day, that one or two just *might* be personal, but I didn't want George's reputation to be sullied at Acme Beepers or whatever the company was called so I said, "Well, I am so sorry that *Agent Hanna* wasn't here to greet you personally and perhaps provide an autographed picture of himself receiving a page, but rest assured, I will convey all that you have shared."

Yes, the legend of George Hanna never dies.

On September 1, 1993, the new director of the FBI, Louis J. Freeh, who had been in the class one week ahead of me at the FBI Academy, and was briefly a squad mate in 1977, was sworn in as the new FBI director.

President William J. Clinton was present for the ceremony at FBIHQ and made some remarks.

I was out of the office that same afternoon and upon returning I saw a message on my desk from a former Queens office support employee, Susanna Mullaly.

Susanna was born in Dublin, Ireland, and we got on great. She had taken a transfer to FBIHQ for a better paying position and a change of scenery. I hadn't spoken with Susanna for several years, so I was quite curious.

"Hi Susanna, it's Neil, how are you getting on down there?" I asked.

"Oh my God, Neil, it's so good to hear your voice. Did you know President Clinton mentioned you in a speech today during the new director's swearing-in?"

"What—what did you say, Susanna? Why would he mention me?"

"I'm not sure what he said. I was there, but couldn't hear him that well, but I distinctly heard him say Neil Moran of the New York office."

Well, Susana turned out to be correct.

In the early portion of his remarks, President Clinton said the following:

> *There are many heroes who do their work in the ordinary course of business: people like Special Agent Daniel Miller of Minneapolis, who subdued an armed bank robber by hand to ensure that no one else got hurt; Special Agent Neil Moran of New York, who was severely injured when he used his car to block a suspect's getaway vehicle rather than risking wounding his colleagues with gunfire; people like the 45 others who received Agency medals over the past 3 years. All of you have served well, and America is justly proud of you.*

When I learned of President Clinton comments, I was deeply touched.

And yes, there are many heroes that do their work every day in the ordinary course of business, but I certainly didn't consider myself one of them.

Hundreds of thousands of courageous men and women have given their lives in service to their nation, city and local municipalities. Count among them servicemen and women, police officers, and firefighters to name a few. Thousands more are permanently disabled and can no longer enjoy life's daily pleasures.

On June 5th, I didn't do anything that the numerous FBI agents, detectives, and police officers wouldn't have done in a comparable situation.

So, again, an honor to have been recognized by the president, but leave the hero moniker to those that truly deserve that distinction.

Shortly after he was sworn in, Director Freeh travelled to New York and presented Dawn Smallwood, Steve Braus, and Steve Shiner with the FBI Medal for Meritorious Achievement for their actions on June 5, 1992. I was awarded the FBI Medal of Bravery and the FBI Star, for being injured in the line of duty.

As much as things looked quite bleak for a time following the events of June 5th, as Grandma Moran used to say, "When God closes one door, he opens another."

I eventually transferred to Jim Abbott's squad, where I spent the remainder of my career.

Count Jim as another one of the genuinely great bosses for whom I had the good fortune to work. He assembled an experienced and a cohesive group of wonderful people with whom I was enormously proud to be a part.

When Jim decided to retire to become the deputy commissioner of the Suffolk County Police Department, not only did I take over his position as an adjunct professor at St. John's University but was fortunate to become the new supervisor at USOU until retiring in May 2000.

Neil Moran with Director Louis J. Freeh, Sept. 1993, Awarding of Medals.

Medal recipients, left to right: Dawn Smallwood, Steve Shiner, Neil Moran, Steve Carbone (supervisor, non-recipient), and Steve Braus—Sept. 30, 1993.

Members of the Moran family at the medal ceremony

STORIES

THE WHITE HOUSE
WASHINGTON

October 1, 1993

Special Agent Neil F. Moran
29 Hemlock Street
Floral Park, New York 11001-3002

Dear Neil:

    Thank you for your kind letter. I want to congratulate you on being awarded the FBI Shield of Bravery and the FBI Star. Your actions exhibited a courage and a grace under pressure that go far beyond the call of duty. You have my deep admiration and heartfelt appreciation.

    Best wishes for a speedy and complete recovery.

Sincerely,

Bill Clinton

October 1, 1993 letter from President Bill Clinton to Neil Moran

CROWN HEIGHTS

On August 19, 1991, in Crown Heights Brooklyn, two children of Guyanese immigrants were struck by a driver running a red light while following the motorcade of Grand Rebbe Menachem Schneerson, the leader of Chabad Lubavitch, a Hasidic Jewish religious movement.

One child, Gavin Cato, age seven, died of his injuries and his cousin, also seven, was severely injured.

In the hours following this tragedy, angry African Americans gathered several blocks away from the site of the accident. A crowd of between twenty and thirty people began assaulting local Jewish residents with some shouting, "Let's get a Jew" and "An eye for an eye."

A visiting twenty-nine-year-old University of Melbourne rabbinical student, Yankel Rosenbaum, was surrounded by the mob, severely beaten, suffering a fractured skull and several stab wounds which ultimately proved fatal.

Struggling to cling to life, Mr. Rosenbaum was able to identify the person who stabbed him as Lemrick Nelson, Jr., who was arrested, charged, and ultimately acquitted of murder on state charges.

Mr. Rosenbaum's older brother, Norman, became an advocate for his late brother. He was an outspoken critic of the U.S. Department of Justice for its failure to charge Mr. Nelson with federal civil rights violations.

On January 25, 1994, with continued pressure from Mr. Rosenbaum following the acquittal of Mr. Nelson, then U.S. Attorney General Janet Reno announced that the FBI would be investigating the death of Yankel Rosenbaum.

I had been transferred to the Undercover and Sensitive Operations Unit working for Jim Abbott over a year ago and was enjoying my new assignment.

January 28, 1994, was much like any other Friday. It had snowed earlier in the week, followed by bitterly cold weather, causing a deep freeze.

It was early in the afternoon when my wife called the office.

"Neil, we have water coming into the basement. It's pouring in from the outside. I'm getting ready for work and don't know what to do."

Ah yes, the American dream. The joy of owning a home.

Lemrick Nelson, Jr.

After a little back and forth with my wife, I said, "I guess I'll have to come home. I'm on my way."

I told my boss of my plight and that I was taking the remainder of the day.

I arrived home to an absolute mess. Some of our daughter's old toys, including several popular Cabbage Patch Kids dolls, were afloat and the water was pouring in non-stop.

The frozen snow was acting as a ramp for the rain, which continued to come down quite heavily and was gliding directly into our wells and the cellar. A few whacks with a shovel to break up the ice outside quickly alleviated the problem.

Thank goodness for "wet vacs," I thought, as I began the tedious process of getting rid of the water. I had shut the vac off several times thinking that I had heard our phone ring. As it turned out, it wasn't my imagination.

"Neil, it's Jimmy," my supervisor said.

"How's it going out there?"

Wow, I thought, *how considerate.*

"Under control boss, but I'm just trying to get up the water. It's a real mess."

"Listen, I know you're up to your eyeballs and this is not a call I wanted to make, but I just received word from upstairs that you've been transferred. You and Bob Joyce have been tapped as co-case agents for the Crown Heights case. Neil, I'm so sorry. My hands are tied. Nothing I could do."

Civil rights, I thought. I've never even worked on one case. What the hell are the bosses thinking, selecting my old partner and me to manage this powder keg?

"Jimmy, be straight with me, did you hand me up for this?"

"Neil, you have my word, I didn't. This is the price you and Joyce pay for being solid guys with good work reputations. The bosses know that. They want this handled correctly. It won't last forever; you'll be back soon."

At the Monday morning kickoff meeting, Bob and I stared at twenty-five angry and disgruntled faces, who also received word last Friday that *they too* were being assigned to this investigation.

In addition to the top brass from the office, a representative from the U.S. Attorney in Brooklyn, Valerie Caproni, was also present to give the troops a pep talk and stress the case's significance. Following the conference, Ms. Caproni, with whom our squad had prosecuted many cases, spoke briefly with Bob and me.

"I've made an appointment with the Brooklyn DA's office for tomorrow. They will be turning over all the evidence in the case. It won't be a fun atmosphere with Lemrick Nelson's acquittal in a high-profile murder case. They are not happy down there."

Ms. Caproni couldn't have been more correct.

"What makes the feds think they can get a conviction with a Brooklyn jury after we went through?" one assistant district attorney said to kick off the meeting.

Citing inconsistencies with witness testimony and any future jury pool that would be influenced by the extensive media coverage over the past few years, "You guys will never get a conviction," the ADA added.

The federal indictment of Lemrick Nelson Jr. on charges that he violated the civil rights of Yankel Rosenbaum had renewed hope for those who had spent three years fighting to bring the alleged killer to justice. It was now in the government's hands, with Bob and I playing a pivotal role. Valerie Caproni told us, "Attorney General Reno and all of DOJ are watching."

Even though the case agent's role in an investigation is to direct, oversee, manage, and gather sufficient facts to make a prosecutable case, first things first.

We decided to meet with the hierarchy of the Lubavitch community to elicit their cooperation.

Bob and I began our careers working truck hijackings in the 1970s, then the bread and butter of organized crime.

We had more than one encounter with the other major sect of Hasidim in Brooklyn, the Satmars, based in Williamsburg. Stolen loads of stereo equipment, air conditioners, Benjamin Moore paint, and a million-dollar shipment of Kodak film were among the encounters we had with the Satmars, who frequently made the mistake of getting in bed with the mob. Any follow-up investigation with them was, without exception, met with no cooperation. Could we expect this from the Lubavitch community?

Bob and I arranged to meet with a team of rabbis at the Lubavitch Youth Council, near 770 Eastern Parkway, home to Rebbe Schneerson.

"Gentlemen, you have the full cooperation of the entire Lubavitch community to bring those to justice who murdered Yankel Rosenbaum," Rabbi Moshe Friedman began.

"Anything you need, and we do mean anything, we are available, 24-7."

The rabbi was not exaggerating.

Only days later, Bob and I met with Rabbi Chaim Mandelbaum and his wife at their President Street home, requesting an interview with his son, who was a witness.

Despite our insistence that there was no need to do this immediately, the rabbi instructed his daughter to walk to the nearby yeshiva and tell his son's teacher that the FBI needed to speak with him *now*.

"We've waited far too long for justice for Yankel. We will wait not one minute longer," the rabbi said.

Shortly before the son's arrival, Rabbi Mandelbaum's wife asked us several times if we would have a glass of wine. Explaining that we were appreciative but drinking on duty was frowned upon, we settled for freshly baked honey cake.

After the last wine offer, the rabbi, now irritated, said, "They can't drink. Suppose they have to shoot somebody. Do you want us to be responsible that their careers should end?"

His comment, although a bit dramatic, did save us from seeming unappreciative.

So, this is the way it went for us over the months that followed. Offers for wine at every stop, sometimes even lunch or dinner. We wound up settling for rugelach, Mandelbrot, or macaroons. I was surprised we weren't offered mezuzahs to protect our homes.

I told Bob we should consider opening our own Jewish bakery. Should I consider converting or begin keeping Kosher, I asked myself. We could not have asked for more heartfelt cooperation.

During our investigation, we identified another potential defendant, who the U.S. Attorney asked us to further develop.

Known only as the "bald Black man," by Jewish witnesses, this individual had allegedly incited and encouraged the crowd, which led to Mr. Rosenbaum's death. We learned that WNBC television had recorded footage of the man but would not allow us to view the tape without the proper legal request. Armed with a subpoena, Bob and I made an appointment with the office of general counsel of parent company NBC, at 30 Rockefeller Plaza.

The general counsel's office was represented by four women who had set up the equipment in a conference room and were presumably ready to go when we arrived.

When one of the attorney's pressed "Play," on the VCR nothing happened.

A good three to five minutes went by with the four of them fiddling with every available button and switch.

"They don't have the VCR set to channel three," Bob whispered. "That's it I bet. I'm not going to say anything unless they ask. I don't want to seem like a know it all."

Moments later, one of the women turned and asked, "Would the FBI like to give this a try?"

Bob calmly walked up, switched to channel three and in an instant, we were off and running, much to the amazement of the high-powered legal team.

Lemrick Nelson and the "bald Black man," who we subsequently identified as Charles Price, were ultimately convicted to ten and eleven years in prison, respectively for violating Yankel Rosenbaum's civil rights. It was the ending of a sad chapter in the ongoing struggle between the

Lubavitch and African American communities to peacefully co-exist in Crown Heights.

No one should ever have to die because of their faith.

This poor young man, a visitor to our city to further his studies and enhance his spirituality, was simply in the wrong place at the wrong time.

After initially being disappointed in this assignment, it came to be one of my most gratifying and profound experiences and I believe in the end, I emerged just a little bit better person.

THIS PRECIOUS LIFE

During what I recall was a beautiful summer weekday evening in July 1996, my phone rang.

"Did you hear about the airplane crash?" my boss began.

"A flight out of JFK, just took off and went down off East Moriches. I need you to make your way out there. Looks like we'll all be working on this."

As we would learn in the hectic hours and days that followed, TWA Flight 800 bound for Rome with a stopover in Paris, had crashed in Moriches Inlet off Long Island's south shore killing all 230 passengers, which at that time made it the third deadliest aviation accident in U.S. history.

At this juncture, I had spent twenty-five years in the FBI and had been involved in many high-profile investigations—but this one would be different.

Although the recovery of victims always takes precedence, especially with the possibility that there may be survivors, when those prospects have dimmed, the focus turns to potential evidence and assessing whether a criminal act has occurred.

Quickly, the main staging area where recovered parts of the plane would be transported was secured—A U.S. Navy airplane hangar in nearby Calverton, formerly used by Grumman Aircraft to build and evaluate jets. It was at this facility that an attempt would be made to

Recovery of the tail section from TWA Flight 800. PHOTO CREDIT: FBI.GOV

recreate the downed aircraft from salvageable parts, which now lay at the bottom of the Atlantic Ocean, in hopes that the cause could be determined.

I was assigned to the 11:00 p.m. to 7:00 a.m. shift and it was only minutes into my first tour when several military vehicles backed up to the hangar doors and dumped sections of the aircraft onto the floor.

Huge pieces of twisted and charred wreckage that were once part of this ill-fated flight now lay before us, and it was our task to identify specific portions of the plane to which these fragments belonged. I wondered if my boss mistakenly believed my background was in aeronautical engineering, as I stood beside highly experienced members of the National Transportation Safety Board, who did this for a living.

STORIES

My initial training at the FBI Academy at Quantico and subsequent in-service sessions through the years, never prepared me for anything like this. Loved ones, our national leaders, the airline community, and the general public pined for answers and a quick determination as to the cause of this tragedy, which I prayed was not an act of terrorism.

In the days that followed, the NTSB representative and our FBI boss in New York, Jim Kallstrom, gave daily press briefings on the investigation's developments. Coincidentally, it was about the time I was waking up each afternoon.

I found that by watching these sessions, I was able to keep current on the probe's progress. As anyone who has worked overnights will attest, personnel assigned to what is known as the "graveyard shift" are often the last to know anything.

Wreckage of TWA Flight 800. PHOTO CREDIT: NTSB.GOV

In addition to developments in the investigation, when there is any large loss of life, the media begins to focus on the victims and the impact of their loss on family and friends.

One story that tugged at the public's heartstrings focused on sixteen students, who were members of the Montoursville, Pennsylvania High School French club and their five chaperones. Sixteen teenagers with their whole lives ahead of them ended so suddenly as their plane plunged into the ocean waters.

One afternoon, as I watched the daily briefing, I received a call.

That evening, I would be reassigned to examine the large volume of recovered passenger personal effects with the hope that some items could be returned to their loved ones.

"You know how important this is," my boss said.

"This will be the only thing that some people will have as a remembrance for the rest of their lives."

As I returned to the television coverage after learning of my new assignment, a story aired about a thirty-seven-year-old woman, who was traveling with her two daughters, ages ten and eight.

All three had perished and their bodies were among the first to be recovered. Pamela Lychner was traveling without her husband, who had to remain home for business but was to join his wife and daughters in Europe.

Pamela Lychner, coincidentally, a former TWA flight attendant, had switched careers to sell real estate.

Several years earlier, she was the victim of an attempted kidnapping and sexual assault.

The man charged, a convicted rapist and child molester, received a twenty-year sentence and resulted in Ms. Lychner becoming an advocate of victim's rights and she founded the group *Justice for All*.

Congress would later pass the Pam Lychner Sexual Offender Tracking and Identification Act of 1996, only months following her death in the crash.

This legislation soon established the National Sex Offender Registry.

As I arrived at around 11:00 p.m. that evening, I was directed to an area in the upstairs portion of the hangar, where a large room contained hundreds of pieces of luggage of all sizes, most of which were damp, some even still drenched, after laying at the bottom of the ocean floor for weeks.

Unlike many of my colleagues, who had the unenviable task of morgue duty, thus far I had primarily worked with NTSB, apart from the human aspect of this disaster.

Now, I realized that for me, this could soon become more personal in nature. It began to have an immediate impact.

The items that lay before me were possessions of people of all ages, most of whom probably were destined to enjoy a carefree summer holiday in Europe, never dreaming of the fate that lay ahead.

I began to open some of the luggage and at the outset there were few items amid the clothing and toiletries that I would be able to link to any of the victims.

The feeling of sifting through one's personal belongings knowing they had perished was particularly unsettling.

Then with difficulty, I unzipped a modest-sized suitcase and was immediately struck by the meticulous organization of the clothing. Each item was neatly folded and assembled as if on display at Bloomingdale's.

I thought *this piece of luggage had been blown out of the sky and lay on the ocean floor for weeks but it appeared as though it had just been packed an hour ago.*

I was drawn to a navy-blue windbreaker bearing the name "Jordan" with a winged foot that lay beneath. *A fellow runner,* I thought.

As I removed the jacket from the suitcase, I held it up and saw 800 on the upper portion of the sleeve, which to me, signified "Jordan's" event, the 800-meter run. As I looked in the back, I saw the words, "Montoursville H.S."

I was alone with no one to share this finding and as I stood there holding the jacket I thought, this is one of the sixteen students—he was probably about fifteen years old and would never attend college, never run another race, never have a career, never fall in love or have an opportunity to pursue his dreams.

Reflectively, I moved on.

Shortly thereafter, I came upon a carrying case too small to contain clothing. I looked inside and unsnapped a woman's wallet. I saw a Texas driver's license peeking through the transparent plastic cover and bearing a photo of a young, attractive woman with blond hair.

As I removed the license from the wallet, amid credit cards and additional pieces of identification, I read the name: "Pamela Lychner," which only hours before had been an unfamiliar name, and suddenly I found myself inspecting her personal belongings, which left me numb.

These were not the only instances where after watching short features, like the young couple that were on their way to Italy to be married and another who wanted to become engaged in Israel where I found myself rummaging through their personal effects in the days that followed.

Amid dozens of often wild conspiracy theories, the NTSB inquiry ultimately determined that the cause of the crash was an electrical short circuit, which initiated an explosion of a combustible mixture of fuel and air in the center wing fuel tank.

It's human nature to roll along and take each day for granted. It's something we all do.

This experience and others have often allowed me to pause and be thankful for the opportunities I've had.

I am far more fortunate than most.

Profound experiences like this and others cannot help but have a lasting impact and make one realize that yes, this *is* a precious life.

MY LAST STOP AT THE BUREAU

In June 1993, several months after returning to work, I was transferred to the Undercover and Sensitive Operations Unit ("USOU") which had been created several years prior to lend support to FBI undercover operations in New York and around the country. The group was headed by Jimmy Abbott, who was no stranger to undercover work, and an ideal choice as the FBI continued to move forward with very successful long-term undercover investigations.

Jimmy or "Chief," as he was affectionately known, a Woodside, Queens, native, had joined the NYPD and worked for several years in its elite Tactical Patrol Force before moving over to the FBI.

One of an exclusive club of larger-than-life figures in the New York office and the FBI for that matter, the closest comparison I can conjure up would be Jackie Gleason, of television's popular 1950s sitcom, *The Honeymooners*.

In the mid-1970s, the construction industry in New York City was largely controlled by the five LCN families. Labor racketeering, bid rigging, no show jobs, and shylocking had long been the accepted norm and the FBI, now catching up from many years of its failure to recognize and investigate organized crime, made it a priority.

Through a confidential informant, Jim Abbott (now Jimmy O'Brien) was introduced to several construction industry organized crime figures including Vincent "Vinnie Drywall" DiNapoli, a *caporegime* in the

Genovese LCN Family. Jim portrayed himself as a bagman and enforcer, who would also carry out contract killings—and rest assured, Jimmy looked and was quite convincing in his role.

Unknown to Di Napoli, Jimmy recalled meeting the Genovese captain and his crew for the first time.

"It was a hotel in midtown Manhattan. I was wearing one of the old-fashioned Nagra body recorders, which are much bigger than the micro-cassettes they have now. I thought there was a good chance I would get patted down, so I taped it as far up my inner thigh as possible, thinking these guys will never want to venture too far into that territory.

"The first words out of Vinnie's mouth were: 'You look like a cop.'

"I will admit to being a bit flustered momentarily, but they all got a good laugh and seemed more at ease when I replied, 'I'm actually an FBI agent.'

"They did search me, but my instincts were right, they stopped at about mid-thigh."

This undercover operation, which ran simultaneously with the case depicted in the movie, *Donnie Brasco,* starring Johnny Depp as FBI agent Joe Pistone, were important inroads into the FBI's organized crime investigations over the next several decades, which broke the backs of the five families and saw their influence nearly eradicated.

Jimmy enjoyed a good practical joke, loved to laugh, and always looked out for and had the backs of his people, but his good-hearted and comical nature wasn't to be mistaken for not wanting to get the job done, when he could show he was deadly serious.

I still recall my first day when I sat down with him in his office.

"Neil-O (as he still refers to me today), this is a really good squad and as you'll see, we do a lot of critical things for the undercover program. Always be mindful with whatever you're doing, we can do 999 good things, but all anyone will ever remember is that *one* bad thing that could get someone killed."

Jim created several visionary programs that don't need further clarification here. It's fair to say, FBI undercover agents that were children or weren't even born at that time are reaping the rewards of Jimmy's imaginative and creative ideas today.

He had assembled a veteran agent and clerical support staff with some of the most capable people with whom I would work. Amongst the support folks were Jane Johnson, Kathy Haag, Morphia Papain, Joan Daly, Valerie O'Connell, Brian Harkins, and Debbie Musso. The agents included Pete Melley, Danny Kelleher, Tom Regan, Debbie Vota, and would later be joined by Bill Carden, Artie Doyle, Dick Rudolph, and Steve Winters.

Tom Regan, the youngest member of the squad, was often the target of Jimmy's razor-sharp humor. Tom, who often seemed to carry the weight of the world on his shoulders, in a good-natured way, would often seek Jimmy's counsel in the most trivial of issues.

It was a Monday morning, and Artie Doyle and I were in Jim's office chatting about our respective weekends. Artie, who was suffering from the advanced stages of melanoma, which would take his life within the next year, was trying to remain upbeat as he spoke about his struggle, when Tom burst through the door.

"Chief, I don't know what I'm going to do," Tom belted out, as he plopped down on the couch.

"It's so hard to make ends meet on our salary. My children are costing me a fortune. Honestly, I don't know where the money goes," Tom added.

There was some back and forth with Jim and some additional personal grievances aired by Tom when Jimmy looked square at Artie and said, "Aren't you glad you don't have this guy's problems?"

In 1998, Jimmy asked me to come into his office.

"Neil-O, shut the door," although it didn't happen that often, I knew it meant business.

In summary, Jimmy was retiring and taking the job as first deputy commissioner with the Suffolk County Police Department. He asked me to apply for his position and said that I had his full support. He also asked if I would take his assignment as an adjunct professor at St. John's University teaching a course on Organized Crime.

As it worked out, I was fortunate to succeed Jimmy (huge shoes to fill, in more ways than one) at USOU and at St. John's, two of the most rewarding of my professional experiences.

After spending about two years at USOU as the supervisor, an unexpected opportunity came along and on May 31, 2000, I retired from the FBI, after twenty-eight fulfilling and rewarding years.

Only a week after my unanticipated departure, I would embark on my eighteen-year 'second career' in what's known in the Bureau as the 'private sector.'

Left to right—Neil Moran, Jim Abbott and Bob Joyce at Moran retirement party in June 2000.

JALTF Task Force Members—left to right—George Hanna, Bob Joyce, Neil Moran, Richie Mika, Janet Engel, George Terra, Steve Carbone, Warren Flagg (in background), Mike Ferrandino, Marty Finn, Don Winters and former ASAC Jim Murphy, at George Hanna's retirement in 2004.

George Hanna and Neil Moran at George's retirement.

MR. CHIPS

It was a regular workday in 1997, when my boss summoned me into his office and said, "Please shut the door and have a seat."

Jimmy Abbott loved to talk, and I didn't give much thought other than he probably was about to share something personal.

"I know I can trust you not to say anything. I have a nice job offer which I've accepted. I'm putting in my papers and starting on Monday. This Friday will be my last day. I want you to know that I'll do everything I can to help you take over here."

I was more than a bit surprised. Jimmy was nearing the mandatory retirement age, but he kept this one pretty close to the vest.

"One thing I need to take care of quickly is my teaching position at St. John's. I can't continue with this new job, and I promised the department head I would recommend someone. I'd like you to consider taking it."

This was a lot to swallow in the few minutes or so it took Jimmy to lay it out. He would no longer be the boss; he was going to push for me to follow him as the supervisor and oh yes, he's asking if I want to begin a side gig as a college professor the following Monday.

"Jimmy, I don't know anything about teaching. You can't be serious. I'm very flattered but what the hell would I talk about for ninety minutes twice a week?"

The position was part of St. John's University's College of Legal & Professional Studies, where active members of the NYPD and several federal law enforcement agencies assumed unpaid teaching positions as adjunct professors. Jimmy was teaching a class on organized crime.

"You can tell stories with the best of them. Besides, you've served as an instructor at Quantico and lectured police agencies all over Europe. Honestly, you'll be fine, and I wouldn't be offering this to you if I didn't think you could do it."

The following Monday, at about 7:30 a.m., as I pulled off Union Turnpike into the parking lot at St. John's for my inaugural class, I was terrified. I sat there for a moment staring out into the sea of cars.

What had I gotten myself into?

Why did I let Jimmy talk me into this?

Why didn't I simply say, "No?"

Too late for any of that.

I had purchased a briefcase over the weekend to at least look the part, but certainly, no one was going to mistake me for Mr. Chips. As I made my way to St. John Hall, I thought about what the department head had said when I met with him briefly.

"The students in this department are your future prosecutors, police officers, federal agents, forensics and intelligence analysts and other related fields. We are grooming them for their professional careers. They want to hear about your personal experiences. We do have a curriculum to follow but never hesitate to use your discretion when it's appropriate. Nobody will be looking over your shoulder."

What was my favorite subject in college, I thought, as I walked across the campus? Russian history—our professor had fled the Bolshevik regime of Lenin and enchanted us with stories of the Russian revolution and the hardships he and his family endured. We were on the edges of our seats every class. As I entered the building, I felt a sense of calm and thought, 'Maybe I *can* do this.'

I suppose getting through the first class after a brief introduction, familiarizing myself with the students, their goals and what was expected of them was a major hurdle. It seemed like thirty minutes had passed when I heard noise in the hallway and the students began gathering their belongings. I looked at my watch and it was 9:30 a.m. I had gone over by five minutes! Not that bad at all.

Arriving for eight o'clock class was relatively painless with plenty of room in the parking lot. That's not the case for the next several hours when students fight tooth and nail for the remaining spots. Following my first class and continuing religiously, it seemed like every attractive coed driving a fancy Camaro or five-liter Mustang was looking for parking.

"Professor, are you going to your car?"

"I am," I would reply.

"Hop in and I'll drive you."

My first thought was *How does she know I am a teacher?* and then I wondered, *Is it the briefcase?*

Maybe I do look like Mr. Chips.

Getting into a car with a nineteen-year-old was not the best of ideas. My standard stock answer was that I *was* going to my car and you are certainly welcome to the spot. You'll just have to follow me.

I mixed up the first few sessions with a combination of showing clips from films including *The Godfather* and *Goodfellas*, charts on the hierarchy of the five organized crime families of *La Cosa Nostra* and introduced a glossary of terms like "sit-downs," "Omerta," "opening the books," "wise guy," "paying tribute," and "cement shoes."

"Ladies and gentlemen," I opened one class, "we have front row seats as spectators to the birthplace and continued prosperity of traditional Italian organized crime in this country. The Bergen Hunt and Fish Club, which has been headquarters for the Queens faction of the Gambino Family, is only about five miles from here. Rarely does a week pass when the body of a reputed mobster is discovered in the trunk of a car or dumped in a landfill."

With each class, the students appeared to be more engaged, asking questions and bringing in articles generating discussion.

It was about three weeks into the semester when a student approached me after class and asked if he could write his term paper on the Pizza Connection case.

This investigation focused on local pizza shops that were used as fronts in a massive heroin distribution case in 1984. Twenty alleged members of the American and Sicilian Mafia were convicted.

"And who might you be?" I asked, quite certain that this was the first time the student had attended class.

"Sal, Sal Randazzo, I've been here for every class. I sit in the back mostly."

Having been paid for some time to make observations for a living, I knew I had never laid eyes on this guy.

"Sal, please don't insult me, this is your first class. The semester began weeks ago."

"Okay professor, you got me. This *is* my first class, but I'm going to try to make it more often. I work at the Yankees ticket office in Queens and we've really been busy."

"Sal, I don't care if you come at all. If you don't fulfill the requirements, you won't pass and will have wasted your tuition payment."

"I understand, I'll try, but can I write about the Pizza Connection? My uncle got caught up in it and I know a lot about the case."

Sal was being truthful. He was the namesake of one of the main defendants. I don't ever seem to be able to get away from this stuff I thought.

I rarely saw Sal after our conversation. He was destined to fail the course, but for some odd reason, as promised, he submitted his paper on the Pizza Connection.

"In the pre-dawn hours of April 9, 1984, FBI agents conducted a well-coordinated dragnet involving the arrest of scores of Mafia members in six different U.S. cities," the beginning read.

As I continued, it was evident that this was not Sal's work. Among my collection of books was one on this very case. Sal had copied the inside flap of the book's cover, word for word and the remainder of the paper was copied from various pages in the book.

My note to Sal (including a xerox copy of the inside cover) was that he was receiving an "F" for the paper, another one for the course and was lucky I was not recommending dismissal from the university. A year later I read that Sal and several employees were arrested in a scandal that rocked the Yankees ticket office.

The Sal's of the class were an anomaly as were two women who thought it would be easy to cheat while taking the final. They protested rather loudly after I separated them, but the class chimed in and voiced their objections to being distracted by the ruckus they were causing. The majority were there to learn and did so enthusiastically.

Teaching at St. John's was one of the true privileges and treasured periods of my life. It afforded me an opportunity to influence and provide direction to the students who were still unsure about their career paths and let them know that if they wanted something bad enough, determination would help them achieve their goals. For me, there was no greater thrill.

My goodbye to each class at the semester's end was, "Whenever you read about a gangster being found in the trunk of a car or one with a shot behind the ear or having a canary stuffed in his mouth, I want you to think of me."

"Professor, this is the best class I've ever taken" and "You are the best teacher I've had in four years," were some of the comments I was fortunate to have received from students.

Mr. Chips should have been so lucky.

BDO

It was about two years after retiring from the FBI, having gone to work for a small investigative and security consulting firm, Murphy & Maconachy, that I received a call from my friend at Aon, John Morrissey.

I had met John on a large bank fraud case in Puerto Rico about a year prior and we had travelled to San Juan together several times.

"Neil, I just got a call from one of the major accounting firms, BDO Seidman, do you know it?" John asked.

I did know BDO to be a sizeable company, a bit smaller than the "Big Four," accounting firms.

"They are looking for someone to replace a guy they just lost to Microsoft. He was a retired U.S. postal inspector and an integral part of their consulting group. Apart from tax and auditing, these people get involved in lots of misappropriation of funds cases and all types of insurance fraud. Basically, people who steal money on a corporate level."

An accounting firm, I thought. I had no background in accounting or business. While in the FBI, I never worked on any white-collar crime cases. Those were left to people with a business background in college and experience prior to becoming agents.

"John, this doesn't sound like a good fit; I don't know."

"Look, what's the harm in having lunch with one of the partners? These are nice people. I wouldn't be steering you in this direction if I thought it wouldn't be worth your while. I'm also leaving out something; this could mean a significant bump in the salary department."

All went well and with much trepidation, in December 2002, I joined BDO's consulting group.

I believe it was only my first week after joining BDO, when John Morrissey called.

"Neil, we have a client from the Netherlands who has suffered a $13 million loss in what they have described as a misappropriation of funds. They are flying here to meet with us tomorrow morning. I have already recommended you as being a former FBI agent who works for a major accounting firm. Can you grab someone and plan on coming to the meeting tomorrow? This could be great for you to land this engagement in your first week."

Partner Glenn Pomerantz and I walked to Aon's nearby offices late the next morning and Glenn, still getting to know me, asked for some brief details about my FBI career so he could speak to the clients about our respective backgrounds.

Later, we sat before the visitors from the Netherlands.

"And Neil Moran, although he has only been with BDO a brief time, is highly qualified to investigate such a significant loss. He had a stellar career in the FBI, where he headed the entire New York field office."

I completely cringed as I saw John Morrissey raise his eyebrows and the Dutch nod and smile approvingly.

Head the New York office—had Glenn lost his mind?

I was a supervisory special agent, overseeing a squad which numbered about fifteen people, not the assistant director in charge of 2,000 or so employees, which comprises the largest FBI office in the country.

"You seem to have gotten a big promotion since leaving the Bureau," John uttered when the meeting concluded.

"You looked like you were going to die when Glenn said that. It's not a problem, no harm done. Not to worry."

As Glenn and I walked out of the building, I couldn't hold it in any longer.

"Glenn, what were you thinking? The head of the New York office? I was a squad supervisor. Just one of dozens. The head of the office is a big deal, and I certainly wasn't a big deal."

Glenn took it in stride.

"Just a minor misunderstanding, Neil. I'll take it down a notch next time."

It was about a month later, still feeling my way along as a senior manager in the consulting group, when my boss, Carl Pergola, called me into his office.

"Neil, my neighbor's company in Sunnyside believes they have been victimized by one of their employees to the tune of several million dollars. They've contacted the Queens D.A.'s Office with no success. The loss is so significant that they fear they might lose the company. Do you have any contacts there?" he asked.

One thing a firm like BDO keeps in mind when hiring people who worked in law enforcement was for their 'Rolodexes,' or in the vernacular, contacts.

"Yes, as a matter of fact I do."

It was less than forty-eight hours when we had a conference call with the bureau chief of economic crimes in the Queens D.A.'s office and after learning the details and requesting additional investigation, he said that he would assign an ADA to the case.

My boss's head was spinning.

"Nice work, Neil. This is why you're here."

At age fifty-two, I was now the oldest member of the consulting arm of BDO.

I was surrounded by the most talented group of young people one could imagine. There didn't seem to be anything they couldn't figure out or find when it came to fraud and given their young ages, they were all whizzes when it came to computer skills. Just being around, on a daily basis, I was able to boost my often-lackluster proficiencies.

Retiring from the FBI, where after nearly thirty years, I pretty much knew and felt comfortable with my craft, did not come easily. Beginning a new career in your fifties, and having had no experience in the white-collar arena, was of major concern. This was my first big test to see how this decision played out.

Well, it wasn't more than a week, and the young prodigies of consulting had concluded that the bookkeeper, a single woman in her late 40s, who lived with her mother in Astoria, had ripped off the company to the tune of $5.2 million.

Lavish weekends in Atlantic City with her boyfriend, transported by limousine; tickets to Major League Baseball and NBA regular season and pricey all-star and World Series games in cities around the country (NBA games were all courtside seats); numerous accounts with sizeable deposits for her nieces and nephews; a $60,000 Mercedes Benz as a gift to her favorite niece, and weekly trips to the hairdresser, where she always generously tipped $100, often more than the cost of the actual appointment, were just the beginning.

The most significant expense we learned, and after twenty plus years still boggles the mind, was the $5,000-$10,000 she spent every week on the NYS Lottery!

"We all thought she was so lucky," one employee said during our interview.

"She won $50,000 once and about $75,000 the second time. *Who is that lucky we wondered?* We didn't realize she was spending that much every week, so it was just a matter of percentages."

"She ran the accounting department like Jozef Stalin. She wouldn't let anyone else near or have access to the payroll. Now we know why," another employee added.

And yes, there was a reason why she kept the payroll close to the vest. She created fictitious accounts with "ghost employees" receiving expenses and having them directly deposited into her personal bank account each week.

Rosanne Messina was arrested in February, 2003, and charged with grand larceny and falsifying business records. We had always preached to clients that it was important to exercise "due diligence," when hiring employees, especially those in a position of trust. Had this company done its homework and conducted a simple criminal check for $50, they would have found that Ms. Messina had embezzled $100,000 from her previous employer for which she was sentenced to twenty-six weekends in jail.

Ms. Messina told us, "When I got the new job, I was spending weekends in the Queens House of Detention. On Monday morning, I got out of my jumpsuit, put on a blouse and a skirt, threw some water on my face, combed my hair, and hopped on the train to Sunnyside. On Friday night after work, I was back on the train to Kew Gardens to the Queens House."

The interviews conducted had humorous and not so humorous moments.

The small bodega in Woodside where Ms. Messina purchased and checked her lottery tickets was run by an Indian immigrant.

"I am so sorry to see her in trouble. She was good for business. She spent hours and hours here every week, buying and then checking hundreds of tickets."

The not-so-humorous discussions were with family members who were about to have their suddenly hefty bank accounts depleted and one $60,000 Mercedes Benz seized by the Queens DA.

Ms. Messina was sentenced to five years in prison and then deported to her native Sicily.

There was a case in New Jersey where we were called in to address allegations of financial misconduct by the CEO of a publicly traded company. The CEO was a bit of a bully and appeared to have intimidated many of the employees.

In conversations with Human Resources, I told them we would need to have access to all of the CEO's electronic devices to allow our computer forensics team to capture their contents.

"Who is going to tell the CEO this—he's a mean guy?" the head of HR told me.

"I'll break the news to him. I don't foresee any problem."

"I hope you're right," he replied

The two of us walked into the CEO's office and he was as advertised—a make-believe tough guy.

The head of HR introduced me, and I told the boss we would need access to all his and his administrative assistant's electronic devices and in addition, we would also need access to his office to retrieve anything that might be evidentiary in nature.

Lastly, I suggested that he excuse himself for a short time so our folks could do what they needed to do with minimal inconvenience to him and to allow the company to continue with business as usual—I could not have been more courteous and respectful.

"Should I leave now?" he asked almost meekly.

"Yes, please and the Blackberry on your belt, please leave that as well," I said.

"I will leave an itemized receipt for anything we remove," I added.

He was out of there in an instant.

"I have never seen anything like that in all my years here," the head of HR said.

"He was completely intimidated, and you couldn't have been nicer."

After reviewing all the documents and the CEO's electronic devices, we found what only amounted to approximately $7,500 in misuse of funds. There were several board members that felt for all he had done for the company, they would simply allow him to resign and let him keep a sizeable payout that had been promised.

That was until we found a software program called "Evidence Eliminator," which was installed on his office computer by the CEO's son who was an IT employee at the firm.

Then the board members really flipped out when we found widespread searching of pornographic sites.

Confronting the CEO with both these issues during a lengthy interview fell on me and frankly, I was salivating at the opportunity.

"And sir, there is the matter of someone utilizing your computer and spending significant hours on pornographic sites," I began.

"And how do you know that it wasn't the janitor when he was cleaning my office?" he shot back.

We sparred back and forth a bit and I could see I was getting under his skin. The tough guy was backed into a corner. Out of nowhere he asked, "What kind of sites are you talking about? I have searched online to buy my wife lingerie, if that's what you're talking about."

"What I'm talking about *sir*, to name one, and I am happy to read them all if you like, is *www.teensluts.com*, where I don't believe they are selling women's lingerie."

It was "Evidence Eliminator and the "teen sluts" that pushed the board of directors over the edge. They sent the CEO packing without his golden parachute with a promise not to publicize his departure.

THE TRIP TO TURKEY

It was during the Christmas season in 2016, when BDO was retained by an international non-profit to look into allegations of widespread fraud by members of senior management and their contractors.

After meeting with the non-profit's office of general counsel in New York, it was determined that we would send a team to southern Turkey to investigate the allegations. As had been the case in several other matters during my tenure, given my background and experience, my bosses requested that I travel with our group of young accountants and a computer forensics specialist.

In early January, we convened at JFK Airport to board a Turkish Airlines flight to Istanbul. As I scanned the awaiting passengers at our gate, it was clear that we were among the few and perhaps only American-born persons scheduled for the journey.

I was checking periodically to see who was winning the Alabama v. Clemson football game for the NCAA championship, when suddenly each team member was approached by people identifying themselves as members of the Department of Homeland Security.

"Mr. Moran, what's the purpose of your travel?" the agent asked.

After explaining where our team worked, the nature of our trip, and adding that I was a retired supervisor in the FBI's New York office, the interview sessions wound down fairly quickly.

Following our ten-hour flight to Istanbul as we deplaned, there was a noticeable buzz in the airport. We soon learned from our translator, a member of our firm's Istanbul office, ten people, including eight German tourists, had been killed earlier by a suicide bomber hailing from Syria.

The airport and a great deal of that area around Istanbul were now in lockdown. Scheduled to depart in several hours, we learned that all outgoing flights were presently on hold. My phone was literally exploding with text messages from home asking if we were in any danger.

Approximately six hours later, in the wee hours of the morning, our flight to southern Turkey was finally underway. In addition to our team, there were probably about twenty-five people aboard.

After landing at Atay Airport in southern Turkey at 5:00 a.m., this small venue had minimal staff checking travel documents and luggage.

Given that nearly every type of financial investigation these days involves computers and mobile phones, a member of our computer forensics staff accompanied us. He carried several hard-shell suitcases containing highly technical equipment. As the airport representative saw these bags come through the X-ray machine, and speaking to our translator in Turkish despite the language barrier, it was clear that he was not at all pleased. He was not buying the translator's explanation that we were in Turkey conducting a review of a non-profit.

He then proceeded to confiscate all of our technical devices and said that we would have to explain the situation to law enforcement authorities later in the day, in order to retrieve them.

As we exited the airport, we were met by several armored black SUVs, which were to serve as escorts during our stay. We were under a strong directive from our CEO, that we were not to leave our hotel unless we were traveling to conduct interviews at the client site. Our translator explained that given the proximity to Syria, a country ravaged by longtime civil war, it was not uncommon to hear explosions in the distance that often spilled over the Turkish border.

Having then recently reached my sixty-seventh birthday, I began to think, *What in the hell am I doing here?*

With assistance from our local office, we were able to retrieve our equipment from the authorities later in the day. It probably didn't hurt our efforts when I struck up a conversation with the only official who spoke any English. With considerable difficulty, I did manage to understand him when he asked if I lived in Brooklyn.

Explaining that hailing from the Bronx, a different section of New York, I wasn't from Brooklyn but was quite familiar with the area.

He then said, "My aunt live in Brooklyn. I visit her when I am young."

Having now successfully got my foot in the door, I asked the most logical question I could think of, "Did you visit Coney Island?"

Now clearly beaming at this apparent universal adoration for the landmark amusement park and grinning from ear to ear, he replied, "Yes, yes, Coney Island. I love Coney Island, yes, Coney Island."

Moments later, this now honorary Brooklynite, gathered with his colleagues and after considerable back and forth, we had our equipment.

We remained in Turkey for about a week and interviewed dozens of the non-profit's representatives, as well as individuals who received lucrative contracts through bid rigging. We uncovered widespread fraud which resulted in the dismissals of many members of the non-profit's senior management. All in all, quite a successful endeavor.

I can't ever remember being so excited as our plane flew over lower Manhattan moments away from touching down at JFK.

Forever terrified at the prospect of no longer working, it was after this trip when I began to believe that retiring might not be such a bad idea. International travel at our firm was clearly on the upswing and spending a week in Turkey, after a career of chasing bad guys in New York, I began to think, . . . *Maybe it's time.*

STORIES

When I narrowly escaped a trip to Sao Paolo, Brazil, the following December in the week leading up to Christmas, I knew it was time.

I haven't looked back since.

IT'S A SMALL WORLD

How many times have we uttered or heard the expression, "It's a small world."

Some of us know it as one of the more notable attractions at Disney theme parks throughout the world. I was surprised to learn that the ride originated at the New York World's Fair in 1964, before permanently moving to Disney.

We live in a world exceeding eight billion people, a country approaching 350 million and approximately twenty million New York Metro-area residents. With those staggering numbers, you would think that the odds of running into someone in another city or country or through conversation would be slim, but then we wouldn't have the expression, "It's a small world."

Prior to the onset of Covid-19, I had the privilege of serving as a volunteer tour guide at the Intrepid Air & Space Museum on Manhattan's west side. It was one of the most enjoyable and exciting things I've ever done. Founded in 1982 and attracting over a million visitors from around the world each year, it's a popular landmark for international vacationers. Whether I was assigned to the flight deck, the Space Shuttle Pavilion, the submarine called the *Growler* or the captain's bridge of the WW II carrier, *USS Intrepid*, I met people from every state and countless nations.

Given my natural curiosity of people, places, and things in general, I would ask everyone with whom I interacted, "Where are you from?" The replies ranged from Morocco to Minneapolis, Baton Rouge to Brisbane, and Fresno to Frankfurt. When assigned to the captain's bridge (the section of the carrier from which it was commanded) on the *Intrepid*, the lines of people coming through could be massive. I would often scan the queue to see if I could guess from where people hailed. I was often correct, but there were occasions when I wasn't even in the right hemisphere.

One group where that percentage was quite high was recognizing the Irish. Given our family's close ties there sometimes it was barely a challenge. On a busy, hot August day, I recall a young couple, who turned out to be honeymooners, making their way up the line.

"Are you from Ireland?" I asked.

"We are, yes," the young man answered.

"What part?" I continued.

"Dublin, do you know it?"

"I do, yes, what part of Dublin?"

"Do you know Tallaght?"

"In fact, I do know Tallaght."

With that, the young man kind of gave me one of those looks that said, 'There is no way this guy has any clue where Tallaght is.'

"Did you by chance attend St. Aidan's Community School?" I asked.

With eyes and mouth wide open, the gentleman said,

"How would *you* know St. Aidan's?"

"I would because my cousin is the principal."

"Ms. Quigley? Karen Quigley is your cousin? I loved Ms. Quigley; she was my fourth-grade teacher and one of my mum's best friends. My mum taught there for years. Wait until I tell her."

Yes, it is a small world.

My father was a New York City firefighter from the late 1940s until his retirement in the late 1970s. Although he began his career in Manhattan, he served most of the time in the Bedford Park section of the Bronx, a short walk across Mosholu Parkway from our apartment.

As a 'chauffeur,' he drove the old 'hook and ladder' rigs and as such, was in much demand to fill in for other drivers all over the Bronx. It broke his heart to see much of the borough he loved burn to the ground during the 1970s.

Firefighters, especially back in my father's time, were and still are a tight group. Much like my dad receiving orders to report to some other firehouse in the South Bronx, when someone called in sick or was injured, a replacement would occasionally be sent to Ladder 37 and Engine 79 in Bedford Park.

It was at dinner one evening when my dad announced, "You'll never believe what happened at the firehouse today."

He went on to say that a young firefighter reported for duty on the day tour and as in most firehouses, everyone had gathered in the kitchen. As the young man introduced himself as Neil McGovern, my father detected an Irish accent.

"What part of Ireland are you from?" my father asked.

"Cork, Cork City."

"My aunt lives in Cork City," my dad continued.

"Anywhere near Turner's Cross?" Mr. McGovern replied.

"My aunt lives *in* Turner's Cross on Father Matthew's Road."

"I was born and raised on Father Matthew's Road, number six," McGovern answered.

"My aunt lives at number four," my father said.

"Is your aunt Mrs. Forde?"

"Yes, that's her, my mother's sister," my father answered.

As Mr. McGovern proceeded to talk about growing up next to the Fordes and playing with my father's cousins, my dad said the other firefighters, most of whom were first generation Irish Americans, looked on in amazement.

It was during a recent visit to Ireland that I sat in my cousin Siobhan's living room in Carrigaline, in Cork, and thinking that all the family had heard this story, I was surprised to hear that she had not. When I was done recounting the tale, my cousin said, "When we used to go to Grandma Forde's to visit, my sisters and I played with a younger brother, Joe McGovern. I still bump into him from time to time and he probably never heard this story."

It was several weeks later, when I had returned from my trip, when Siobhan called me.

"I gave Joe McGovern your number. He is so intrigued and is dying to hear more about the story." He told me that his much older brother Neil is retired, now in his 80s, and living in the Woodlawn section of the Bronx.

A short time after I had a Zoom call with Joe McGovern and we spoke for almost an hour. He briefly spoke with his brother, based on what my cousin had told him, and he clearly recalled meeting my father at the firehouse over fifty years ago. Joe periodically travels to New York on business and stays with his brother. He said that he would reach out to me prior to his next visit and hopefully, we could meet for lunch.

Yes, as the song goes, "It's a small world after all."

Neil Moran on duty at the Captain's Bridge, Intrepid Air and Space Museum, New York City—visited by grandchildren, left to right, Aidan, Maeve and Rory O'Neill, February 2019.

SOMETIMES TRAVEL ISN'T SO EASY

For as long as I can remember, I've had a love affair with the journey to Idlewild, now known as JFK Airport.

In the 1950s, when air travel became more common, it was almost a yearly ritual to accompany my grandmother and various combinations of her six brothers, who also settled here, to Idlewild Airport on their trips home to Ireland. In the 1960s, as their travels continued, our Irish relatives began to pay us visits, which always drew a sizeable family crowd at JFK to welcome them.

Many years have passed since, and looking back what now seems like a less complicated and more informal time. I can only visualize what it would be like to have our beloved Grandma Moran, who I never saw outfitted in anything but a dress, removing her heels, broach, handbag and hat for TSA inspection.

I often think about how excited all the cousins were waiting for our respective grandparents to enter the U.S. Customs area upon their return. In an elevated waiting space, we all carried quarters in our hands, furiously tapping on the huge glass windowpanes, trying to get their attention as we watched the arriving passengers below. Days never to be revisited again.

I find today's travel to be very stressful. It appears the airlines answer to no one.

"Our computers are down;" "We are short several people in the flight crew;" "We have overbooked this flight;" and "We are experiencing bad weather," are just some of the many justifications airlines use today in what are often mammoth inconveniences to the public.

In July 2024, as I made my final preparations for what has become an annual trip to visit my cousins in Ireland, my wife made the same comment she does every year.

"I can't believe what a different person you are when you're traveling."

There is no argument from me because it's completely true. I find the entire process to be nerve-wracking.

Even though I leave myself every bit of the recommended three hours prior to departure, I visualize the Belt Parkway being shut down, getting a flat tire on the Southern State Parkway, or getting bumped off the flight. Will the airline's computers die under the severe July heat I wonder? These are not things with which I normally concern myself, but on travel days I transform into a virtual "Mr. Hyde."

Although I'm probably not the person you want heading the next "Space X" launch, technologically speaking, I do everything in my control to make each trip a bit smoother. Having successfully checked in online and obtained a "QR" code on my phone, all I needed to do was visit one of the kiosks and drop off my bag.

Having had little success scanning my passport on prior occasions, I opted for using my debit card at the first available kiosk. Once, twice, three times with no luck. An airline rep apparently noticed my failed attempts and came to the rescue.

"Need some help, sir?" she asked.

"Please, I don't have much luck with these things for some reason," I replied.

"Do you have your passport handy?" she inquired.

With that, I handed her my passport, and within seconds my luggage tag printed and I was on my way.

The security lines evoked memories of young Vito Corleone arriving at Ellis Island in *The Godfather*. The lines snaked in and out in what

Above: Left to right—Cousins/sisters, Daragh Forde, Karen Forde and Orla Forde with Neil Moran at the All-Ireland Senior Hurling Championship pictured outside Croke Park, Dublin, Ireland, September 28, 2013—Cork v. Clare.

Left: Cousin Siobhan Corbett and Craig Casey pictured at Cobh Golf Club, Cobh, County Cork, Ireland.

seemed like a never-ending morass of people hailing from nearly every hemisphere.

Bomb and drug dogs, under the watchful eyes of their handlers, quietly went about their business. It was close to an hour before I removed my shoes, belt, phone, iPad and emptied my pockets.

As I placed my wallet into the gray bin, I noticed my driver's license, where my debit card is normally visible. With my apparent sudden look of anguish, the TSA agent asked, "Something wrong, sir?"

"Yes, I think I left my debit card in the kiosk outside."

I must say, the TSA folks and airline personnel, given how hectic things were at that moment, made every effort to help me retrieve my card but to no avail. It was at least another hour now before I sat down at the gate to report my card missing when I realized that I had no backup credit card.

"What is your card number?" the bank rep asked.

"Ma'am, I have no idea, I'm calling to report it missing."

My regular routine of leisurely picking up various items for my cousins in the duty free' shop was now scuttled with little time remaining and no way to pay for anything. Normally, when boarding and realizing that in six hours I would be in Ireland, I feel as excited as I did when making the trip as a teenager. This was a different feeling for sure.

It was about 9:00 a.m. Irish time when I landed and as much as I tried to convince myself to put on a brave face, I was still very upset.

A little bit of historical fact is important. My family in Ireland are the kindest, most hospitable, and warm people imaginable. No celebrity, sports figure, or member of a royal family could be treated better. I literally want for nothing when I visit. As such, I try to express my thanks by paying for the occasional meal, filling the gas tank when we're on the road, buying flowers, or purchasing 'vouchers,' as they call them, to their favorite restaurants. These efforts are often met with good-natured resistance and many a spirited argument with wait staff as to who should be allowed to foot the bill.

"Don't dare take his money, it might be counterfeit," my cousin Orla once yelled to our server.

"His money is no good here," my cousin Siobhan Corbett has often been known to utter to our server.

After greeting my cousins, as I got into the car, there was no way I could keep this to myself.

"You're not going to believe this. I did a very stupid thing. I lost my debit card at the airport. I have no money. What the hell am I going to do?"

As I was sitting in the front seat alongside my cousin, Karen, who was driving, I saw her grin broadly and glance in the rearview mirror where her sister, Daragh, was seated.

"You have no credit card or any money, Neil, is that what you're saying?" Daragh said.

"Karen, I believe we have the Yank exactly where we've always hoped we'd have him. He's penniless and completely at our mercy."

We laughed at my expense. Mind you, all the way home and for the duration of my stay, I think my cousins told everyone about my misfortune, including the local butcher and baker. Thank goodness there is no candlestick maker in the village of Youghal, in East Cork, or he or she would have joined in on the absolute hilarity as well.

As things have a habit of doing, they are never as bad as they seem. My cousins floated me cash advances so we could continue battling over the bills and it made for many late evening laughs and spirited conversation. Despite a shaky beginning, it was one of the best trips in recent memory.

SUDDENLY A וֶאמסדנאלל (LANTZMAN)

It's been very popular in recent years to have a DNA test performed by a third-party service to determine your ancestral origins and uncover living relatives you may not know.

"Don't do it, Neil," my longtime friend, Tommy Gallagher, told me.

"Here I was living my whole life thinking my roots were 100 percent Irish, only to find out that I'm part German, Welsh, Scottish and English. It was devastating."

"My situation is a little different," I countered.

"Although, I know my roots are solidly Irish on three sides, my maternal grandfather was adopted and apparently knew little, if anything, about his parents. So that part remains a mystery. I think I'm going to give it a try anyway."

So, after ordering the kit from the service, '23 and Me,' providing a saliva sample, and answering a few basic questions, I shipped it off in early to mid-June and awaited the results.

It was the first few days of my trip to Ireland, in July, when the subject came up.

"Neil, that's fascinating," said my cousin, Daragh.

"Do you think you'll get the results while you're here?"

"A good chance," I replied.

It was only days later as I awoke and began to check my email when I saw "23 and Me—Your Results are In," as the caption.

I was barely awake but could feel a rush, fully aware that there was a potential bombshell awaiting.

"European 100%—Northwestern European—81.6% Irish, Central and Southern Ireland" read the first segment.

Eighty-one, and six tenths' percent, I thought, what about the other 18.4%?

As I scrolled down, I next saw, "Ashkenazi Jewish, 16.6%"—Central European and Western Ukrainian Jews—Eastern Polish and Western Ukrainian Jews."

I was and even now am still stunned.

How was this possible?

There must be an error. They must have gotten my saliva mixed up with another person.

Nearly frantic at seeing this and seeking further explanation, I continued to explore the options. I clicked on Family and Friends and my mother's brother and fraternal twin, now ninety-nine years old, appeared. Amazingly, my uncle had submitted a sample with the same provider.

In a series of questions under "Family Background" he was asked to provide information which included, 'Family Surnames.' My uncle included two, 'O'Shea,' my grandmother's maiden name and 'Schwartz.' *Schwartz,* I thought, *where could that have possibly originated?*

What in the hell is going on here?

As I now heard stirring in the kitchen, I knew my cousins were up and would be floored hearing this quite stunning news.

"I'm 16% Jewish," I began.

I can't possibly capture the looks on their faces.

"Jewish is it," Daragh said.

"That's absolutely brilliant."

How could this be humanly possible, I wondered?

This had never been discussed. My mother had passed away several years ago at ninety-three and surely would have shared this revelation had she known. I had to get to the bottom of this.

I began by emailing my cousin, Madeline, one of my uncle's children. I explained everything in detail and asked if she could shed any light on things. I received a prompt response with a letter attached explaining that she was under the impression her father had shared it with my mother.

The 1993 letter was addressed to my uncle in response to his inquiry, written by a nun from the Sisters of Charity at the New York Foundling Hospital. It explained that in 1891, my grandfather, Richard Schwartz, was brought to the facility by a woman identifying herself as his birth mother, who indicated that she was unable to care for him. He was six weeks old.

"The only information recorded in our records," the letter reads, "concerning Richard's natural mother is that she was Jewish."

Her name, age or place of birth were not furnished. No additional information, including his father or any siblings or immediate family were provided.

The letter indicated that on the day after my grandfather was brought to the Foundling Hospital, he was baptized by a priest.

"In 1893," the letter continued, "Richard was placed in the home of Mr. and Mrs. Patrick Owens in the Bronx, who eventually adopted him and changed his surname name to Owens."

According to the Foundling Hospital records, in 1913, my grandfather visited the facility seeking his birth and baptismal certificate. Although he was provided with proof of his baptism, they had no knowledge of a birth certificate ever being recorded.

So, there you have it, a mystery of sorts that now may never be solved. My extended family and most of my friends are still in shock, while my Jewish friends, much like my Irish cousins think it's fabulous. I'm suddenly looked upon in a whole new light.

"So, Neil, you said you recently began taking Irish lessons," my friend Eric said.

"Why not add Hebrew and/or Yiddish and at least become conversational."

"Instead of a trip to Ireland next year, why not consider the Holy Land," Doris suggested.

I received an invitation from a friend in Brooklyn to attend Rosh Hashanah services at his synagogue and candle lighting and a festive meal in the evening. I've even taken to reaching out to Jewish friends on the sabbath wishing them "Shabbat Shalom" and "Good Shabbos."

I really don't see myself abandoning my Catholicism at this juncture, but suddenly an entire new world has been opened to explore.

Grandpa Owens in military uniform circa 1917—he was in the Fighting 69th renamed in WW I to the 42nd Rainbow Division 165th Infantry Division.

Grandpa Owens at my parents wedding at St. Philip Neri Church in the Bronx, in February 1948.

SOMEONE ELSE PERHAPS

At one time or another, especially when growing up, we probably have all imagined that we would like to be someone or do something else. Perhaps a beautiful leading lady like Vivian Leigh or a dynamic leading man like Clark Gable. A distinguished statesman like Winston Churchill, who steered his country through such difficult times. Maybe it was to have a brilliant mind like Albert Einstein or to rock and roll like Elvis, box like Muhammad Ali, sing like Barbara Streisand, paint like da Vinci, or dance like Fred and Ginger.

From a very young age, I idolized Hollywood's James Cagney. I watched every one of his movies and imagined that I could be a tough guy just like him. Hours were spent watching his every on-screen movement and memorizing the famous lines from his movies. At family gatherings as early as age ten, I was always asked to give my latest Cagney rendition.

In the waning moments of Super Bowl XXIII, trying to rally his team to a come from behind victory, while in the huddle, with millions of people watching all over the world, hall of fame quarterback Joe Montana calmly said to his teammates who were awaiting instructions for the next play, "Look who's in the stands watching us, John Candy (the legendary comedian). Pretty cool huh; I love that guy."

Yes, we've all fantasized about standing in someone else's shoes, but what about when someone tells *you* that they wished they could trade places—be you and do what you do? As happened to me, it might take your breath away.

Volunteering at the Intrepid Air & Space Museum was one of the most enjoyable things I have ever done. I simply couldn't wait to board the railroad each Monday, zip into Manhattan and respond to the eager tourist's questions. The museum sponsors many annual events, one being a Thanksgiving dinner for those in need, who reside in Hell's Kitchen. Having considered myself most fortunate in that I have always enjoyed a warm and plentiful Thanksgiving, I unhesitatingly volunteered to work at that event.

Talk about being assigned to maybe the most unflattering of stations, I was tasked with serving creamed corn and Brussel sprouts. While those doling out the perfectly carved slices of turkey, stuffing, yams, bread pudding, and cranberry sauce were doing a robust business, it seemed at times, even though I was standing, that I was in danger of nodding off.

"A little creamed corn and a few Brussel sprouts to go with that drumstick sir?" I asked. A very polite "No, thank you," seemed to be on auto repeat each time I inquired, in vain. It didn't seem all that long when I decided to use the restroom, honestly, in hopes that my luck would change. Lo and behold, when I returned, a new steward now stood over these ill-considered trimmings. Things were looking better as I now was assigned to the final station which contained hard and soft rolls. Business was now brisk.

"Hi, my name is Mike," the poor soul standing over my prior domain said.

"Hi Mike, Neil Moran, a pleasure to meet you." "Did you serve on the Intrepid?" he asked. I had hoped that Mike didn't think I served with the carrier during its most active years in a war in which my father fought. "No, I'm not a veteran," I replied. "I volunteer once a week."

"Are you retired?" Mike continued.

"I am, yes."

"What did you do?"

"I was with the FBI, here in New York."

"The FBI, wow, that's amazing. You mean you were an actual FBI agent?"

"I was, yes."

"I've never met an FBI agent before. I can't believe this. It's something I really considered at one time. Let me ask you a question, one of my favorite movies is *Goodfellas*. Did you know any of those guys that robbed the Lufthansa terminal at JFK Airport that were portrayed in the movie?"

"Yes, I was assigned to the squad that handled the investigation. All the people portrayed in the film, Jimmy "The Gent" Burke, Tommy DeSimone, Paulie Vario, and Henry Hill were all truck hijackers and that's how my career began, working on that squad. We had encountered or arrested all those guys prior to the Lufthansa robbery. Our squad put Henry Hill and his wife Karen into the witness protection program when they decided to cooperate."

"I just can't believe that I'm talking to someone who was in the FBI," Mike said. "It sounds like it must have been exciting."

Obviously very flattered that Mike seemed to be so taken with my former career, I was now quite anxious to switch gears. Mike was quite tall and looked to me to be in his mid-50s. I then asked, "How about you, Mike, how did you wind up here tonight? What do you do for a living?"

"I consult with the museum on the Space Shuttle Pavilion. I am a professor at Columbia University and a former member of NASA."

"*NASA*," I said. "Wow, what did you do for NASA?"

"I was in the astronaut program."

"You mean you were an astronaut?" I blurted out, now in a state of shock.

"Yes, I was." Mike clearly had my interest and full attention. *How many of us have ever met an astronaut,* I thought. "Did you go on any space missions?" I inquired.

"Yes, I was part of a team that performed two separate updates to the Hubbel telescope and during those missions I had two spacewalks."

As my Irish cousins would say, "I was gobsmacked," utterly and completely amazed that I was speaking to an astronaut who, only moments ago, gushed at the fact that I used to lock up bad guys for a living.

As I was now aboard the train for the ride home, I couldn't wait to power up my phone and have a closer look at this unassuming gentle giant. As I scanned his bio, I saw that he was raised in Franklin Square, Long Island. *Franklin Square,* I thought. Astronauts aren't from Franklin Square. Astronauts are from places like Waterloo, Iowa, or Broken Arrow, Oklahoma, or Ohio like John Glenn. Mike Massimino received three master's degrees and a PhD in mechanical engineering from MIT. In addition, his two spacewalks totaled over fourteen hours, his spacecraft orbited the Earth 165 times and covered 4.5 million miles in in 262 hours. He is an accomplished author, having written a *New York Times* bestseller, was awarded two patents, and even appeared as himself in a recurring role on the television sitcom *The Big Bang Theory.*

I suppose it's simply human nature for people to have natural curiosity as to what it would be like to be someone or do something else. No matter how smart, accomplished, or successful one might be, some of us will always think, *"I wonder what it would be like to be that guy?"*

Former NASA astronaut Michael Massamino.

THE REGIFT SAGA

Have you ever "regifted" something? Some would never consider doing so while others wouldn't think twice.

Perhaps a sweater of which you already have too many, or a pair of gloves that you know you'll never wear, simply because you don't like them.

My personal feeling would be that even though it's probably not always the most pragmatic approach, if someone took the time to shop for a gift, I could never imagine or allow myself to pass it on to someone else.

Just imagine the total embarrassment of someone asking, "How you are enjoying the sweater I gave you for Christmas? I bet you're getting plenty of use out of it with the cold winter we're having. I struggled so much when deciding what to get you, but when I saw that sweater I said to myself, 'I know he will love that.'"

What's the response?

If you can come up with one, I'd be interested to hear it. I'd have no idea what to say.

Regarding regifting, *Town and Country* magazine recommends:

> "You can only regift something if the gift has never been opened before, and if both people in the situation (the

one who gave you the gift and the one receiving the regifted item) will never find out. And finally, the type of present also determines if you can regift: if it's something generic, like a box of holiday chocolate, then you can recycle it.

You can also regift if you already have the exact item you received (or something similar), if the item doesn't fit, if it's not your sense of style, or if you simply have no use for it."

I so look forward to what have become annual trips to visit my cousins in Ireland. Their kindness, charm, hospitality, and good humor are indescribable. Each trip is more memorable and enjoyable than the last. We are constantly on the go from the moment I arrive until I'm dropped at Dublin Airport for the trip home. Through the years, I've even gotten to know many of their childhood friends with whom they are still close.

So here we were only days before the end of my most recent trip when, following our dinner, we were visited at my cousin, Orla's house by Miriam and her husband, Ger, for tea. As would be normal practice for most people when dropping in, they brought a cake. Not technically a gift, I suppose, but fairly close.

"Just to be clear," Miriam began, "I'm regifting this cake. Friends dropped by yesterday with it and no one was interested, so I decided to bring it to your house."

It was a vanilla cake with white creamed frosting, but having just finished dinner, no one was interested.

The next day as we packed up for the three-hour ride from Cork to Leixlip in County Kildare to head to my cousin Karen's house she said, "We should bring the cake. I'm sure we'll eat it at some stage."

Generally speaking, on the last full day of my trip, we take the bus into Dublin and I spend several hours buying gifts for the family. My cousins, Daragh and Karen, act as my consultants and stylists, making recommendations as to what I should purchase for my wife, daughters and grandchildren.

My cousin Siobhan, who operated her own clothing business for decades, outfitting many Cork children with their school uniforms, also could spot good value for an Aran sweater or a beautiful scarf.

I would add that they are always spot on with their selections. We had tentatively planned that once we got back to Karen's house, we would walk to one of the restaurants in Leixlip for dinner.

"Oh, my goodness," Karen said as we passed beautiful Phoenix Park on the bus ride home.

"Here's a text from Aisling saying that Tommy and Sheelagh want us to come to their house for a barbecue this evening. Now what shall we do?" she asked.

As it was growing late and we kicked it around, we all agreed it would be "good craic," or fun as the Irish say, to accept the invite.

With the baker in the village already closed, we pondered what to bring.

"We can bring the cake from Miriam," Daragh said. "Absolutely not," I chimed in.

"We can't possibly bring that cake. It's at least three or four days old."

About an hour later, we packed a few bottles of wine and the regifted cake into bags and walked up Captain's Hill to Tommy and Sheelagh's.

"Oh, what a lovely looking cake," Sheelagh said as we arrived. I thought I would die on the spot.

Hours later, with dinner concluded and everyone appearing to have had their fill, Sheelagh surprisingly announced, "I don't know about anyone else, but I'm going to try a piece of that lovely cake."

With that, she went inside and moments later emerged with cake in hand saying, "This does look delicious."

With the cake providers eerily silent, Karen bravely proclaimed, "Sheelagh, full disclosure, my friend, Miriam, brought us this cake on Tuesday after someone had given it to her when visiting the prior evening. We make no guarantees."

"The cake is fabulous," Sheelagh said, already digging in for a second bite.

"Does anyone else want a piece? I have the kettle on, and we'll have tea in a moment."

"I'll have a piece," Orla announced, followed one by one from everyone in attendance. In about twenty minutes, not even enough for the ants remained.

Although *Town and Country* did seem to make allowances for "... something generic, like a box of holiday chocolate," I wonder what their take on the saga of the regift cake might have been?

We all ate the cake at Sheelagh and Tommy Malone's house in Leixlip, County Kildare, Ireland. Left to right—Allyn Quigley holding son Cillian, Orla Forde, Sheelagh and Tommy Malone, Daragh Forde, Karen Forde and Aisling Malone.

RETIREMENT AND DEAR ROSE

Since retiring in June 2018, what I had always feared might be a struggle has turned out to be just fine. I say with all honesty that I'm not on the edge of my seat every day, but there are very few occasions where I find myself without some challenge or opportunities to feel a sense of accomplishment.

Now, the thought of commuting by car as I did into Manhattan and Queens for twenty-nine years, followed by another eighteen of taking the LIRR into Penn Station is almost unthinkable.

Following an automobile accident in 1992 that left me with some physical limitations, I no longer was able to run, which to this day, I truly miss.

"Why don't you take up golf?" my father suggested at the time.

"You can play with your brother and me. It's really not as difficult as you might think."

Although I think my dad was a bit askew on the degree of difficulty in playing golf, I followed his recommendation and was happy to have played with him and my brother regularly before he passed away.

I wish I could say that now getting out one or two times a week, I am ready for the Champions Tour (the PGA tour for professionals over fifty), but I'm still just another frustrated hacker out there often mumbling to myself from hole to hole. I do really enjoy being out with friends and having a few laughs and I've even have gotten confident enough to show up at a course alone and get paired with people I don't know.

Shortly after I stopped working, I read a small notation in the 'Library News,' that the non-profit, Literacy Nassau, was looking for volunteers to teach English as a second language. This past September marked my seventh year teaching ESL.

Rarely have I done anything so gratifying. Imagine packing up and moving to a new country and not being able to continue your profession because you can't speak the language?

I have had teachers, police officers, engineers, MDs, prosecutors, and scores of other professionals in class with the goal of becoming citizens and returning to their respective professions. The profound thanks and appreciation the students show at every session, especially when they have landed a job, has often left me teary-eyed.

Several years ago, after getting requests from friends who were former prosecutors and now partners at law firms, to assist them in fraud cases, I decided to start my own limited liability company.

I continue to work periodically, primarily investigating so-called geniuses out there who steal money and somehow are under the delusional impression that I can be outsmarted. It continues to be great fun.

About three years ago, I decided to become a Eucharistic Minister at my church. Our job is to help the priests distribute Holy Communion to parishioners at Mass.

About a year after I started, I received a call from the coordinator of the program asking if I would be interested in bringing Holy Communion to people who are home bound and can no longer receive the Eucharist.

"Some of these people are deeply religious and have attended daily Mass throughout their lives. Now, they've been cut off from doing so and really appreciate being able to receive the sacrament," she said.

Why not, I thought. I'll give it a go.

At first, I filled in occasionally for people who were on vacation or unable to make their home visits due to illness. The coordinator was spot on—the recipients were all so grateful.

I was soon asked to regularly visit Rose, an eighty-five-year-old blind woman from Haiti. With a son living in south Jersey, who couldn't visit regularly and a live-in aide who she didn't like, I suddenly became one of Rose's regular connections to the outside world.

In our long conversations every Sunday, I learned that while a young girl in Haiti, Rose became a novice, a period of study on the path to becoming a nun. Before taking her final vows, she decided that the religious life, on a permanent basis, was not for her. After immigrating to the U.S., she began working in a research laboratory, which she did until complications with glaucoma took her sight.

Given her physical restrictions, Rose was prone to periods of depression and on occasion when I arrived, she would be in bed. No matter what her mood, whenever I walked in and said, "Hi Rose," she would rocket out of bed, extend both arms and give me a big hug.

"Hello, sweetie," she would always say greeting me. "I am so happy you're here."

We would talk and laugh endlessly. I felt like I had known her for many years.

Rose was a woman of deep faith and spiritual commitment. We prayed together before and after I would distribute Holy Communion to her.

"Please God, help me see one day. Please do that before you take me," she would often say.

On one Sunday, I noticed a sizeable book (over 1,500 pages), *The Roman Missal*, alongside Rose's bed.

"Do you see the book on my nightstand, Neil? I want you to have it," she said.

"Rose, I can't. This looks like something you should give to your son or grandchildren. I really can't," I replied. Even a call to her son, Patrick, fell on deaf ears.

"You have gotten to know my mother, Neil. You know how strong-willed she is. She cares deeply for you and wants you to have it. Please don't even give it a second thought."

Recently, Patrick texted me saying that Rose had been rushed to Mercy Hospital after suffering a heart attack. The prognosis was not good. I thought perhaps I would be able to speak with her one last time when I visited Mercy, but she remained unconscious. A few days later she was gone.

At her wake, I met Patrick for the first time. After giving me an extended embrace he told me, "You should know as my mother was being loaded into the ambulance no less than three times, she reminded me, 'Patrick, you must call Neil. He will be bringing me Holy Communion. I don't want him to come unnecessarily. Please ask Neil to pray for me.' It was a great comfort knowing that you were with my mother every Sunday," he added.

Yvrose M. Austin

"I can never thank you enough for being such a great friend to my mother."

Yes, retirement certainly does have its often-unexpected rewards.

LOOKING BACK

As the years have flown by *"faster than a speeding bullet,"* as the intro went in the *Superman* television series, I now find myself 'going back' and reflecting more frequently on a life well-lived.

Although I often think about the carefree years of my youth, it seems that when I embarked on my career and started a family, I now look back on those occasions more frequently and fondly.

It was about two years after getting married that my wife, Maureen, and I attended our first Lamaze class, in anticipation of the birth of our first child. Having seen a number of bloody crime scenes and dead bodies, attending natural childbirth class was not something I gave a second thought. That's until our initial meeting, when the nursing staff at Albert Einstein Hospital, in the Bronx, showed a film depicting an actual birth.

"Mr. Moran, Mr. Moran can you hear me? Mr. Moran are you alright?" asked the RN overseeing the session as I lay on the floor slowly regaining consciousness, with expectant mothers, husbands and partners looking on.

Talk about total and dreadful embarrassment. Of course, at the beginning of class we had all introduced ourselves, as well as our respective professions and when I announced mine as working for the FBI there were the normal "oohs and aahs," which now as I lay prostrate, certainly elevated the level of humiliation. I should have said I was a carpenter or unemployed.

Several months later, on a steamy August afternoon and two weeks past her due date, Maureen's water broke, and I immediately ushered her into the back seat of our 1969 non air conditioned Volkswagen for our trip from Long Island to the Bronx. As I sped toward the Throggs Neck Bridge, with my wife timing her contractions aloud and letting out an occasional, "Hurry, Neil, please," I wondered if the collector and I would be assisting in the delivery at the upcoming toll booth.

Standing by Maureen's side as she was wheeled into delivery, of course, as luck would have it, the RN who oversaw the Lamaze classes now on duty took one look at me and said, "Mr. Moran you shouldn't go in there. We can't be attending to you if you pass out again."

I couldn't miss this experience and given it was our first, Maureen was understandably nervous and did want me with her. "You have my word, if I feel the slightest bit woozy, I'll walk out immediately," I pleaded.

Fifteen minutes later with the nurses yelling, "Just one more push, Mrs. Moran," as I held her hand, someone blurted out, "Wow this is a big one. It looks like we have a truck driver here, a woman truck driver as a matter of fact. Mr. and Mrs. Moran you have a beautiful daughter."

As I squeezed Maureen's hand, I said, "Honey, you did it, you did it."

I will never forget the utter joy I felt at that moment and the mixture of exhilaration and exhaustion on my wife's face. As my eyes filled up with complete attention focused on Maureen, moments later she said, "How come she's not crying?"

As I shot a quick glance to the attending physician and the delivery team, all focus was on our newborn daughter. They seemed to be far from finished with their movements now almost bordering on frantic. The umbilical cord was lodged around our daughter's neck, and she had yet to take a breath.

"Everything's going to be ok, Honey," as I tried to reassure my wife with euphoria quickly turning to extreme unease. What was only probably a short time, but seemed like minutes, went by and still no utterance from our future truck driver. My eyes were now riveted on the team when one of the nurses looked up at the doctor as if to say, "What's happening? What's wrong? Are we going to lose her?" The doctor said nothing, nodded abruptly at her to renew her efforts and moments later, our daughter let out a cry worthy of a burly teamster.

In the four years that followed with the births of two more daughters (none of whom decided to enter the trucking profession) and with nowhere near the drama of our first, I was at Maureen's side during the deliveries and happy to say I remained upright at all times.

It's difficult to fathom that in the blink of an eye our 'truck driver' is now forty-seven, and our other two daughters, now also in their 40s, will soon be "going back" and recalling their special and tender memories.

THE NEXT GENERATION

It was almost sixteen years ago when our daughter, Colleen, announced that she was pregnant. This wasn't entirely unexpected. Colleen and her husband had been married less than a year and of our three daughters, she was the one who loved playing with dolls and was never without a baby carriage. My wife and I thought that it was only a matter of time before she would be pushing a pram for real.

I knew my siblings, Ellen, Cathy and Terry would be thrilled at the prospect of becoming aunts and an uncle, so I called to spread the joyous news. My sisters were naturally thrilled, but also not surprised.

My brother, a confirmed bachelor and ever the smart aleck said, "Wow this is quite a year for you, you'll be sixty and a grandfather all in one shot."

Pretty saucy from the then forty-seven-year-old.

Full disclosure, the oldest of four, I had recently expressed reservation in turning sixty. My brother, even though his comment sought to get a rise out of me, was pretty much on target. Turning sixty was traumatic enough, but now I was venturing into genuine senior citizen terrain in becoming a grandfather.

My wife and I have been blessed with three wonderful daughters.

Our oldest, Meghan was good at every sport she ever tried and was the most (and still is) competitive of the three. Her favorite pastime and the one she enjoyed the most was basketball. Fortunate enough to play in college, she is still on the all-time top ten list in many of the record categories at Adelphi University. She was also the Nassau County coach of the year after winning the NYS Federation high school championship while at Bishop Kellenberg High School.

Colleen, our doll and baby carriage devotee, never had a competitive bone in her body. A bit on the quiet side, she is the softest and most thoughtful. Although she swam competitively in high school, we've often recalled watching her playing girls' softball when she was about eight or nine as she adjusted the ribbon in her hair with line drives whizzing past.

Our youngest, Patricia, the toughest of the three and also highly competitive, was a four-time first team Division II All-American lacrosse player, a prestigious Tewaaraton Trophy nominee and a member of a national championship team at C.W. Post. Patricia is in the Post athletics hall of fame and enjoyed a successful college coaching career before switching vocations to nursing.

So now we come to the "next generation."

Colleen's daughter, Kate, in the blink of an eye is sixteen and a junior in high school. Kate is the epitome of her mother—quiet, soft, thoughtful and the perfect likeness to my late sister, Cathy. Given the proximity of everyone, if needed, I try to make myself available for after school and sports practice pickups, homework, or school projects. Several years ago, I recall helping Kate with her homework when I discovered what I believed to be an error in the teacher's instructions and wrote her a brief note. The next day my phone rang.

"Dad, what are you doing writing notes to Kate's teacher?" my daughter bellowed. The teacher shared the note with Colleen, adding that it was her first correspondence from a grandparent, adding that her father was indeed correct.

One of the proudest moments in recent memory was when Kate asked if I would participate in career day and speak to the classes at her school. Surrounded by doctors, nurses, police officers, firefighters, a chef, a fashion designer, and even a funeral director, all thirty years younger, Kate was beaming as I walked into her class for my presentation. In her yearbook, when asked of her most noteworthy memory of the past year, she commented, "When my grandpa came to speak at career day."

Kate's brother, Kevin, at twelve is a lot more curious than children his age. Recently, he spoke about the world's evil dictators including Vladamir Putin, Kim Jong-Un, and Ali Khamenei.

"We better be careful, Grandpa. These people are dangerous."

Kevin has gone on record stating that he wants to make enough money someday so all our immediate family can live in the same house.

Our daughter Meghan's children, to no one's surprise, are as competitive as their mother.

In the midst of Covid, when meeting a friend at a high school track for some exercise, I could see Meghan in the distance with the three children running up the bleacher stairs in her best Vince Lombardi mold, as if she was running the Green Bay Packers through game preparation.

Aidan, the oldest at fourteen, is as smart as a whip. The scope of topics we discuss while in the car range from his latest science project to a question he asked when he was a bit younger, which nearly had me run off the road, "Grandpa, what's cleavage?"

His sister, Rory, loves hanging out with the boys so it won't come as a shock that she is a member of an all-boys ice hockey team. At twelve, the hitting/checking allowed is minimal, but we've witnessed games that can get a bit rough.

Last year, while playing a team from Brooklyn, it was evident after the first five minutes that the opposition was serious. Following the decking of Rory's teammate which resulted in stoppage of play and his removal from the game, Rory immediately went after the assassin giving him a check heard in Manhattan. In the parking lot following the contest, a parent overheard Rory's victim utter, "Wait till we play them again, I'll kill that blond bitch."

Our youngest grandchild, Maeve, at ten, is equally at home playing with her collection of dolls as she is running up and down the basketball court, lacrosse field or making her way in a swim lane in the pool.

Another potential scholar, I recently was pressed into action to help with a project detailing her Irish heritage.

Yes, we are truly blessed to be such an integral part of our children and grandchildren's lives. They genuinely do seem to enjoy being with us. My wife and I could not be more delighted and prouder to have played a small role in molding the 'next generation.'

Our Family

STORIES

AFTERWORD

At age 21, when I started working in the FBI office in New York, it was only a short time before I realized that I was happy with my career choice.

Surrounded by so many people with whom I had much in common, first as a clerical employee and then as an agent, I will forever look back fondly on those early days in my long and wonderful professional journey.

As I assimilated myself into the office, I was often stunned that many of the older agents, now at the end of their careers were the essence of what author and longtime broadcaster Tom Brokaw described in his book, *The Greatest Generation*.

My longtime friend and former colleague Tommy Gallagher, a war history buff of sorts, and former U.S. Marine, seemed to know many of the senior agent's accomplishments.

"See that guy, he was shot down over Germany and was a POW in a concentration camp for over a year."

"This guy coming down the hall flew thirty bombing missions over Japan."

Generally, these men were often the most unassuming agents in the office and true to Mr. Brokaw's book, almost never shared tales of their hardships, sacrifices and heroism.

It seemed like in only a few years I was surrounded by a new and perhaps our own *greatest generation* of FBI agents with whom I was very proud to serve. Many of them were combat veterans of the Vietnam War, others were accomplished attorneys, bankers, accountants and some had been clerical employees like me. We all had many things in common: similar upbringings, dedication to our profession, a passion for our work and a belief that in some small way we were contributing to the common good.

No, we weren't in it for the money. As I look back, I wonder how many of us made it on our meager government income. Having said that, I'm fairly certain that an informal poll of retired agents with whom I worked would reveal that given the opportunity to turn back the clock and switch professions, very few, if any, would choose to do so.

There are many of my colleagues and contemporaries that have similar and certainly more interesting and exciting stories to tell about their experiences in the FBI than I have shared in my book.

With regard to all my associates, I hope that I have captured these stories in such a fashion that makes you proud to have been part of the FBI and the outstanding people with whom we worked.

Many of my former colleagues and I have been saddened in recent years to see the FBI at the forefront of the political arena—something it had successfully managed to elude since its inception. We can only hope that the Bureau can restore its once trusted and deserved reputation and continue to fulfill its mission to serve the American people.

www.ingramcontent.com/pod-product-compliance
Lightning Source LLC
Chambersburg PA
CBHW060450170426
43199CB00011B/1152